Helping Adults Learn

*A Guide to Planning,
Implementing, and
Conducting Programs*

Alan B. Knox

Helping Adults Learn

Jossey-Bass Publishers · San Francisco

HELPING ADULTS LEARN
A Guide to Planning, Implementing, and Conducting Programs
by Alan B. Knox

Copyright © 1986 by: Jossey-Bass Inc., Publishers
350 Sansome Street
San Francisco, California 94104

Library of Congress Cataloging-in-Publication Data

Knox, Alan Boyd (date)
   Helping adults learn.

   (The Jossey-Bass higher education series)
   Bibliography: p. 227
   Includes index.
   1. Adult education. 2. Continuing education.
I. Title. II. Series.
LC5219.K574   1986   374   86-45629
ISBN 1-55542-023-0 (alk. paper)

Manufactured in the United States of America

The paper used in this book is acid-free and meets the
State of California requirements for recycled paper
(50 percent recycled waste, including 10 percent
postconsumer waste), which are the strictest guidelines
for recycled paper currently in use in the United States.

JACKET DESIGN BY WILLI BAUM

FIRST EDITION
HB Printing   10 9 8 7 6 5 4

Code 8641

The Jossey-Bass
Higher Education Series

Contents

Preface

Several million Americans helped adults learn last year in a wide variety of part-time and short-term educational programs. The number of such programs—and of instructors in them—has been increasing steadily for the past century. This growth is likely to continue as lifelong learning becomes an essential feature of our educative society.

Most instructors in adult education programs are expert in the content they teach, but they usually have little preparation in the process of helping adults learn. The aim of this book is to assist such instructors to find ways they can strengthen and broaden the teaching methods they use.

Helping Adults Learn provides the most comprehensive overview to date of specific procedures for helping adults learn in various settings. It covers continuing higher education as well as human resource development programs provided by employers. Various other settings are also considered: museum education, adult basic education, continuing professional education, and adult religious education.

This book reviews many procedures for planning, conducting, and evaluating educational programs for adults and provides specific examples of techniques instructors can adapt and use in their situations. In addition, it aims to help instructors develop a clear rationale for selecting ideas and practices that will strengthen their teaching efforts and fit their individual content areas, teaching styles, and program settings.

This book is designed for instructors and teachers in all types of educational programs for adults, whether they are called instructors, teachers, trainers, facilitators, mentors, docents, or discussion leaders. Coordinators and supervisors of adult education programs will also be able to use the ideas and examples offered in this book to help instructors improve their methods. In addition, *Helping Adults Learn* will be a source of useful readings for association workshops and university courses on teaching adults. Its comprehensive treatment, varied practical examples, discussion questions, and citations to scholarly and practical writings would be particularly useful in such a context.

In addition, this new book draws on a base of over a thousand pertinent study reports, books, and articles, most of them from the past decade. The reference list is designed to function as a selected bibliography, and thus as a guide for readers who wish to pursue any topic in greater detail.

Each chapter focuses on a particular aspect of helping adults learn, which allows readers to select chapters according to their needs or interests. Most chapters contain checklists and practical examples from various settings, again to enable readers to adapt suggestions to their own situations.

Helping adults learn has been described as a spiral developmental process in which participants move through topics and later return to them at higher levels of understanding. Chapter One provides an overview of the process of helping adults learn. It is based on the premise that successful instruction depends on well-planned and carefully implemented educational programs. The chapter examines the various aspects of program planning, which include needs assessment, context analysis, selection of objectives and learning activities, program evaluation, and related arrangements.

The core of program implementation is the teaching-learning transaction, which involves engaging each learner, sequencing activities for progression, and assisting participants with application. Chapter One explains how effective instructors

use various types of program support and assistance for counseling, marketing, personnel, finance, materials acquisition, staff
development, and the like. The chapter concludes with an
example that shows how the various components of a program
are interrelated in the planning and implementation stages.

Chapter Two is based on the premise that effective teaching depends on being responsive to the learners in the program,
not to adults in general. For example, finding out what the participants already know about the subject is one of the most valuable first steps instructors can take. Further, instructors can
help provide varied learning activities so that participants can
select learning methods as well as broaden the ways in which
they learn effectively. Chapter Two examines these and other
ways instructors can balance support and challenge—and use
performance as a vehicle for learning.

In addition to content mastery, teaching style affects
learning significantly. An instructor's teaching style is based in
his or her fundamental ideas about helping adults learn and is
linked to specific procedures. Chapter Three discusses the varied
teaching methods that can facilitate active learning by participants. It also looks at the inherent limitations of such methods,
including restricted time for instructor presentations. Nonetheless, flexible selection of a progressive sequence of objectives
and activities, and feedback on their effectiveness, can serve to
increase participants' confidence and ability to guide their own
learning.

Chapter Four examines three components of program
planning—needs, context, and objectives—and suggests modifications that can be made in each of these procedures. For example, deciding on the extent and type of needs assessment to use
in a specific instance depends in large part on what additional
information about participant needs and expectations is essential for planning.

Context analysis considers major influences, such as societal trends and issues and the mission and resources of the
provider organization. Such data, combined with information
about needs, can help instructors and participants analyze and
agree upon feasible learning objectives.

Chapter Five provides insight into how instructors can

select and organize a sequence of activities likely to encourage participants to persist until their objectives have been achieved. Activities may be related to instruction, inquiry, or performance, and may be individually or group paced. The chapter also considers the importance of planning and scheduling to ensure successful arrangements for resource persons, finances, materials, facilities, and the like.

Whether educational materials are purchased or developed by instructors, the main selection criteria should be that they serve the group's educational purposes and that they pertain to learner backgrounds and interests. Chapter Six shows how the choice and use of materials can both contribute to active learning and provide repetition for practice and mastery. It explains how evaluation can be used as a two-edged tool to enable participants to compare their progress with their goals and also to help instructors modify and refine the materials. This chapter also provides guidelines for planning the *sequence* of materials to use at each stage of a program.

Chapter Seven looks at various ways instructors can help participants become committed to the program. Because learners' reasons for participating in a program may vary considerably, it is important for instructors to test their assumptions about participants' needs and expectations. Sound information will help instructors decide what needs assessment procedures to use. The chapter also considers ways to establish a supportive and challenging climate for learning, such as selecting conducive facilities, arranging for instructor and participants to get to know each other, providing warm-up activities, sharing information about backgrounds and expectations, providing an overview of the program, periodically obtaining participant reactions, and encouraging persistence.

Chapter Eight focuses on the teaching-learning transaction, which includes both activities and evaluation. Among the issues discussed are the value of questions and examples, the importance and quality of practice, ways of sequencing learning activities for progression, and reinforcement.

Chapter Nine describes ways evaluation can be focused on feasibility as well as on such specific program components as objectives, participation, facilities, and the like. The chapter discusses how various kinds of evaluation can be useful regarding program accountability and justification and how instructors and participants can use findings to make educational decisions. Guidelines for conducting evaluations are included along with suggestions for identifying evaluation activities that provide sound findings and that promote commitment to use of the findings.

Chapter Ten examines the various ways instructors can help participants apply what they learn. Among the issues discussed are how to emphasize and be responsive to the improvements that participants want to make. Standards of achievable best practice, procedures for reinforcement and encouragement, and feedback and evaluation regarding progress are also considered.

Chapter Eleven describes the surprising number of sources of support and assistance available to instructors as they help adults learn. These include coordinators and specialists in marketing, counseling, personnel, finance, and materials. Such people can help instructors attract and retain the numbers and types of adults for whom their programs are especially intended.

The concluding chapter reviews highlights from the book and poses questions about what instructors can do to strengthen the process of helping adults learn. In each section of the chapter, readers are encouraged to reflect on their current practice, select promising new ideas, try them out, evaluate the results, and share new insights with the rest of us. In addition, this chapter encourages readers to combine professional reading with observations of exemplary instructors and discussions of promising practices with colleagues.

Helping Adults Learn provides a comprehensive overview of all major aspects of planning and implementation of educational programs for adults. It includes examples and references from many types of educational programs for adults that can benefit any instructor. This book can enrich the perspective and stimulate the initiative of instructors to strengthen specific aspects of teaching in order to benefit learner achievement and instructor satisfaction. Special attention is given to ways to include participants in the selection of program goals and procedures. Instructors will also find practice standards they can use to assess and guide their improvement efforts.

It is my hope that this book will encourage instructors to strengthen the procedures they use to help adults learn. I also hope it will encourage widespread communication on evaluation for program improvement. This book does not advocate a single approach to teaching adults. Instead, *Helping Adults Learn* provides readers with a comprehensive overview on which to reflect regarding specific aspects of instruction as well as the rationale for instructional decisions.

Madison, Wisconsin   Alan B. Knox
August 1986

The Author

Alan B. Knox has been professor of continuing education at the University of Wisconsin in Madison since 1981. He received his bachelor's degree, two master's degrees, and his doctorate (1958) from Syracuse University, from which he received the Distinguished Alumnus Award in 1980. His scholarly activities are focused on leadership of continuing education and on helping adults learn.

Knox has published more than one hundred articles, chapters, and books on many aspects of continuing education of adults, including some in international journals such as the *International Review of Education* (1977), *World Yearbook of Education* (1979), and *International Encyclopedia of Education* (1985). Among Knox's published books are *Teaching Adults Effectively* (1980), *Developing, Administering, and Evaluating Adult Education* (1980), and *Leadership Strategies for Meeting New Challenges* (1983). Between 1979 and 1984 Knox served as editor-in-chief of the quarterly sourcebooks on continuing education published by Jossey-Bass. He received two Okes Awards, one in 1977 for Outstanding Research for *Adult Development and Learning* and one in 1980 for coauthoring *Last Gamble on Education,* from the American Association for Adult and Continuing Education, which he served as president during 1984-85.

Knox has held teaching, research, and administrative positions at various locations, including Syracuse University, University of Nebraska, Teachers College Columbia University, and University of Illinois at Urbana-Champaign, where he served as associate vice-chancellor for academic affairs and director of continuing education and public service between 1973 and 1977. He also chaired the Commission of Professors of Adult Education in 1975-77.

Each year, Knox's activities include talks, workshops, and leadership of special projects in various parts of the United States and in other countries. Recent international activities included two weeks in Yugoslavia for the United States Information Agency and serving as a delegate at the Buenos Aires World Assembly for Adult Education of the International Council for Adult Education.

Helping Adults Learn

*A Guide to Planning,
Implementing, and
Conducting Programs*

ONE

The Process of
Helping Adults Learn

Every time you set out to help adults learn, you have the opportunity for a unique and fulfilling experience. In this statement, the word *unique* deserves special emphasis. That is because the rich mixture of varying content, learners with distinct needs and life experiences, and your own instructional approach creates the potential for infinite variety and unending challenge. For this reason, it is unlikely that everyone will agree on one best way to help adults learn.

Most people who instruct adults do improve. In part, you improve by means of trial and error: You learn from experience and apply your insights to your practice. You also improve by example, by emulating other instructors whom you admire. And you improve by reading about teaching. By reading descriptions of innovative practice and rationales for improvement, you can benefit from the insights gained by others. Such insights help you make your own instructional decisions. Equally important, they help you understand the significance of those decisions. In the following pages, we explore both the "hows" and "whys" of helping adults learn.

Your Instructional Role

If, as in other complex interpersonal relationships such as friendship or administration, there is no one best way, how can you benefit from the experience and insights of other people? One way to benefit is to have a robust metaphor for your in-

structional role—a way to describe that role that encourages you
to view your current teaching style as evolving and open to useful ideas. A second way is to understand the *process* of helping
adults learn; combined with your mastery of subject matter
content, this understanding enables you to become an even
more effective instructor. A third way to benefit from the insights of others is to commit yourself to using some of their
ideas about helping adults learn to enhance your current instructional proficiencies.

There are various metaphors for helping adults learn. For
some, the process is like serving as a guide for people on a trans-
formational *journey*. You can aid them in their search for meaning and mastery by discovering the goals, maps, and proficiencies they already have and then helping them clarify their goals
and improve their maps so they can become their own guides. Is
this how you view your role? For others, helping adults learn is
like facilitating a *spiral* developmental process in which the assistance produces benefits appreciated by the learners in the
form of ever higher levels of understanding and problem solving.
For yet others, it is like the *mobius strip*—a flat strip that, when
given a half turn and the ends attached, becomes a curious loop.
As with the inside of learning and the outside of teaching, when
you run your finger along the inside of the mobius strip, sud-
denly it is on the outside and then on the inside again.

Your reading of these words reflects your commitment to
strengthening your own instruction and perhaps that of colleagues who instruct adults. This book provides an overview of
generalizations and examples about the process of helping
adults learn. A parallel between teaching and learning helps connect the two. The same concepts and procedures you use to
help *other* adults learn can also help *you* learn how to become a
more effective instructor. Also, the adult learners whom you instruct can help you learn how to teach them more effectively
and can serve as learning resources to one another. Writings
about helping adults learn can enrich your practice. You can
also report your insights and discoveries, thus enriching the professional literature for the rest of us.

The many topics that pertain to helping adults learn can
be grouped in various ways. As you read this book, your under-

standing of adult learners and of your own contribution provides a perspective on the procedures you use and your efforts to strengthen them. This perspective should contribute to planning educational activities and materials and conducting the teaching/learning transaction. Throughout that process, the provider organization for which you instruct (educational institution, employer, association) should have program support services that can assist you (for example, in marketing, counseling, finance, materials, or staff development). These topics are both the major contents of this book and decision areas as you seek to strengthen your instruction.

Your attention to these topics is not like a series of steps but instead like the interrelated components of a record player or tape player. Most people instructing adults for the first time arrive with at least rudimentary components in place. Your mastery of subject matter content is probably well advanced, because this is usually the main criterion for hiring. Other basic components are satisfactory interpersonal relations and verbal facility. As you make decisions to plan and implement your program, and as you enhance your proficiency at doing so, the process is typically more spiral than linear as you give attention to one component and then another and their relationships.

As the process progresses, ideally your attention to a component each time enhances its quality and fidelity. Refining and upgrading the system in this way enables you and the participants to make beautiful music. Defective components (such as misjudging participants' backgrounds and interests, an unsupportive or unchallenging learning climate, or irrelevant and overwhelming materials) can diminish the outcomes even though the rest of the system may be excellent. As you read this book, be alert to components of your instruction that you especially want to upgrade. Have any come to mind already?

The varied examples in this book parallel the variety of provider agencies and program formats in which people help adults learn. There are examples from continuing higher education programs (extension, outreach) of colleges and universities. There are also examples from human resource development programs (training, in-service) provided by employers.

In addition, the generalizations throughout the book

should apply to adult and continuing education instructors in many other organizational settings. These include local public school or community college adult education programs, adult religious education, continuing professional education provided by associations, and educational programs for adults by libraries, museums, and community agencies. In most of these organizations some organizational unit is concerned mainly with educational programs for adults and is viewed as the provider. For which of these providers have you helped adults learn? Such part-time and short-term educational programs for adults are referred to in various ways, including "adult education," "training," "extension," "in-service," "outreach," and "staff development." I will be referring to all of them as "continuing education."

From your standpoint as an instructor (teacher, trainer, professor, discussion leader, tutor, mentor, or specialist in organization or community development), such distinctions in terminology or organizational setting are probably of less consequence than the format of the program (course, workshop, coaching session, meeting) in which you instruct. You may help adults learn individually, in large or small temporary groups, or in the context of their organizational or community life. You may refer to the learners who participate in your program as "students," as "trainees," as "members," as "learners," or typically as "participants" (to emphasize their active roles as adult learners). But the essential ingredients in the process of helping adults learn are basically the same.

Throughout this book, the ideas that seem to apply to instructors in most settings, and the examples that show how and why they occur in particular settings, should suggest how you can select useful ideas and adapt them to your own situation. That is what professionals do in any field. They use their familiarity with practice to select and adapt general concepts and procedures to work in their own unique circumstances. This praxis back and forth between knowledge and action is central to your increasing effectiveness as an instructor. And it is also what many of your participants seek from your program.

How do you view your interaction with adult learners

and subject matter content? There are many possibilities. Instructors variously describe their role as "guiding discovery," "dispensing information," "facilitating sharing," "enforcing standards," or "stimulating a search for meaning." I find it helpful to think about the process as a *transaction*. My main responsibility is to ensure that the basic program decisions are made and implemented—not necessarily to make them all myself.

The *transaction* is the essence of our role; the specifics vary. Involving learners and specialists in decisions about planning, implementation, and application helps raise the quality of the educational program and encourages continued involvement. Sometimes I serve as content expert and designer of program (curriculum) and related materials. At other times I begin with some adults with compatible educational needs and draw on my familiarity with some pertinent experts and materials to orchestrate the planning and implementation process. Thus, the core of our role is the *transaction* as we interact with learners, content, and other people and materials to plan and implement an educational program.

I use the term *instructor* to refer to all that you do to help adults learn. You may think of yourself as a teacher or discussion leader. Sometimes you may receive help from instructional designers, materials developers, content experts, or the adult participants themselves. At other times you may handle most of the tasks and decisions yourself. In any case, the person who has the main responsibility for planning and conducting an educational or training program for adults should ensure that sound program decisions are made. The goal is to enhance learners' proficiencies. This is why, besides mastering content and process, it is important for you to understand adults as learners.

Ideas About Process

Did you ever wonder why some of those adults are in your program? Besides their responses when you ask them why, generalizations about adult development and learning can deepen your insight into their backgrounds and aspirations. Their characteristics, in contrast with the many potential participants who did not take part, reflect an outlook and readiness to learn that can powerfully affect their persistence, achievement, and application. Generalizations about adult learners are valuable to you as an instructor, mainly *as they guide your understanding of the individual participants in each program.*

The most valuable information you can obtain in order to help adults learn something is about their pertinent current proficiencies (knowledge, skills, attitudes). Many continuing education programs aim to help participants advance from their current proficiencies toward their desired proficiencies. Understanding discrepancies between their current and desired proficiencies helps you make your program responsive. You and your participants can then deal better with the diversity of backgrounds and aspirations, assess readiness, clarify aspirations, progress to higher levels of learning and development, provide relevant materials, and encourage application. By appreciating the multiple influences on participation, you will be better able to reduce barriers, encourage initial participation and persistence, and provide counseling assistance.

Desirable as it may be to understand participant proficiencies and interests, the difficulty is probably *how* to obtain such information. How do you do so? Ways to estimate current proficiencies include self-assessment inventories, performance records, supervisory reports, direct observation, tests, and interviews. Ways to discover expectations and preferences about desired proficiencies include checklists, essays, and interviews with participants and sometimes with other people such as family members or work supervisors whose expectations are also important. Collecting parallel information about current and desired proficiencies lets you identify discrepancies, which can focus your responsiveness in the ways mentioned above.

It is also important to understand your own contribution as an instructor. This includes content mastery and general teaching style as well as use of particular instructional procedures. Content mastery enables you to be flexible and responsive as you respect both content standards and participants' proficiencies, purposes, learning styles, and search for meaning. Your teaching style includes the instructional procedures you typically use, as well as personality characteristics and interpersonal relations. How would you characterize your own typical teaching style? Consider such features as enthusiasm, details, practice, examples, participation, flexibility, and application. A question on which to reflect as you complete each section of the book is: What are the implications of that section for enhancing your approach to helping adults learn?

Your understanding of adult learners and of your role can enhance all aspects of program planning and implementation, which should blend together. Your experience from past programs and ideas from resource persons can contribute to flexible plans that enable you to be responsive as you select ideas, methods, and materials that best fit the flow of the program.

Most program-planning tasks can be grouped within six interrelated components: needs assessment, context analysis, objective setting, learning activities, program evaluation, and related arrangements. In best practice, these components are first outlined in a preliminary way. Then they are progressively refined so they fit together. An overview of these components can serve as a checklist to help you identify satisfactory program aspects and those that you want to modify or strengthen in the upcoming program. Each section of the book constitutes an overview of various ideas and procedures from which you can select those that seem useful to you.

Needs assessments identify discrepancies, or gaps, between participants' current and their desired proficiencies as perceived by themselves and others. *Context analyses* identify influences such as societal trends, competing or complimentary opportunities from other providers, and the mission and resources of your own provider organization. Information about both needs and context can be used to set satisfactory educational *objectives*. These objectives (including the content they reflect), along with learner characteristics and your perspective, can be used to select *learning activities*. The sequence of learning activities should encourage participants to persist until they have achieved their objectives.

Program evaluation can be used for planning, improvement, and justification. The evaluation procedures that you select should reflect evaluation purposes, audiences, and issues as you describe and judge the worth and effectiveness of aspects of the program that are selected for evaluation. Each of your programs is evaluated informally by yourself, the participants, and other people associated with the program. Formal evaluation can increase the soundness of the judgments and the likelihood that conclusions will be used to benefit the program.

Planning guidelines can also help you select, develop, and sequence educational materials. Major considerations include program purposes, content, and organization, along with learner backgrounds and interests. Effective materials focus on important matters, are relevant to a variety of participants, and encourage active and flexible use and repetition for practice and mastery. Guidelines for sequencing include specific program objectives at each stage, responsiveness to preferred learning styles, learner selection and pace of materials, and focus on fundamental concepts and procedures.

Effective planning of program activities and materials should strengthen the teaching/learning transaction. This includes engaging the learner, guiding growth and change, and encouraging application. When planning, remember that *early program sessions are crucial.* The highest attrition typically occurs at this stage. Early program sessions should help participants clarify their expectations and help you decide what you hope to accomplish. At this early stage, it is important to establish a supportive and challenging climate for learning and to obtain agreement on specific objectives. Ways to establish such a climate include selecting conducive facilities, providing an overview of the program, and arranging for introductions that reveal backgrounds and expectations. Ways to gain agreement on objectives include agenda building, learning contracts, group discussion, and planning committees.

From the first session to the last, the teaching/learning transaction is the dynamic core of helping adults learn. The satisfaction that you and participants gain from the program experience depends on how you use questions and examples, provide practice opportunities, sequence activities for progression, pace the program, give positive reinforcement, and allow for program evaluation that provides useful feedback to you and to participants. Both activities and evaluation are integral parts of the teaching/learning transaction. One way to increase use of evaluation conclusions is to involve in the evaluation process the people who should use them.

One crucial aspect of the teaching/learning transaction is the way you *sequence* learning activities for progression. This might begin with an overview of fundamentals followed by help for participants to progress toward higher levels of understanding.

Understanding can be increased by stages. At lower levels of understanding and problem solving, learners process information in fragmentary ways without organizing concepts or themes. At a somewhat higher level, they deal with central concepts but without relation to supporting facts and details. At a still higher level, they understand relations among concepts and facts. A more inclusive level of understanding occurs when learners use deep processing of integrating themes to go beyond the context of information presented to provide reasons for similarities and differences and to explore alternative views.

In some educational programs for adults, encouraging and assisting with *application* is an important part of the teaching/ learning transaction. Ultimately, participants' application of what they learn in your program depends on themselves and other people in the settings in which that application might occur. However, there are various ways you can increase the likelihood of such application: by responding to pertinent participant aspirations, by clarifying performance standards, by including application-oriented materials for practice and ongoing assistance, and by reinforcing and evaluating progress. You can also arrange for assistance with application.

Many sources of *program support* and assistance, inside and outside the provider organization, are available to continuing education instructors—coordinators, for example, and specialists in marketing, counseling, personnel, finance, materials, and staff development. Such assistance may benefit any aspect of your program planning and implementation. How much support your program receives is likely to depend mainly on your initiative in identifying, selecting, coordinating, and evaluating such staff assistance.

As indicated earlier, these components of planning and conducting educational programs for adults are not a series of steps but an interacting system. Most people who help adults learn have done so before. They start planning a program with a general idea (distilled from past experience) of how the major parts of the upcoming program are likely to fit together. So the planning process does not begin with a blank slate. Some ingredients (such as instructor, location, budget, objectives, or participants) may be set, which means that other ingredients must be planned around them. In this way, the implementation experience from similar past programs influences the planning process for the new program, which is further modified as it is implemented. Decisions about any component affect other components also. Such interrelationships are illustrated by the following brief example about conducting an in-service program for nursing supervisors cosponsored by the hospital where they work and a nearby university school of nursing.

Sue Barton, a recently appointed assistant professor of nursing with experience as a hospital director of nursing, agreed to conduct a series of six in-service sessions for nursing supervisors in area hospitals, based in the university's main teaching hospital. Sue had grown up assuming that she would become a nurse—and she did! She had never thought that she would become a professor of nursing and would conduct in-service sessions—but she did!

Sue jumped at the opportunity to conduct this series of in-service sessions because the purpose was to help supervisors understand how and why to strengthen cooperation among various health professionals engaged in delivery of health care in area hospitals. Problems related to staff cooperation were her pet peeves as a nurse and as director of nursing, and she had focused on this issue in her recent graduate study.

Although Sue had never directly studied adult development and learning, her study of human development in nursing school, along with her experience with patients of all ages and backgrounds and some reading of popular articles on aspects of adult development, had given her an appreciation of topics, such as career development and "teachable moments," that might be included in the program. She therefore invited someone with such expertise to join an informal advisory committee to help plan the program.

The combination of formal study and extensive experience related to the supervision focus of the proposed program made Sue confident about most of the likely subject matter content. However, she did not think of herself as a teacher, although she had conducted some in-service sessions over the years. Consequently, she found herself thinking about the teaching style and approach of instructors she had admired.

Enthusiasm for a program for nursing supervisors about cooperation among health professionals increased as a result of a conversation Sue had over lunch with a nursing supervisor with whom she had worked some years before at an area hospital. In a flush of enthusiasm after lunch, each of them talked with one or two nursing supervisors at other area hospitals for their reactions to the idea. These supervisors were positive enough that several agreed to participate in the advisory committee. Sue thought their involvement might also help enrollments. The following month, at a meeting of the state nurses' association, Sue mentioned the idea and was again pleased with the interest.

From later conversations with colleagues in the school of nursing and with staff from the teaching hospital, Sue found out about several articles on ways to achieve greater cooperation among members of various health professions working in hospitals that program participants could use as prior readings. One older article described a bicycle approach to organization development in hospitals, using information from staff performance reviews to focus educational activities that were then evaluated for improvement in performance. Sue decided that some organization development features might be included in the program.

The list of program objectives submitted to the state nurses' association for approval to award continuing education units (CEUs) included such phrases as "understand facilitators and barriers to cooperation among various health professions" and "formulate supervisory strategies likely to increase interprofessional cooperation," which were intended as participant outcomes. However, even as Sue submitted the plan, she felt that it didn't really capture what she wanted to do. The plan for six weekly two-hour sessions seemed long on understanding and short on action.

A professor of hospital administration with whom Sue discussed the plan suggested that she change the format to have three weekly sessions, then a month break before the fourth session, then another month break before the final two weekly sessions. The idea was to encourage the program participants from each hospital to meet together during the first three weeks to plan a two-month action learning project in their hospital, which would include staff from other health professions associated with that hospital. Each project would focus on increasing interprofessional cooperation that a nursing supervisor might help to achieve and would be modest enough that substantial progress might be expected in two months. The fourth session would allow for progress reports from the project teams from the hospitals represented.

The first session began with introductions

(brief, because most of the participants knew each other). The program objectives and plan were discussed and modified, some basic issues from the prior readings were discussed, and the project teams met for the first time. (The registration materials had asked enrollees to start thinking about concrete ways to increase interprofessional cooperation.) Sue conducted the session, and several members of the advisory group served as resource persons to help each project team select a coordinator and begin planning its action learning project.

At the second session, each project team discussed and analyzed a case example based on one of the articles distributed before the program. Sue provided some discussion questions in case the team coordinators wanted to use them. At the end of the session, participants completed an opinionnaire to let Sue and the advisory committee know how the program was progressing for them. Sue summarized responses soon afterward and distributed a summary to the advisory committee and then, at the third session, to the participants. The third session was devoted to discussing ways to conduct the action learning projects.

The fourth session was a lively affair with much sharing of progress reports on the projects and discussion of how to make them work better and why they were being approached as they were. Sue and several advisory committee members agreed to serve as informal consultants to the project teams, and several times they were called to discuss an issue or were asked to attend a brief meeting of the team members. Other hospital staff members who were not program participants became associated with the team projects, and specialists on materials and on evaluation from the university office of continuing education assisted Sue.

The final two program sessions discussed the largely incomplete projects, how the augmented team members planned to continue beyond the program sessions, and what participants had learned about both the content of interprofessional cooperation and the process of planned change. Several months after the sixth and final session, Sue conducted brief follow-up phone interviews with most of the participants to assess the extent and type of impact the projects seemed to have achieved in the hospitals. She sent the summary of her conclusions to the advisory committee members with a note asking for their ideas about possible future programs.

The foregoing example illustrates not an ideal program but one that shows interrelationships among program components and how each decision or choice affects others. How might you have approached a similar opportunity to help adults learn? In what ways might Sue's program have been strengthened?

The following chapters explain concepts and procedures related to all aspects of the foregoing example. Perhaps you will discover some that can enrich your practice when you help adults learn.

TWO

Understanding Adult Learners

What do you know about adult learners that typically guides you in planning and conducting an educational program for adults? Many instructors recall their own experiences as learners, pertinent readings, and impressions of past participants in similar programs. Such recollections and impressions tend to blend together, and it may be difficult to extract implications for specific program decisions. The following generalizations about adults as learners may reinforce some of your current understandings and perhaps provide additional insights.

Adult learners have many characteristics related to past experience, current abilities and roles, and future aspirations that influence adult learning and teaching (Knox, 1977). You cannot take *all* these characteristics into account, even when assisting one learner, as in on-the-job training. Effective instructors recognize that there are some general characteristics associated with adult learning that enable them to be especially helpful to learners in each instance. Understanding such characteristics can enable you to *organize adult learners' activities around their backgrounds and aspirations.* This chapter presents some generalizations about characteristics of adults to take into account when helping adults learn. They are grouped in four sections: on enhancing proficiencies, development and learning, influences on participation, and the importance of active learner participation.

Enhancing Proficiencies

Adults engage in learning activities mainly to enhance their proficiencies. You can use information about proficiencies to assess educational needs, encourage persistence, and relate new learnings to old (Knox, 1980a; Knox, 1985). Proficiency is the capability to perform effectively if given the opportunity and typically entails a combination of knowledge, attitudes, and skills. In most adult life roles and tasks, actual performance reflects both the individual's proficiency and the influence of other people. As an instructor, you can help adults acquire desired proficiencies, but you cannot assure satisfactory performance.

Proficiency-oriented adult learning is similar to competency-based preparatory education for young people: both give attention to specific objectives, mastery learning, and evaluation of learner achievement of objectives. However, whereas competency-based preparatory education emphasizes achievement of minimal standards of performance in educational tasks, proficiency-oriented continuing education emphasizes achievement of optimal standards of proficiency related to adult life roles. This is especially apparent in continuing professional education.

An understanding of discrepancies between current and desired proficiencies is useful in several ways. Awareness of such a discrepancy can motivate an adult to engage in a learning activity. Specification of such a discrepancy is the main purpose of an educational needs assessment, whether performed by the learner or by someone else as part of the program development process. Program evaluation includes assessing the extent to which educational activity is enhancing current proficiencies so that they more closely approach desired ones (and sometimes assessing the extent to which even more desirable ones are recognized). Effective educational activities and materials help learners build on current proficiencies and progress toward desired proficiencies. Thus, an understanding of discrepancies between current and desired proficiencies helps to explain motives of adult learners and enables those who help adults learn to do so responsively and effectively.

As an instructor, you should understand that the impact of your program is affected by many influences on proficiency and on motivation to enhance proficiency. An adult's profi-

ciencies change developmentally over the years. Unused proficiencies diminish. Adults who engage in work, family, and community activities in reflective ways gradually become more proficient in those activities. Evolving proficiencies result from
personal and situational influences—past, current, and even
prospective. Past influences include not only the individual's
abilities, education, and experience but also opportunities and
encouragement, which are sometimes related to social class.
These past influences enter into an adult's general sense of being
a proficient person, and this self-perception, along with current
proficiencies, contributes to an individual's outlook regarding
the risks and benefits of future efforts to enhance proficiency.
This outlook interacts with current and evolving performance,
as the adult and others who care about his or her performance
form a sense of the adult's proficiency. Many personality-
related characteristics, such as values, interests, self-concept,
and attention to stability and change in the process of decision
making, affect a person's striving to enhance proficiency. Especially for older adults, physical condition and health can modify an adult's efforts to enhance proficiency. Hopes and expectations for the future are major spurs to growth for some adults.

Gradual adjustments of proficiencies and tasks result in a
fairly stable equilibrium for most adults most of the time. This
stability tends to be interrupted by major role-change events,
such as a job change, a family change, or a move to a new community, which require some adjustments and typically heighten
readiness to learn. Rapid increases in proficiency can result, followed by periods of relative stability. Responsiveness to such
teachable moments can increase the impact of your program.

An understanding of the transactional and developmental
process by which proficiency evolves can be helpful in various
ways to adult learners and to those who help them learn. The
evolution of proficiency is developmental in that past characteristics influence current proficiencies, which influence future
choices, and it is transactional in that it results from the individual's social interaction. An understanding of the process by
which proficiency evolves can enable an engineer who confronts
a new and different assignment to anticipate the requisite profi-

ciencies, select relevant learning activities, and thus apply what is learned to improve performance. Such understanding can enable a farmer engaged in an extension computer project on farm records to clarify agribusiness goals and related educational objectives. Hospital staff members can use concepts regarding proficiency to guide a practice audit comparing current practice with achievable standards of best practice in order to focus on needed improvements and monitor efforts to achieve them. Attention to participants' proficiencies can help an expert conducting a workshop relate new ideas to their current knowledge and encourage them to persist in the workshop and apply what they learn. A supervisor in a financial institution can use concepts regarding proficiencies to improve the annual performance review for employees so that supervisor and employee agree to growth goals for the employee to which both are committed.

A developmental understanding of current and desired proficiencies can also help individual adults in their self-directed learning efforts. Concepts about proficiencies can help individuals use their experience and aspirations to assess their educational needs, clarify their educational objectives, select educational materials, and evaluate their progress. The result should be challenging—but not overwhelming—learning projects that address the questions, problems, and opportunities that concern the learners, enhance their proficiency, and encourage them to apply what they learn to improve performance.

In some instances, such as self-directed learning projects on a leisure interest or learning activities on personal health and fitness, undertaken by adults with much experience with and leaning toward education, almost all of a learning project may be pursued on a self-directed basis. In other instances, such as orientation sessions for new entry-level employees with little understanding of procedures and expectations, most of the learning activity may be guided by the supervisor. Even so, self-directed learning can be a supplemental activity for some highly motivated new employees, and encouragement and assistance with self-directed learning during the coming months can be an objective of the orientation experience. In most instances (such as continuing professional education) direction of continuing education activities is a shared responsibility of the learner and others able and willing to help.

Use of ideas about proficiencies is illustrated by the experience of Tyler Springfield, a state library administrator.

> Tyler Springfield conducted a five-day workshop for two dozen librarians who had recently assumed administrative responsibilities for staff development, cosponsored by a university library school and an association of librarians. Findings from a recent survey had alerted Tyler to the similarity of tasks and educational needs for most categories of library personnel, with the exception of administrators. The workshop participants' recent career transitions alerted Tyler to analyze gaps between current and desired proficiencies.
>
> Tyler and the other workshop instructors were committed to help participants strengthen proficiencies that were new and important in their staff development roles. Because workshop registrations were confirmed a month ahead, Tyler was able to send a brief questionnaire to be completed for summary and use in the final planning process. Without this early preregistration, he would have distributed the questionnaire when participants arrived and had it summarized during the first session.
>
> Because he and the other workshop planners were familiar with such participants, the staff development roles they were entering, and typical adjustments that people make in such career transitions, the questionnaire was quite selective. It requested information about pertinent experience, aspirations in the new role, self-confidence, major perceived barriers, and perceived sources of assistance.
>
> Tyler used the summary of questionnaire findings and other background information to orient workshop instructors regarding the main gaps between participants' current and desired profi-

ciencies. The summary was also used to select
workshop materials and activities likely to connect
new learnings to old and encourage persistence in
learning activities during and after the workshop.
After the workshop, participants were given their
questionnaire statement of what they hoped to
gain from the workshop as a basis for their evaluation of the extent to which those gains had occurred and for their planning of follow-up activities.

Development and Learning

Of course, adult development extends far beyond proficiencies—so far, in fact, that you may be tempted to throw up
your hands and wonder why, as an instructor, you should pay
attention to adult development at all. After all, even when you
work individually with adult learners, you are not a counselor
helping them cope with life crises. And when you work with
groups of participants, they are so varied, how could you pos-
sibly have the time and expertise to comprehend their unique
backgrounds and aspirations? You couldn't, of course.

But it is just that diversity that makes generalizations
about adult development and learning so useful to you—not for
individualizing your instruction to respond to all the differences but, rather, for helping you decide what options to provide: alternative materials and activities for groups of participants, specialized learning projects for individual participants.

Generalizations about various learning styles and interests
that reflect developmental tasks and personality development
warrant responsiveness and individualization. The highlights
about adult development in this section suggest dynamics that
give rise to teachable moments in your participants' lives, moments that contribute to participation, motivation, and application. The concluding example of in-service teacher education
suggests a few of the ways instructors can select and use developmental generalizations.

Learning Style. Adults vary in how they approach and
use learning activities. The characteristic and preferred way in

which an adult engages in learning activities is termed "learning style" (Claxton and Ralston, 1978; Cross, 1981; Dunn and Dunn, 1972; Gregorc, 1979; Holtzclaw, 1985; Kalamas, 1986a; Krupp, 1982). Intelligence, personality, age, formal education, and previous specialized experience all contribute to the great variety of learning styles within the adult population. These characteristics are associated with development generally. Thus, to understand and guide adult learning, it is important to understand adult development (Hultsch and Deutsch, 1981; Knox, 1977; Krupp, 1981; Merriam, 1983, 1984; Schaie and Geiwitz, 1982; Troll, 1982; Whitbourne and Weinstock, 1979).

A developmental perspective helps explain how adults acquire their learning style, what prompts learning activities, and how teaching style can both accommodate learning style and guide its further evolution. For example, change events, such as a job change, loss of a loved one, or even buying a new car, heighten readiness to learn and often trigger participation in educational activities (Aslanian and Brickell, 1980; Chiriboga, 1982; Glustrom, 1983). Understanding such events can enable you to offer educational activities that are responsive to those developmental tasks, publicize educational programs in ways that help potential participants recognize how the program is likely to aid in their developmental adjustment, and select relevant and helpful educational materials and activities.

Learning ability and style change gradually throughout life. Most adults can learn almost anything they want to if they are willing to devote enough time and attention and if they receive some assistance. However, the mix of learning abilities and interests evolves during adulthood, as some learning activities increase in attractiveness and ease of learning while others decline. The result is a stable plateau of general learning ability through most of adulthood, but with shifts in what seems important to learn and in how easy it is to master various types of learning tasks.

Regarding ability, for example, performance in learning tasks that benefit from accumulated experience, such as those that entail vocabulary, general information, and fluency in dealing with ideas, continues to improve during most of adulthood.

By contrast, performance in learning tasks such as rote memory, discovering figural and mathematical relations, and inductive reasoning steadily declines from young adulthood into old age. Consequently, as adults grow older, they tend to substitute wisdom for brilliance when dealing with intellectual tasks. These shifts in learning style reflect developmental trends in intelligence (Cattell, 1971; Horn, 1970).

Shifts in learning style also reflect developmental trends in personality during adulthood. Aspects of personality associated with learning style include cognitive style and growth, ego development, and moral development. Adults tend to evolve from unquestioning conformity to recognition of multiple viewpoints to deliberate commitment to application of universal principles and appreciation of relationships, both human and cognitive (Fowler, 1981; Kohlberg, 1973; Loevinger, 1976; Perry, 1970; Weathersby, 1981). However, people change in various directions, sometimes associated with differences in social class, gender, experience, and motives and perceptions (Baruch, Barnett, and Rivers, 1983; Gilligan, 1982; Loewenthal, Thurnher, Chiriboga, and Associates, 1975; Rubin, 1976; Weathersby, 1981). An appreciation of these trends and influences can enable you both to recognize major features of an adult's current learning style and to help adults enhance their learning style so that it will serve them even better in the future.

You can assess participants' preferred ways of learning in various ways. Informal ways include asking them on a registration form or in conversation to express their preferences. You can also provide a variety of methods and note choices and reactions, and you can ask them to share their reactions as a part of their program evaluation comments. Smith (1982, Appendix A) contains a review of learning-style inventories for those who want to use a more formal procedure. Providing participants with the results of any of these ways of assessing learning style helps them to clarify preferences and to make more informed choices in the future. Summaries of their preferences can guide your instructional decisions.

Various dimensions of cognitive style define characteristic modes of mental and creative functioning that people typically use for perceiving, remembering, thinking, and problem solving (Brown, 1978; Gubrium and Buckholdt, 1977; Steitz, 1985). One dimension is an analytic, impersonal approach to problem solving versus a more global, social orientation. Another dimension is cognitive complexity and abstraction (which enables people to view social behavior in ways that are highly differentiated, finely articulated, and flexibly integrated so as to accommodate diversity, conflict, and inconsistency) versus cognitive simplicity and concreteness (in which people function best when dealing with consistent information).

A third dimension is impulsivity (that is, using the first answer that comes to mind even if it is incorrect) versus reflection (pondering several alternatives before deciding). A fourth dimension is convergent thinking (which emphasizes logical conclusions and conventional best outcomes) versus divergent thinking (which emphasizes originality, variety, and quantity of relevant results).

Developmental Changes in Learning Style. The foregoing dimensions help characterize how an adult compares with other adults in typical cognitive style. By contrast, some dimensions, such as style of conceptualizing, seem to be developmentally ordered: Younger people have relational styles that rely on routine use of thematic or functional relationships, and as they become older some of them develop more analytic ways of conceptualizing descriptive relationships, and with age and experience some go on to develop more categorical inferential styles (Messick, 1984).

If you understand these or other cognitive-style dimensions, you and the learners themselves can select and organize learning activities most likely to be useful (DeNovellis, 1984, 1985; Dixon, 1982, 1985; Holtzclaw, 1985; James and Galbraith, 1985; Myers and Myers, 1980; Schwen and others, 1979). Some of these dimensions contribute to more general cognitive development that sometimes occurs during late adolescence and young adulthood. For example, some college students progress from a simple dualism based on authority and division of meaning into two realms such as good versus bad, right versus wrong, and we versus they, through discovery of multiple perspectives and relativism, to the development of commitment within an awareness of relativism.

It is likely that cognitive style and development, with its focus on intellectual tasks such as perceiving, thinking, and problem solving, is related to the developing sense of self, with its focus on feelings about self, impulses, aspirations, and relations with other people. Like cognitive development, ego development continues into adulthood, and some adults continue to evolve in their sense of self and their approach to decision making.

Early stages of ego development tend to be impulsive, self-protective, and conformist, characterized by dependence, opportunism, manipulation, belonging, and stereotyping. Some adults never outgrow these stages of character development and interpersonal style and so experience difficulty when dealing with learning activities that entail dealing with complex patterns of ideas and making clear distinctions between process and outcomes. Several more advanced stages in the evolving sense of self entail increased awareness of one's own standards, appreciation of relationships between the self and others, and concern for communication and collaboration to deal with problems, opportunities, motives, and achievement. Cognitive styles at these stages of ego development are characterized by multiple perspectives and complex patterns of ideas. People who achieve individualistic, autonomous, and integrated stages of ego development become more attentive to relations between feelings and action, respect for individuality, interdependence, causation, self-fulfillment, inner peace, and identity. Their cognitive styles are typically characterized by conceptual complexity, recognition of distinctions between process and outcomes, tolerance for ambiguity, broad perspective, and objectivity.

There is ample and growing evidence that ego development continues well into adulthood (Bandura, 1982; Block, 1981; Hentges, 1983; Lasker and Moore, 1980; Weathersby, 1981; Wortley and Amatea, 1982). Furthermore, views of education shift with increasing levels of development, from an emphasis on practical benefits and occupational advancement, through broadened uses for personal coping and growth, to an intrinsic valuing of lifelong learning for self-fulfillment and social concern (Houle, 1984).

You can use an understanding of developmental orienta-
tions of adults to select appropriate learning activities. For
example, prespecified objectives, packaged content and materials, and achievement testing, when they entail a passive learner
role, and an educator role as transmitter of knowledge and
judge of learner achievement may be comfortable for adults at a
conformist stage of development or lower. However, such procedures may be dysfunctional for adults who have progressed
to self-awareness or autonomous stages or beyond. For them,
more active and self-directed learner roles (self-assessment, contract learning, discussion, simulation) may be more appropriate.
Providing such options allows participants to select types of activities that seem best for them.

Learners prefer educational settings that fit their preferred learning style. However, in some instances the intent of
continuing education is to help adults make transitions to higher levels of personal and cognitive functioning. The challenge is
to help adults master an active process of praxis in which learners alternate between current proficiencies and a search for
higher levels of understanding and mastery (Daloz, 1986; Flavel,
1976; Ford, 1981; Heffernan, 1983; Kolb, 1984; Richards and
Perri, 1978). In such instances, teaching entails helping learners
process ideas more deeply, confront discrepancies between current and desired proficiencies, recognize differing perspectives,
examine assumptions and values, and consider higher-level reasoning. Such a transformation is more likely when adults gain a
broad view of themselves as learners with goals to pursue and
efficacy in the learning process. Their conviction that lifelong
learning is essential to a continuous process of becoming helps
them appreciate how their learning abilities (related to learning
strategies and personal attributes) combine with their learning
difficulties (related to content and task demands) to affect their
learning performance.

A general instructional goal is self-actualization of learners. You encourage actualization and growth toward "what can
be" when you take a holistic approach toward enhancing a
range of proficiencies related to various life roles, in contrast
with narrow skill training. Instructors' emphasis on creativity,
excellence, and self-directed learning enables learners to gain

mastery, self-esteem, and confident use of learning procedures (Connell, 1981; McAlindon, 1981; Rinke, 1985).

How do you think about such developmental transformations in your own instruction? Can your program contribute to longer-term participant goals such as career development, public leadership, or enrichment of family life? If so, progress seems more likely if you and the participants consider relations between program objectives and participant goals. Do you want to help participants progress to higher levels of understanding and problem solving? If so, explicit attention to learning how to learn may help.

A related aspect of personality is moral development. With age and experience, people expand moral judgments from a personal focus on their own needs and on demands from rules and people in authority to increasingly take other people into account: the group, the society, and finally all humanity. People vary in how fast and how far their moral development progresses. Those who achieve higher levels of moral development do so in part because of experience with adult choices and responsibilities. Such experience, and reflection about it, contributes to a commitment to principled justice that acknowledges various viewpoints and contexts. In this developmental process, a person can question assumptions and beliefs, and some people progress beyond problem solving to problem finding. In almost any content area, your teaching can assist adults with this type of transformation.

An understanding of learning style is useful in recognizing and selecting conditions under which adults with various characteristics are likely to learn effectively. In many instances this process entails matching educational activities to learning style. However, learning style evolves throughout life, and the effectiveness of learning strategies varies with the learning task. From adolescence through young adulthood, many people shift from *acquisition* of basic concepts and learning abilities to *specialization* (which is reflected both in the selection of an occupation and in the learning associated with that occupation) to *integration* in which ways of learning that were set aside during the earlier emphasis on specialization are now developed and combined with the dominant learning style to enhance career, life-style, and general creativity (Kolb, 1984; Schaie and Geiwitz, 1982).

In addition to these subtle shifts in learning style during adulthood, there are broad and sometimes dramatic changes in performance and personality that affect the learning activities in which adults engage. Understanding these developmental tasks can enable you to recognize emerging educational needs, select relevant materials, and encourage application of new learnings to improved role performance. Recognizing developmental tasks characteristic of each stage of adulthood can help explain the educational activities that adults voluntarily select (Darkenwald and Knox, 1984; Knox, 1979b; Okun, 1982; Snider and Houser, 1983). For the educational programs that employers provide for their employees, information about developmental tasks and work requirements can be combined to match organizational and individual needs (Schein, 1978).

Developmental tasks vary across the population, but for middle-class adults during the late teens and early twenties, typical developmental tasks include achieving emotional inde-pendence, developing an ethical system, preparing for marriage and family life, and choosing and preparing for an occupation. These concerns are reflected in the sizable enrollments of young people in educational activities related to work generally, career planning and preparation, assertiveness, personal development, consumer education, and human relations (Darkenwald and Knox, 1984).

Through the twenties and early thirties, the emphasis shifts to such tasks as starting a family, starting an occupation, managing a home, and assuming civic responsibilities. These de-velopmental tasks are reflected in enrollments in educational activities related to occupational advancement and specializa-tion, marriage and parenting, managing home finance, and vol-unteer leadership of youth groups.

Time perspectives change with the onset of middle age, and adults revise career plans and redefine family relationships. These developmental tasks are reflected in educational activities about career advancement, supervision, midcareer changes, parenting teenagers, relating to aging parents, marriage enrichment, and dealing with divorce (Knox, 1979b).

In middle adulthood, there is increasing attention to tasks associated with maintaining a career or developing a new one, restabilizing family relationships, making major civic contributions, and adjusting to biological change. Resulting educational activities include executive development, midcareer transition, human relations, social issues, stress management, and preparing for retirement.

Beyond retirement, there are tasks associated with adjusting to retirement, declining health, changing living arrangements, and the loss of loved ones. These concerns are reflected in educational activities related to finances, health, values, and leisure (Okun, 1982; Peterson, 1983).

How well do the foregoing generalizations fit your participants? If they are from families with average levels of formal education and above, the generalizations probably fit fairly well, because those are the adults most often studied. If not, what developmental tasks are most widespread and important for your participants? How could you use this information to increase program relevance?

Many continuing education activities are related to concurrent adult roles and responsibilities. This accumulating life experience both helps and hinders educational activity (Knox, 1985). It helps because such experience gives rise to the aspirations that motivate adults to participate and the current proficiencies on which they can build. It hinders because it creates competing time demands that can interfere with progress in educational activities. Examples include family health problems or major changes in work assignments that can cause adult learners to drop out or to interrupt their educational activity. Practitioners can provide responsive educational programs by being flexible in helping participants accommodate competing time demands (Brundage and Mackeracker, 1980).

Occasions for New Learning. Many adults experience major developmental changes from decade to decade. By contrast, from year to year, adult life is very stable as a result of personality, habit, role responsibilities, and other people's expectations.

However, this stability is periodically punctuated by role-change events. Examples related to occupation include starting a new type of work, job change, temporary unemployment, and retirement. Change events also occur in relation to family (marriage, children, loss of spouse) and other life roles (organizational leadership, move to new community). Such changes reflect both external influences and adults' own strivings.

Change events require adaptation, which produces teachable moments. These transitions trigger educative activity that may have been needed or desired for some time, because the change makes the discrepancy between current and desired proficiencies sufficiently apparent that the individual is ready to do something about it (Aslanian and Brickell, 1980).

In addition to widespread use of educational activities to adjust to external demands and to achieve educational objectives set by the situation, some adults use education to discover new objectives, to decide which proficiencies are desirable. Programs that seem interesting may be selected to explore what their topics actually entail. In such instances, the adult learner considers assumptions, alternatives, standards, implications, and influences related to desired proficiencies. For such purposes, the adult's aspirations become especially important. Practitioners with such a broad view of adult development help learners discover more important questions to pursue and problems to solve as well as resolve those they had earlier recognized (Argyris, 1982; Eble, 1983).

Responding to Learners' Diversity. As people grow older, they become both more similar and more different. They become more similar in that they confront more and more of the widespread dilemmas of society and in that their essential self becomes more apparent. They become more different in that their specialized circumstances, abilities, and experiences produce among all adults an increasing range of individual differences within each increasing age cohort (Knox, 1977).

Those who effectively help adults learn necessarily deal with this diversity. Because stereotypes about learners' backgrounds and interests tend to be quite inaccurate, effective practitioners find out about participants through such procedures as

conversations, registration forms, organization records, and the
initial sessions of an educational program. Recognition of pertinent individual differences can enable you to individualize materials, to provide alternative sections, and to encourage participants to share experiences and insights with other participants
who have common concerns. The typical result is more specialized educational activities, materials, and self-directed study
arrangements in an effort to maximize responsiveness and application. Sometimes, however, continuing education programs address common themes from diverse perspectives in an effort to
promote a more comprehensive sense of self for the individual or
greater solidarity for the organization. Humanistic approaches to
general education for adults address the former goal, and organization development activities concerned with communication,
conflict resolution, and team building address the latter.

Collaboration by school and university educators to provide in-service education for teachers illustrates uses of adult development concepts for helping adults learn (Knox, 1985;
Steitz, 1985; Warnat, 1980). A key concept is the transactional
and developmental nature of adult development in which personality and change events can combine to trigger motivational
energy and educative activity for teachers to assume responsibility for dealing with boredom, challenge, coping, problem solving, and especially overload and stress. If you conduct such in-
service programs, it would be helpful to understand and guide
self-directed learning activities focused on discrepancies between
current and desired proficiencies, in ways that enhance self-
concept and self-esteem.

If you were helping to conduct in-service sessions for
teachers on dealing with stress in classrooms, how might you
use concepts about adult development to recognize and accommodate individual differences? You might begin by recognizing
variations in the ways people deal with stress. Unlike reactive
approaches to stress reduction, proactive mastery approaches to
learning and problem solving under conditions of stress include
investing energy, using resources, interpreting and formulating
the problem, and responding constructively. Depending on optimal levels of stress for each participant, constructive responses
might emphasize managing stress, changing a stressful environ-

ment, analyzing one's situation to identify alternatives to avoid stress, and channeling excess energy into constructive activities that can reduce tension. A developmental perspective could help distinguish such variations.

Perhaps instead of just discussing stress and burnout, you could help the participants make decisions about learning activities, which might encourage them to persist and to apply what they learn. You might do so by having them use their own classrooms as living laboratories for learning and problem solving related to stress. Their familiarity with their work settings would enable them to consider their current performance and proficiency in relation to expectations of people in related roles, standards, resources, and likely reactions to proposed changes. You and other resource persons from school and university might contribute by providing participants with perspectives on what might be, clarifying discrepancies between what is and what ought to be, identifying useful learning resources, and facilitating progress in dealing with stress and gaining a more positive sense of self and optimism about this aspect of professional practice. A developmental perspective could help in planning activities for growth during and after the program.

Influences on Participation

One use of generalizations about proficiency and development is to increase initial and continued participation by adult learners in your program. What do you know about the reasons participants are in your program and the reasons some drop out? What appear to be some major influences on their participation? Is this an area of concern? If so, this section may contain some useful ideas.

In addition to generalized influences on educational activity, such as developmental trends and change events, there are some very specific influences on participation that reflect the adult's current outlook and major demands and constraints in the current situation. These influences are important to understand because they suggest how to encourage adults to participate and persist.

For example, in employers' education and training departments, trainers know that both organizational expectations (such as increased productivity) and individual aspirations (such as career advancement) influence the educational program. Organizational expectations for outcomes such as increased productivity, reduced costs, improved morale, or a pool of people prepared for promotion are usually translated into objectives that educational activities can achieve. Likewise, personal aspirations for advancement are translated into enhanced proficiencies that make promotion more likely and performance after promotion more effective. Of special interest to the instructor are learner motives that contribute to both learning and application. For education in the work setting, the instructor and work supervisor can consider multiple influences that affect an employee's performance, participation in educational activities, and application of what is learned.

A barrier to learning can be learner attitudes that the content is irrelevant. For work supervisors a way to reduce this barrier is use of quality circles that connect learning activities to higher-quality performance. A quality circle is a small group of employees doing similar work who voluntarily meet periodically on work time to discuss problems related to quality, explore causes, suggest solutions, and take corrective action. Supervisors help employees learn about communication, measurement, quality strategies, and problem analysis techniques. Motivation to learn comes from the intrinsic value of contributing to improvement plus released time and social interaction (Yager, 1980).

By contrast, a community college continuing education instructor might be interested in understanding influences on participation to better encourage enrollment and persistence. Human-interest stories about why similar adults enrolled and the benefits they gained can be persuasive to an adult who is undecided about whether to participate. Such information can also help instructors select relevant materials and examples. Findings from dropout studies can suggest ways to increase the persistence rate.

For almost any topic and setting, adults engage in educational activities for multiple reasons (Boshier and Collins, 1985).

Some reasons, such as upward social mobility or generalized dissatisfaction, may be subtle and diffuse but nonetheless powerful. Major reasons identified by adults in many programs include occupational advancement, content interest, compliance with external expectations, service to others, enjoyment of mental stimulation, and interaction with other participants. For an individual participant and a given topic, one of these reasons is likely to be paramount and several others also influential. Multiple motives are common. When many alternative activities are available, those for which there are multiple reasons are typically selected over those with only one reason, unless it is very powerful. Knowing widespread reasons that adults generally participate in educational activities can enable you to more readily identify why individual adults do so and to adjust program offerings accordingly.

Practitioners have found it useful to think about educational participation as the result of a combination of personal and situational facilitators and barriers. Most of these influences are filtered through the individual's subjective perception. A supervisor's suggestion that an educational program seems desirable may be regarded by one employee as an order and by another as an irrelevant whim. Salient personal influences include gender, intelligence, family social-class level, level of formal education, and role changes that produce a heightened readiness to learn (Fingeret, 1983; Havighurst and Orr, 1956). The personal characteristic most highly associated with extent of educative activity is level of formal education (Johnstone and Rivera, 1965; Anderson and Darkenwald, 1979). However, the extent of association is moderate and there are many other influences. Salient situational influences include awareness of opportunities, encouragement by other people, recognition of benefits from participation, and lack of obstacles such as distance or expense. Each variable can serve as a facilitator or as a barrier, depending on its extent of match with learner characteristics. For example, a high level of education is associated with much participation (as background, facility in learning, and benefits of doing so provide incentives, assistance, and rewards), whereas a low level of education is associated with less participation.

However, in some important respects, barriers are not just a lack of facilitators. For example, in contrast with well-educated and highly motivated volunteers for learning who look forward to educational achievement and beneficial use of new learnings, some nonparticipants experience personal, situational, informational, and institutional barriers that are not likely to be overcome by more attention to facilitators (Darkenwald and Larson, 1980; Darkenwald and Valentine, 1985b). However, once recognized barriers can sometimes be reduced. Personal barriers include physical ones such as poor vision or hearing and psychosocial ones such as extreme anxiety or fear of failure. Many adults with insufficient confidence as learners experienced numerous failures and few successes as students, so early success experiences in the program are especially important. Situational barriers include difficulties of transportation, competing role responsibilities, and active discouragement by other people. Information and encouragement for coping with such obstacles can be very helpful. Informational barriers, such as lack of information about relevant educational opportunities, procedures, and benefits, can be reduced by marketing efforts by continuing education providers. Institutional barriers, such as scheduling educational activities at inconvenient times and locations, can be reduced by more responsive arrangements.

Some of the foregoing influences on initial participation also affect persistence. Learners who are adversely affected by such influences tend to withdraw, physically or psychologically. The following list suggests what you can do to encourage persistence by participants as you and they become aware of such negative influences. (For more detail on the counseling function, see Chapter Eleven.)

- Those who have difficulty with educational procedures, such as studying, writing reports, or taking tests, might receive suggestions, materials, and assistance regarding study skills and other aspects of learning how to learn (Apps, 1978; Maxwell, 1979; Moore and Poppino, 1983; Walter and Siebert, 1982). In addition to what you can do as an instructor, participants who need more such help can be referred to specialists in the parent organization or the community.

- Those who are apprehensive, lack confidence as learners, or fear failure might be helped to achieve some early success experiences to increase their optimism and sense of mastery (Daloz, 1986; Hvitfeldt, 1986).
- Those who are uncertain about whether they are making satisfactory progress might benefit from more feedback and activities that enable them to assess their achievement (Brookfield, 1984).
- Those who encounter outside problems that affect their study, such as transportation or family difficulties, might be referred to people who can help them cope more effectively (DiSilvestro, 1981).

Encouraging Active Participation

How active or passive are the participants in your programs? Active learning takes many forms in which participants help clarify preferences, make choices, ask questions, seek answers, select activities, practice procedures, and give you feedback on their progress and satisfaction. How important is such active learning? How satisfactory is the extent of active participation in your program? What indications do you look for as you seek to maintain an optimal level of participant involvement?

Many adults prefer active roles as *users* of education instead of *recipients* of education. Even those who are apprehensive about assuming major responsibility for their learning appreciate options that allow them to select learning activities that fit their backgrounds and interests (Brockett, 1985; Kalamas, 1986a; Knowles, 1975). This preference for active involvement reflects their self-images as independent people, their natural inclination for informal learning, the importance of their active involvement for learning how to learn, and the major contribution of personal interest to lasting and pervasive learning.

An early way to be responsive to adults' preferences for active participation is to include them in the needs assessment and objective-setting process. You can do this by asking them their expectations and reasons for participation. Include attention to both what they want to accomplish and why. Only some of their expectations may match the purposes and contribution of your program, but it is useful for both you and the participants to recognize the expectations that match and those that do not. They will appreciate the relevance of the program objectives that you value to the extent to which those objectives relate to their purposes. Because trying to change can be threatening, helping to set goals can give participants a sense of security, ownership, and responsibility for their learning.

Learning activities provide prime opportunities for active participation. Assumption of major responsibility for the learning process facilitates learning. In addition, if you can minimize external threats (such as severe criticism from other people or dire consequences of trying and failing), it becomes easier for learners to explore and change. Helping adults relate their past experience to current learnings contributes to an active search for meaning and sharing with other participants. Performance provides a useful vehicle for learning many types of content. You can use performance (as instructors do in the arts, athletics, agriculture, and on-the-job training) by demonstrating, observing participants' performance, showing appreciation of their approaches, suggesting improvements, observing practice and progress, and providing further feedback and reinforcement. In group learning settings, participants can choose options and prepare plans for implementation. In most instances, active learning entails trying to clarify and reconstruct concepts and procedures.

Your efforts to encourage learning can be reflected in an educational setting conducive to learning that you help to create, as well as in your assistance to participants in dealing with general societal influences on their educational activities. It helps if you can organize content around themes relevant to problems and opportunities important to the learners. Varied learning activities are vehicles for inquiry, sequenced practice, and positive reinforcement (Anderson and Faust, 1973; Ausubel and Novack, 1978; Bigge, 1982; Burton, 1958; Wlodkowski, 1985a). You can pay special attention to participants with learning disabilities due to any cause, such as cultural deprivation, aging, or sensory handicaps (Anderson and Niemi, 1969;

Brown, 1982; Gray, 1981; Ostwald and Williams, 1985; Peterson, 1983). Awareness of possible learning disabilities can alert you to barriers that you may be able to reduce (Lean, 1983). For example, general trends toward increased introversion and excitability among older adults may have action implications for you if these trends characterize the older participants in your program. In addition, you can do something to reduce problems associated with declining vision and hearing by ensuring excellent illumination, large-scale visuals, and good acoustics.

Active learner involvement in evaluation is also important. In addition to participant cooperation that helps you with program evaluation, self-assessment helps learners become more independent, creative, and self-reliant in future self-directed learning activities. Your feedback can help them realize how their ability and effort contribute to their educational achievement.

Enabling participants to become more active learners can be a special problem when they have little formal education— and that, some years ago, when, as youngsters, they were expected to be passive. Rose Carmella confronted this problem as a community college developmental education instructor working with adults seeking to achieve a high school equivalency.

In spite of her initial efforts to get her high school equivalency learners involved, Rose was surprised at how much they resisted active participation. It seemed that many participants didn't know how to take responsibility for their own learning and feared failure in unfamiliar activities. As a start, Rose helped them select some problems they wanted to solve, such as filling out a job application form, reading a story to their children, or balancing a checkbook. She then helped each adult select relevant and interesting materials and activities where the chances of success were high.

Each participant had a folder in Rose's filing cabinet to keep these plans, materials, and evidence of achievement. Periodically, Rose talked with each person about questions, progress, materials, and plans. Self-assessments and Rose's evaluations were combined, as they discussed satisfaction and concerns regarding both the process and the results of learning. Gradually, many of the adults began to assume increased responsibility for their own learning. This pleased Rose, because one of her goals was to enable them to have the motivation and ability to do so after they completed her program.

Conclusion

This chapter highlighted many generalizations about adults as learners. Clearly, they do not fit neatly together and result in specific implications for practice. Then why bother? What might you do with any of these ideas?

Paradoxically, generalizations about adults as learners are useful not so much to guide your teaching as to guide your understanding of the individual participants in each program. *Effective teaching depends on being responsive to the learners in the program, not to adults in general.* Generalizations about adult development and learning suggest what information you might obtain about a participant's discrepancies between current and desirable proficiencies to help assess needs, encourage persistence, and facilitate application. As with other aspects of developmental interweaving of stability and change, insights about evolving proficiencies can help you and the learners themselves make decisions about educational goals and procedures.

The most valuable information you can obtain in order to help people learn something is what they already know about the subject. How do you do this in your program? Understanding discrepancies between current and desired proficiencies enables you and the participants to deal with diversity of backgrounds, assess readiness, clarify aspirations, and pursue their transformation to higher levels of learning and development. What gaps are important in your program? Understanding of adult life-cycle role performance and expectations of participants and people with whom they interact can be used to heighten interest, to provide relevant materials and examples, and to encourage application. To what extent do you do this? Familiarity with participants' preferred learning styles can be used to provide varied learning activities that enable them to select preferred methods and broaden the ways in which they learn effectively. What options do you provide? What ones could you add?

Appreciation of multiple influences on initial and continued participation can help you attract, retain, and assist a higher proportion of the adults that you seek to serve. You can build on positive personal characteristics and aspirations, as well as organizational expectations and societal images. You can at least partly counter some of the barriers to participation and persistence. Some of this counseling assistance, you can provide as a part of your instructional role; for some purposes referrals to specialized counselors will be preferable. Is enrollment and persistence a concern? If so, what influences on participation seem pertinent, and what might you do?

Throughout, a more fundamental understanding of adults as active learners can enable you to enhance their motivation, achievement, application, and continued inquiry. As you create supportive and challenging settings for adult learning that use performance as a vehicle for learning, and as you encourage sharing of insights among participants, if the adult learners are active partners in planning, conducting, and evaluating their learning activities, they can help individualize the process. Subsequent chapters explore concrete ways to do so.

THREE

How Instructors
Can Enhance Learning

There are many effective ways to help adults learn. The desired result is that participants will persist in effective learning activities in pursuit of worthwhile goals. Your willingness to share your content mastery with adults who seek it is one of the two major ingredients in your success; the instructional methods that constitute your teaching style are the other. For instructors whose aim is to empower participants with the desire and ability to guide their continued learning beyond the program, instructional mastery and style are intertwined components of the teaching/learning transaction.

How do you view your contribution as an instructor? How much of it seems to come naturally without making deliberate choices? If you were explaining your rationale for instruction to someone else, what would you emphasize? How important would your mastery of subject matter content be, and how does that emphasis affect the programs you conduct? What attention do you give to instructional procedures, and why? This chapter explores aspects of instructional roles to encourage you to consider how they fit together, before analyzing each aspect in more detail in the subsequent chapters.

Content Mastery

Your effectiveness in guiding the teaching/learning transaction can be greatly influenced by your content mastery. The phrase *content mastery* refers to all aspects of the proficiency to be acquired or enhanced by participants. These include knowledge, psychomotor skills, and attitudes.

Desirable levels of content mastery by an instructor depend in part on how much proficiency the participants have when they enter the educational activity. For example, if participants enter with very little proficiency and do not expect to go beyond an introductory level, it may be unnecessary and even undesirable for the instructor to have a very high level of content mastery. A too-expert instructor may tend to introduce very advanced topics that may be interesting to the instructor but beyond the participants. However, it is essential that the instructor have substantial mastery of the content with which the participants will be dealing so as to be able to diagnose participants' current proficiencies, emphasize fundamental concepts and procedures, and begin with learning tasks that are most important early. By contrast, when at least some participants enter with fairly high levels of proficiency, although they can make some instructional contributions to aid less knowledgeable participants, they expect the instructor to be more proficient than they are, in part as a source of challenging learning activities (Eble, 1976; Gullette, 1982; Lowman, 1984; Miller, 1964).

High-level content mastery by teachers of adults is very desirable for several reasons.

1. Content mastery allows instructors to focus on important aspects and to avoid trivial ones. Many topics adults seek to learn about are complex because of detailed procedures or relationships, major value questions, and variations due to specific contingencies. An instructor with inadequate content mastery may be unable to clarify fundamental aspects and provide a sequence of challenging learning activities.

2. Some aspects of facilitating learning about a content area are specific to that content—for example, raising helpful substantive questions and selecting useful methods of learning. Consider the distinctive contributions of content mastery by instructors in welding, music appreciation, or world affairs. Performance skill seems important to demonstrate welding. The music appreciation instructor's content mastery helps participants enrich their enjoyment through greater appreciation of

the structure of music. The world affairs specialist, though seldom a world leader, should be someone who can illuminate the
complexities of foreign policy issues.

3. Teachers typically want to provide participants with
standards against which to compare their own proficiencies.
This may occur through modeling by the instructor or by selecting people or materials that provide such standards. A high level
of content mastery is sometimes necessary to judge and provide
such standards.

4. A major and often recognized benefit of content mastery is the freedom it gives instructors to be flexible and responsive to adult learners. A teacher who is scarcely more proficient
than the participants typically plans learning activities that
occur in the narrow margin between his or her proficiency and
theirs. By contrast, a very proficient instructor may be able to
respond to unanticipated questions and directions of inquiry
and to encourage learners to pursue their varied interests related
to the content. The instructor does this with helpful answers,
information about useful resources, and suggestions about problem-solving strategies.

5. Educational objectives constitute an implicit intent to
change. The type of change expected may be quite specific and
well recognized by most participants (as in many occupationally
related educational programs) or may be quite diffuse and implicit (as in adult basic education or liberal education for
adults). However, in most instances value judgments are included in the hoped-for changes, from the perspective of participants, educators, and the larger society. An instructor with a
high level of content mastery should appreciate the implications
and value judgments associated with the educational objectives
and thus be able to help participants recognize and deal with
them as well (Apps, 1981; Cross, 1976; Eble, 1983; Langerman,
1974; Rogers, 1971).

How would you characterize your level of content mastery? How does that level compare with the proficiency levels of
the participants? Do you use your content mastery in any of
the foregoing five ways? To the extent that you do so, how
much does this contribute to program success? Are you inter-

ested in increasing your content mastery or using it differently in your instruction? If so, how might you do so? In addition to reading and workshops, consider observations and conversations with outstanding instructors who use their content mastery effectively to help adults learn.

Components of Teaching Style

Your teaching style consists of the characteristic ways in which you help adults learn. Your main contribution is to encourage participants to make useful decisions about their learning activities (Joyce and Weil, 1972; Lenz, 1982; Milton and Associates, 1978; Robinson, 1979; Travers, 1973). This requires a match between your encouragement and assistance and the participants' decisions and learning activities. Teaching tends to be quite intuitive and implicit, largely reflecting the instructor's personal qualities and habits. This section suggests ways to make your teaching style more explicit so that you can more easily share instructional decision making with the participants and learn from and improve with your experience in helping adults learn. As you make explicit the "why" as well as the "how" of your instruction, this rationale can guide your instructional decisions as well as your efforts to improve.

Your teaching is more likely to be satisfying for you and the participants if you are confident in and comfortable with your teaching style. However, helping adults learn is difficult as well as satisfying, and you are likely to become even more effective if you reflect on your characteristic teaching style to identify aspects that might be strengthened. This section contains an overview of procedures that effective instructors of adults have found useful. (In a sense, the entire book consists of more detailed suggestions for effective teaching, but this section emphasizes ways to interact with learners. That interaction includes your efforts to match participants' characteristic learning styles with the most valuable contributions you can make.)

Responsiveness. As indicated in the previous chapter, many characteristics of adults as learners have implications for helping them learn. Some characteristics are especially pertinent

to needs assessment or program planning generally. The following summary emphasizes characteristics likely to have implications for your teaching style and ways in which you can be responsive to those characteristics.

Respect. Participants want respect for themselves as
adults. Regard for them as people with something to
offer contributes to their sense of stability, worth,
and confidence. Responsive teaching styles are supportive and encourage participants to be resources for
the learning of others as well as active agents of their
own learning.

Reasons. Adults have multiple reasons for participation,
and the reasons that are especially important will vary
greatly among your participants. Typically participants' current proficiencies also vary greatly (although
dissatisfaction with current proficiencies may be widespread). Responsive teaching styles accommodate participant needs and expectations that fit program purposes, let participants know early where their reasons
and program purposes match, and help them seek resources and assistance to meet needs that some learners may want to pursue beyond your program.

Options. Adults vary in ways other than confidence and
reasons for participation. Included are experience, ability, and resources. Responsive teaching styles will help
participants understand their characteristics related to
learning and will provide options for individuals as well
as the group. Self-assessments of preferred learning
style help adults to select learning strategies that they
prefer and to broaden their repertoire. Summary information about variations in learning style, ability, experience, and access to resources can enable you to provide
options that are responsive to such individual differences.

Proficiencies. Information about adults' current proficiencies related to program objectives is especially valuable. Responsive instructors use such information in se-

lecting examples, concepts, and procedures likely to be helpful to the participants at their current stage of development.

As you seek to be responsive to adult learners, to what extent do you consider characteristics such as these four? How does this affect your teaching style? Does it seem desirable to increase your responsiveness in any way? If so, how might you do so?

Procedures. Your answers to the following questions about your typical ways of helping adults learn will characterize your teaching style. The comments following each question suggest desirable ways to handle that aspect of teaching style. Later sections of the book deal with each aspect in greater detail. Aspects for which there are substantial discrepancies between your current practice and suggested approaches indicate topics that may be of special interest to you; readings and professional development efforts can help you reflect on the assumptions and beliefs that constitute an implicit rationale for your instructional decisions.

1. *Presentation.* What emphasis do you give to presenting content and your ideas? Most teachers spend more time presenting content than they realize. Does the balance between your presentations and more active learner involvement seem satisfactory as reflected in participant feedback and your instructional goals? If not, what might you do to achieve a better balance?

2. *Active learning.* What opportunities do you provide for participants to engage in active learning, such as discussion, practice, and problem solving? Teachers encourage active learning by raising questions that participants can discuss individually or in small groups and by providing opportunities for learners to explore or practice the concepts or procedures they seek to master.

3. *Meanings.* How do you assist learners in their search for meaning related to the topic of your program? It is important that participants discover and remember the important

meanings that the content has for them, as well as the images and words. Doing so helps them establish the validity
of new concepts and procedures, understand relationships,
and remember what they learned.

4. *Variety.* How varied are the methods you use? An optimal
    variety fits the requirements of the objectives and content
    and prevents boredom for participants. What other meth-
    ods might you add?

5. *Stages of the program.* How does your role shift from the
    beginning through the middle and end of your program? As
    participants enter your program, first impressions should
    emphasize an accepting but challenging climate. During the
    middle part of the program, a sequence of activities should
    be provided that help participants progress and persist.
    Toward the conclusion, greater emphasis should be given to
    understanding the context in which application will occur.
    As your program proceeds, how satisfactory are the ad-
    justments you make?

6. *Affective and cognitive elements.* In what ways do you at-
    tend to both cognitive and affective educational objectives
    and aspects of your role? Cognitive aspects include intel-
    lectual content and well-prepared and well-organized pro-
    cedures. Affective aspects include attitudes, feelings, and
    emotions (Gladis, 1985).

7. *Interpersonal relations.* How much and what type of at-
    tention do you give to interpersonal relations with and
    among participants? Instructors can take into account
    typical cognitive styles and other participant characteris-
    tics to encourage friendly and supportive interpersonal
    relations.

8. *Past and future.* How do you help participants relate con-
    tent to their current proficiencies and to the applications
    they intend? How important are such past and future rela-
    tionships for your participants? If they are important,
    finding out participants' current proficiencies and intended
    applications can enable you to increase relevance.

9. *Purposes.* How do you discover and respond to the rea-

sons that participants enrolled? Needs assessment and inclusion of participants in objective setting are ways to do so.

10. *Support and challenge.* How do you combine an informal and supportive climate for learning with content and procedures that are sufficiently challenging and demanding that achievement and satisfaction occur? You can give attention to both throughout the program, and most participants appreciate the combination.

11. *Models.* How do you provide models and examples of the proficiencies you hope participants will acquire? In addition to serving as a role model and demonstrator by letting participants know you and how you think and perform, you can arrange for other people and resources to be available.

12. *Self-direction for learners.* What attention do you give to helping participants learn how to learn, explore, and assume responsibility for direction of their learning activities? Most instructors want participants to be interested in learning and able to learn fairly independently after the program. What assistance do you provide to make this likely?

13. *Confidence among learners.* How do you help participants become more confident in their roles as learners? A strengthened sense of educational efficacy can motivate adults to venture and accept the risk entailed in trying to learn and change. Success experiences from mastery of increasingly difficult tasks can increase self-confidence.

14. *Feedback.* How do you provide for feedback to learners? Effective feedback provides encouragement and direction. Questions and answers can be used for feedback that encourages further questions and answers.

15. *Flexibility.* How flexible are you and your plans and procedures to adapt to opportunities or problems that arise? Plans can be made to accommodate unexpected developments, as by including uncommitted time to allow last-minute scheduling of people and topics that arise.

In addition to discovering additional instructional procedures to use, reflecting on these questions can help you clarify why you make the instructional decisions you do. When you recognize practices that do not fit your educational values, you may select other practices that do.

Interaction of Learner Characteristics and Teaching Style. The foregoing list of questions may give the false impression that your concern with teaching style should be restricted to your performance. This narrow view would ignore the dynamic features of the teaching/learning transaction. Rather, in assessing your teaching style, it is desirable to take into account learner characteristics, content, educational goals, and the surrounding context, especially as it is likely to affect learners' application efforts.

To illustrate how you might consider learner characteristics when you assess the appropriateness and effectiveness of your teaching style, there are various ways in which you might mix and match your teaching style and the participants' preferred learning styles (Beder and Darkenwald, 1982; Brophy and Evertson, 1976; Conti, 1985a, 1985b; Gorham, 1985b). The most desirable approach is a combination of the following three strategies, depending on the objectives and circumstances (Messick and Associates, 1976). Each strategy assumes that you have estimated participants' preferred learning styles and that you seek to respond to a category of participants with similar learning styles.

One strategy is *correction.* You use your assessment of learning styles to identify weaknesses and then help participants to strengthen inadequate learning procedures. For example, if some participants don't read well and you believe they avoid reading (even though it is important for achievement of program goals), use remedial procedures to strengthen vocabulary, along with materials to increase reading speed and comprehension. You might also challenge them to improve their reading and reward them when they do.

Another strategy is *compensation.* You use the assessment results about learning-style weaknesses, to avoid them. You might do so because you conclude that the time and effort required for remediation cannot be justified given a short program, low participant interest in reading improvement, and different but very important objectives that are not very compatible with remedial reading. Therefore, you provide or use methods and materials that deemphasize reading for participants with this weakness in their learning style.

A third category is *capitalization.* You assess learning style to identify strengths and then build on them by using methods and materials with which participants learn best. This entails providing varied materials to allow participants to select those best suited to their learning styles. You can enable participants to do so by helping them discover the ways in which they learn best.

As indicated earlier, you can use a combination of strategies. For instance, you can use a compensatory strategy for sessions for the total group, a capitalization strategy in the learning activities for which participants can select preferred sessions or materials, and a corrective strategy for participants whose learning-style weaknesses interfere with achieving their objectives and who want to correct those weaknesses.

Alliances. In your own instruction, do you consider relationships between your role, style, and assistance, on the one hand, and the participants' needs, styles, and aspirations, on the other? Various relationships between instructor and learner roles have been termed "alliances." As indicated briefly earlier, and as discussed in more detail later in the book, many quite different alliances can be established between teachers and learners (Epperson, 1974). The alliances vary in the needs that are emphasized (ignorance, incompetence, inner conflict), the resources that are especially helpful (knowledge, skills, insight), and the philosophical perspective on human development (rational humanism, progressivism, humanistic psychology). Each alliance is an effort to match learner needs and instructor assistance, through a distinctive relationship between instructor and learner roles.

Useful considerations in the matching process include types and quality of general intended program goals and outcomes, types and scope of learner needs to be addressed, priorities set by the parent organization or other sources external to the teaching/learning transaction, clarity and scope of specific educational objectives, and logistical demands and constraints. Considering such influences in an individual instance can reassure you that your intended alliance is likely to enable you to provide what learners need and what the situation will allow—or that you can select another alliance that is more likely to do so.

For example, you may assume from past experience with management development programs that it is appropriate to use an alliance between instructors and learners to provide knowledge of supervisory concepts and procedures. However, as you discover that the potential participants have less experience and face different circumstances than their predecessors, you may decide that an alliance that gives far more attention to participants' feelings about their new supervisory roles is more appropriate. As a result, instead of being a presenter of concepts and examples that participants are prepared for and able to apply, your most appropriate role may be as a facilitator of discovery learning through role playing and discussion.

It seems useful to think about the process of matching learning styles and needs with teaching styles and assistance as a series of provisional choices. The choices can occur at the program or at the session level. Examples of program-level choices that program coordinators might make include a lecture series, a workshop, and on-the-job training. Once begun, such choices are more difficult to change than an instructor's selection of an alliance for a session or two.

In seeking a satisfactory match, you should recognize your own characteristics as a teacher as well as the participants'. Your pertinent characteristics include aspects of personality and attitudes as well as your areas of expertise and content mastery. For example, personality characteristics often identified as characteristics of effective teachers of adults include enthusiasm, humor, cultural awareness, clarity of explanation, and memorable comments (Eble, 1983; Wlodkowski, 1985a). Some of these characteristics are central to differing teaching styles. For instance, enthusiasm is a central feature of a flamboyant style, while clarity of explanation is a central feature of an organized style (Solomon, Bezdek, and Rosenberg, 1963).

Some personal attitudes and habits related to teaching are also likely to influence your style. One of the most influential is your willingness to devote the time and effort required to prepare for use of methods that enlarge the ways you can help adults learn (Chickering and Associates, 1981; Jain, 1981; McLagan, 1978). Diversity of methods increases your flexibility and responsiveness to participants' needs and preferences. Other personal attitudes and habits likely to influence your teaching style include your appreciation of the importance of encouraging learner persistence until mastery and of using methods that encourage application and use of what is learned, along with your recognition of how influential you are on the meanings that learners extract from their educational experiences and on their use of what they learn. They respond to your style, character, and interpersonal relations. Although teaching is a helping profession, most teachers could be more helpful than they are. Attention to the match between teaching style and learning style is one step in that direction.

The concept of teaching style extends beyond the extent of organization or flamboyance in presentations and discussion (Brockett, 1983; Conti, 1985b). For example, in university professional education, style may include elaborate simulations to enhance problem-solving capability (Barrows and Tamblyn, 1980). The following example comes from problem-based medical education. Its essential features can be adapted to most areas of continuing professional education or other areas in which helping adults master high levels of problem-solving proficiency is important enough to warrant the preparation entailed.

In problem-based medical education, learners who want to master diagnosis and patient management for a particular health problem begin with reading about pertinent clinical practice and related medical science topics. A number of participants engage in the learning activities (to justify the preparation time), but they do so individually. A carefully coached person simulates a selected set of symptoms, and each participant seeks to diag-

nose them in a videotaped interview and examination, which culminate in a diagnosis and a prescrip-
tion for a plan of action. Computer-simulated lab
tests and other pertinent information can be obtained as part of the diagnostic process.

The participant then views a prepared videotape in which the same simulated patient with the
same set of presenting symptoms is examined by
an expert diagnostician. Participants can then view
their own videotapes and compare their strategies
and conclusions with those of the expert in this
specialty. For important discrepancies, particular
readings or clinical experiences are recommended,
after which the participant examines another simulated patient with a different set of presenting
symptoms related to the same general type of
health problem. After each examination, the simulated patient can comment on interpersonal relations from a patient's perspective, which is so important for diagnosis, compliance, and patient
education.

Throughout this process, the underlying intent is to upgrade the learner's problem solving, using standards, practice,
and feedback combined in ways designed to improve actual
practice, not just to increase knowledge. In such an instance,
your teaching style includes your orchestration of all types of
learning activities included (even provision for small groups of
participants to discuss the problem-solving process), even
though you may never make an oral presentation or lead a discussion.

Conclusions

This chapter highlighted several aspects of your instructor role, which will be analyzed in more detail in subsequent
chapters. How useful are such concepts as content mastery and
teaching style? As broad concepts, they can help you interrelate

many specific ideas about participants, content, yourself, and instructional procedures.

Your contribution to helping adults learn reflects your content mastery and general teaching style as well as specific procedures in interacting with adult learners. Content mastery allows you to be flexible and responsive as you focus on matters important to the content and the participants; it also enables you to emphasize pertinent standards and help participants deal with underlying value judgments. Responsive instructors show respect for participants by providing options suited to their current proficiencies, multiple purposes, and preferred learning styles.

Although there are great variations in teaching style, effective instructors tend to undergird their specific procedures with some fundamental ideas about helping adults learn. Included are the beliefs that constitute your rationale for selection of methods and procedures. Varied methods provide opportunities for active learning, which requires restricting time devoted to instructor presentations. Helping participants relate cognitive and affective content to their past proficiencies and intended applications contributes to their search for meaning. Supportive interpersonal relations allow use of challenging standards, models, and examples. Flexible selection of a progressive sequence of objectives, activities, and feedback can increase participants' confidence and ability to guide their own learning. Instructor characteristics such as style and character interact with particular instructional procedures to produce effective teaching/learning transactions. Mixing and matching teaching and learning styles can contribute to effective current learning outcomes as well as enable participants to learn even more effectively in the future.

FOUR

Assessing Learner Needs and Setting Program Objectives

When you are planning an educational program for adults, where do you start? The starting point could be intended outcomes, learning activities, educational needs, organizational expectations, or evaluation results the last time the program occurred. It doesn't make much difference as long as you touch on all of them early, because they are so interrelated.

What do you have to go on when you begin to consider each of these planning components? As you decide, what ideas and evidence do you include beyond your own assumptions and beliefs? How do you decide when it is important to go beyond your own experience and ideas to obtain additional opinions and facts? What other people do you involve in the planning process? Why? For each program, how do you decide how much planning to do? How do you distinguish between planning and doing?

In the process of helping adults learn, program planning and implementation should blend together. As you are planning a program (course, workshop, coaching session), it is desirable to use impressions, evaluations, and materials from similar ones in the past with special attention to what worked well and what could have been improved. If resource persons will assist with the program, it is desirable to involve them in the planning process to have the benefit of their ideas and their commitment to a coordinated effort. As the program proceeds, it is desirable to have planned for likely contingencies, so you can be flexible and responsive by selecting ideas, methods, and materials that best fit the unfolding flow of the program (Becker, 1980; Bell and Putnam, 1979; Bowren and Zintz, 1977; Caffarella, 1985; Carnarius, 1981; Houle, 1972; Knowles, 1980; Knox and Associates, 1980; Nadler, 1982; Sork and Buskey, 1986; Torrence, 1985; Wedemeyer, 1981).

This chapter and the next together cover program planning; the following one, materials. They emphasize the preparation and planning you do before the program begins. The subsequent four chapters emphasize implementation during the program, including engaging the learner, the teaching/learning transaction, program evaluation, and ways to encourage and support participants' efforts to apply what they learn.

The major sections of this chapter are needs assessment, context analysis, and objective setting. The next chapter covers learning activities and related arrangements. These two chapters explore interrelated components that in best practice are outlined in a preliminary way and then progressively refined so they fit together. However, those components are described separately in these two chapters to suggest some of the options you might consider in a given instance and to provide examples from practice. Experienced instructors can use these chapters as a checklist of concepts and practices to consider when refining an instructional plan.

Needs Assessment

How do you usually decide on the educational needs your program will address? How formal or informal is the process, and how satisfied are you with it? To what extent do participants help assess their own educational needs? Why? Do you distinguish between educational needs and other needs? How dependent are you on your own assumptions and beliefs?

Practitioners make assumptions about learners' educational needs based on their experiences as teachers and learners. Effective practitioners use their familiarity with content and learners (including the context in which learners will apply what they learn) to decide which assumptions seem warranted in a particular instance and which should be explored through for-

mal needs assessment procedures (Scherer, 1984). Formalizing
the process is especially important when you plan to work with
a type of learner with whom you have not previously worked.

Adults may be unaware of some of their educational
needs, which may be implicit in their attitudes and choices, and
may be aware of other educational needs, which they can state
explicitly in response to your questions. You will find it helpful
to use needs assessment procedures to confirm and discover
both implicit and explicit needs important to adult learners
(Kopp, 1986a; Pennington, 1980). This section suggests why
needs assessment can strengthen your planning to help adults
learn, lists some concepts and procedures you can use, and indicates how you can use the findings to improve your teaching.
As you read this section, note desirable changes in your needs
assessment procedures.

Reasons for Needs Assessment. Familiarity with concepts
and use of procedures in continuing education needs assessment
can help in several ways.

- A checklist can help you easily review your assumptions
  about potential participants' educational needs. If the assumptions seem sound, you can proceed with assurance. If
  not, you can decide how much and what type of formal
  needs assessment is warranted.
- Information about educational needs can help you select
  topics, materials, and examples so that the program is responsive to the participants.
- Descriptions of your program that emphasize its responsiveness to the major educational needs of potential participants
  will increase the likelihood that they will participate.
- The program focus on meeting learner needs will encourage
  participants to persist, learn, and apply what they learn.

What other benefits of needs assessment have you discovered? Which reasons for needs assessment are most important to
you? As you review the following concepts and procedures, pay
special attention to those that are desirable and feasible given
your purposes and resources.

Concepts in Needs Assessment. It is useful to think of educational needs as gaps between current and desired proficiencies. Beyond the evident benefit from awareness of typical educational needs among the program clientele, you usually want to clarify the specific educational needs of your participants. This contributes to their motivation and responsibility for learning as well as to the decisions you make.

The learners themselves are the sources of two major kinds of information about educational needs: information about their stated *preferences* for the topics they want to study and the proficiencies they want to enhance and about the *choices* they make when given opportunities to participate in educative activities. Two other kinds of information come from other people (teachers, supervisors, experts) who identify unsatisfactory proficiencies by comparing potential participants with adults generally or with the expert's standards of desirability. In all four approaches to needs assessment, adults' current proficiencies are compared against standards of desirable proficiencies to identify discrepancies, or gaps, to be closed. In the first two approaches the learner makes that judgment, while in the latter two the judgment is made by other people. In all instances you can arrange for relevant information to be considered and useful judgments made. Usually judgments about educational needs are most valid when multiple sources are used so that both the adult learners and other people contribute.

Formalizing needs assessment procedures contributes to agreement among learners, yourself, and other people associated with the educational program about the needs on which to focus (Franco, 1985). As the program is planned and conducted, participants meet some needs and discover others, and perspectives shift regarding the pertinence and importance of needs. Therefore, needs assessment should be an ongoing process, consisting in evaluation for purposes of planning. Plans for needs assessment should include attention to who requires further information about needs, what those persons want to know, how beneficial such information is likely to be, how much and what type of information is warranted, and what should be done to encourage use of findings.

Procedures and Uses. Many writings about planning and conducting continuing education activities include needs assessment procedures as an important component. Some procedures are large-scale and enable program administrators to decide whom to serve and what programs (courses, workshops, on-the-job training) to offer. By contrast, instructors appreciate small-scale procedures that help them decide which topics are most important for individual learners, the learners' current proficiencies, the standards or expectations that constitute their desired proficiencies, and the relative priority of various needs (Birnbrauer and Tyson, 1985). Following are some of the major needs assessment procedures, with indications of how you and learners could use the findings.

- Observing and analyzing performance and tasks to clarify discrepancies between current and desired proficiencies. (Task analysis, familiar in work settings, also occurs when the focus is on homemaking, recreational, or leadership activities.)
- Discussing findings of performance review with learners to agree on educational objectives to which all those associated with the review are committed.
- Reviewing organizational records for evidence of adequacy of performance and proficiency, which has implications for unmet educational needs. (Examples of such evidence from systems analysis include audit findings; records on productivity, attrition, absenteeism, errors, accidents, and dissatisfaction; and recognition for outstanding performance.)
- Obtaining opinions of experts and people in helping roles to identify needs they perceive as widespread among participants.
- Using standards of achievable best practice (such as examples, role models, and formal standards) to help you and learners agree on desired proficiencies.
- Administering instruments to assess current knowledge, skills, and attitudes. (Examples include achievement tests, exams, self-assessment inventories, interest checklists, observation guides, and projective tests such as sentence completion.)

- Comparing responses to voluntary program offerings as a basis for estimating responses to similar future offerings.
- Discussing alternative topics with participants to identify widespread interests.
- Reviewing past provider experience with teaching similar adults and topics to project likely future trends.
- Surveying organizational or community opinions to identify additional clienteles and needs.
- Considering new developments and trends that are likely to create educational needs. (Examples include new technology and equipment, changing laws and expectations, and shifting relations among organizations, communities, and nations.)
- Reading about adult development and learning to recognize pertinent characteristics of similar adults that suggest likely needs of participants.
- Reading professional literature about trends, issues, and procedures to suggest possible unmet needs.

The wide variety of methods for educational needs assessment makes it difficult to choose those that are best in a particular instance. Newstrom and Lilyquist (1979) provide a rationale for such decisions, especially in work settings. The methods they review include advisory committees, assessment centers, attitude surveys, group discussions, interviews with potential participants, management requests, observations of behavior, performance appraisals, organizational records, questionnaires, and proficiency tests. Although such methods are described for use in deciding which programs to offer, they can be used on a modest scale to help you decide which topics to emphasize in your program.

Newstrom and Lilyquist present a contingency model that includes four criteria for selecting a combination of methods:

> *Learner involvement.* Including potential participants in assessment of their own educational needs will provide them with insights about their strengths and weaknesses that can motivate them to engage in learning activities to meet their needs.

Organizational commitment. Including supervisors and
other people from the organizational settings where
participants' needs occur and where they might apply
what they learn will enable the supervisors to share valuable insights about participant needs and will encourage the supervisors to support both the educational activities and application of enhanced proficiencies.

Time and cost required. Instructors want needs assessment procedures which are efficient of their time and
expense as well as the learners' and which produce conclusions worth the needs assessment effort.

Relevance and quantifiability. You and other people who
make program decisions usually want to base conclusions on information that is reasonably objective and
relevant to the decision to be made so that estimates
are valid.

In addition, the combination of methods selected should
complement one another. This occurs when perspectives of
both experts and potential participants are included and when
the strengths of one method compensate for the weaknesses of
another, such as participant opinions combined with organizational records (Schein, 1978).

Another approach to selection of procedures
for gathering information about educational needs
occurred when Dorothy Olsson prepared to conduct her first adult religious education class after
years as a participant. Informal conversations with
congregation members identified some topics of
widespread interest, but Dorothy felt that those
topics might have reflected familiarity with past
programs. A religious education conference provided a convenient opportunity to get opinions
from two additional sources. Conference speakers
and planners identified some emerging trends and
issues likely to kindle enthusiasm. Experienced instructors from similar congregations told Dorothy

about topics and discussion materials that had generated a large and spirited response. Dorothy selected a program topic mentioned by peers and leaders at the conference as well as by members of her congregation who seemed likely to participate.

Analysis and Use of Findings. Having such an array of procedures for collecting data about educational needs is very helpful, but it is only part of the process of needs assessment. Other major parts are selecting data-collection procedures to use, analyzing the data to specify needs, using the findings to plan and modify learning activities, and involving in the needs assessment process people who should use the findings so as to increase the likelihood that they will do so.

Criteria for choosing data-collection procedures include appropriateness to the topics and clientele, efficiency so that the benefits exceed the effort, and involvement so that use of findings is encouraged. Most needs assessments use fairly basic research and evaluation procedures for data collection and analysis (Grotelueschen, 1980). Such procedures include questionnaires, tests, interview guides, observation checklists, and guidelines for content analysis of materials or summary of information from records. Data analysis includes both summary of information and making judgments and conclusions based on comparisons of data summaries in relation to the objectives of the particular needs assessment. Basic procedures for summary of quantitative data include frequency distributions, contingency tables for cross-tabulations, computing percentages, and indications of association between two or more variables (such as a correlation coefficient). Basic procedures for summary of qualitative data include inductive classifications of common themes from open-ended responses and content analysis. Fortunately, most continuing education providers have materials for and people with expertise in such data-collection and data-analysis procedures to help with needs assessments.

By contrast, your effectiveness in involving learners, resource persons, and coordinators in the needs assessment process and in encouraging them to use the findings for program planning and improvement will depend on your understanding and use of concepts related to this interpersonal aspect of needs assessment. The following concepts can enable you to conduct focused needs assessments that strengthen your efforts to help adults learn.

The relative importance of the educational needs identified tends to be judged in light of expectations of learners, yourself, and representatives of organizations. It is the participants in your program who learn, and the needs that will mainly influence their learning activities are those that pertain to proficiencies *they* want to enhance. Thus their involvement in the needs assessment process is important both for their motivation to change and for their decisions about their ongoing learning activities. Specification of current proficiencies helps both learners and instructors recognize the extent to which learners already have prerequisite abilities. For many educational objectives regarding leisure, family, and citizen roles, learners' perceptions of their own needs are the main basis for educative activity.

In some work, organizational, and community roles, however, other people's expectations are also important. For example, expectations about quality standards held by supervisors and recipients of service are clearly relevant to the assessment of educational needs of physicians and pilots. Accountability requirements result in multiple expectations—for example, in deciding which needs not to respond to and which should receive high priority. Organizations sometimes tend to identify educational needs as deficiencies when performance does not measure up to standards. A positive emphasis on growth to achieve desired proficiencies is preferable because it increases motivation and decreases defensiveness associated with participating in a program for people who are deficient. In addition, you can extend the needs assessment process beyond acquisition of technical knowledge and interpersonal effectiveness to fit in with existing organizational and societal expectations, by exploring needs to challenge such expectations and values, sometimes in order to help learners become emancipated from inequitable or inhumane restrictions and to renegotiate more mutually desirable goals and relationships.

When you help adults enhance their proficiencies in applied performance areas such as work or recreation, it is important to focus on the source of the problem, not just symptoms. One type of needs assessment that can help you do so begins with functional analysis of high-frequency tasks that are critical to successful performance. Among the ways to identify critical proficiency areas are observations of and interviews with beginners, suggestions by supervisors and experts, and conclusions from research studies and literature reviews. Within each proficiency area, you can then describe specific proficiencies and indicate how they contribute to successful performance (Zemke, 1982).

Obtaining information from several sources (triangulation) helps to identify various levels of expertness for important proficiencies. For occupations in which tasks are relatively complex, such as managerial and professional occupations, the proficiencies may be fairly abstract. A survey of managers' educational needs found that communication abilities were the most widespread needs, followed by control and leadership. In that instance it was decided that the educational activities should be highly individualized (Thomas and Sireno, 1980). By contrast, in less complex occupations a skills audit can specify minimum levels required for more concrete tasks, to help employees and their supervisors recognize deficiencies as a basis for remedy and excesses as a basis for advancement (Jons, 1980).

Especially in work settings, needs assessment can include a mastery model against which to assess discrepancies in relation to current proficiencies. Barr (1980) reports an example from newly appointed first-line supervisors in the Bell system. Their approach included relative weights for the importance of remedying discrepancies for major generic supervisory tasks. In declining order of importance, those tasks were planning, controlling, problem solving, performance feedback, coaching, motivating, time management, oral communication, self-development, written communication, career counseling, and conducting meetings. The development of the mastery model included comparing highly proficient, experienced supervisors with those who were newly appointed on performance, task complexity, frequency, time, key decision points, and deficien-

cies noted. Based on the model, a diagnostic test was prepared
to assess need for targeted educational activities and materials.

Sometimes educational needs assessment can be combined with other activities such as personnel selection and development. This is illustrated by the assessment center technique
(Byham, 1980). This technique is typically used to identify the
potential of first-level supervisors for advancement to middle
management positions, especially those that include unfamiliar
areas of work. Usually the technique entails several days of
varied assessment and learning activities, such as business games,
in-basket exercises, self-assessments, discussion groups, and
(especially) interview simulations. Such activities enable participants to demonstrate their skill at management tasks and to receive feedback useful for selection and development.

The assessors are usually middle managers, several levels
removed from the supervisors being assessed. This position contributes to assessors' familiarity with the supervisor's roles and
to top management's acceptance of the technique. Assessors
benefit educationally as they develop interviewing and observing skills, and they increase their understanding of management
and human behavior as they compare their assessments with
those of other assessors. After the supervisors leave, the assessors stay on to evaluate the supervisors' potential, including
strengths and weaknesses on tasks related to managerial success.
The resulting evaluative feedback to participants helps them develop and implement written plans for professional development activities. The feedback mobilizes them for particular
changes, and its detail increases with management level. Supervisors can disprove negative conclusions through actual work
performance.

Management acceptance of the technique reflects findings
from evaluation studies that show its validity and the savings of
time and money that result from the combination of assessment
and development. Use of the assessment center during the past
two decades is part of an increasing emphasis on analysis of job
performance as a basis for needs assessment for continuing education.

By contrast, many nonoccupational needs assessments for

which the potential participants are the main beneficiaries consist only of a brief self-assessment inventory, composed of a few questions about expectations on a registration form or a few comments about expectations by participants when they introduce themselves at an initial session.

Instructors typically prefer needs assessment procedures that produce sound and useful results with modest time and effort. Although there is some trade-off between effort and results, it is possible to scale down the usual ambitious guidelines for needs assessment to a manageable size and still get useful results (Birnbrauer and Tyson, 1985; Kopp, 1986a; Pennington, 1980). The key to going beyond symptoms and assessing educational needs with a modest effort is to be very clear about the purpose and audience of the needs assessment. Are the findings only for your use to attract hard-to-reach adults to your programs or to revise materials to better serve current participants? Knowing the types of decisions to be based on needs assessment findings allows you to be very selective in the people and other sources of information you call on, the information you collect, and the procedures you use for data analysis and reporting of findings.

Dave Oliveira, a community college instructor, was thinking of offering a new noncredit course for adults. He discussed his idea with a few instructors who had taught similar courses, and he looked at available course evaluations. In some brief reading he located a few conclusions from similar needs assessments and some useful examples of questionnaires. He pretested a draft form with a dozen people, representative of potential participants, and was pleased at how much this questionnaire contributed to satisfactory coverage, clarity, and face validity. Next he adapted it for use in brief phone interviews with a few people who work with potential participants.

Dave used standard guidelines for keeping in perspective what he already knew about the in-

terviewees and the potential participants, along
with effectively handling the opening, data collection, and closing points of each interview. He felt
that these guidelines contributed to sound and efficient results. Formulating the questionnaire for
efficient hand or computer tabulation of responses
helped him compile, analyze, and report results in
a timely and useful way. Selection and interpretation of findings, including identification of important needs and program implications, were based
on the questions that were important to Dave and
others who planned to use the findings.

In your instructional planning, the main point is that you
include an amount and type of needs assessment that is warranted by each individual program. The result may be a major
needs assessment project for a new program for an unfamiliar
clientele when the disadvantages of an unresponsive program
would be much greater than the costs of the needs assessment.
However, for a familiar program and clientele, a modest needs
assessment effort may be sufficient.

Context Analysis

Your decisions about program objectives and emphases
benefit from analysis of influences on your efforts to help
adults learn and on their efforts to learn and to apply what they
learn. When you plan a program, what do you consider regarding the purposes and resources of your provider organization?
Are there topics to be covered or materials to be used? And
what do you consider regarding situational influences on participants' learning and application, such as encouragement by
supervisors and discouragement by peers?

This section identifies major contextual influences and
suggests how you can use an understanding of them in your situation to strengthen the ways you plan and conduct educational activities for adults (Keaveny, 1983; Schein, 1978).

Given your content expertise and objectives related to

the educational needs of the adults you want to teach, a useful starting point in context analysis is an understanding of major influences in the setting where the learners are likely to apply what they learn. Adults' motivations to learn and to apply what they learn are influenced by their perceptions of standards, opportunities, and expectations related to enhanced proficiencies. In addition, their and your understanding of context can contribute to decisions on using learning activities to strengthen problem solving, specifying mastery levels (as for contract learning), and helping learners use educational strategies that enable them to use or deflect influences that encourage or discourage them to learn and apply. For example, in work settings, analysis of current tasks and likely technological and societal trends that affect one's work can suggest how to avoid obsolescence and benefit from supportive reference groups. Your conclusions about context can also help you decide whether to emphasize individual, temporary group, or organizational learning formats. (Organizational formats are for people whose interaction over time in the same organization is considered when assessing needs and planning application. Typical examples are curriculum study for school staff and performance audit for hospital staff.)

Another set of influences relates to your proficiencies and preferences as an instructor and your awareness of other providers. Emphasizing your abilities and interests enables you to make distinctive contributions and enhances your satisfactions. Knowing about the process and outcomes when other people have conducted similar or related educational programs for adults enables you to build on and incorporate that strength and assistance. If you teach for a large and varied provider (such as a company's training and education department or a university's continuing education division), there are typically many people who can assist with planning and conducting your program. This is especially useful when you are teaching a new category of learners or dealing with a new content area. Especially in smaller providers (such as a community agency or an association), familiarity with comparable programs of other providers in your service area can enable you to build on their offerings, provide information to people engaged in educational brokering and counseling for adults so that they can refer interested adults to your program, and in general increase support and reduce opposition from other providers.

A contextual influence that probably affects decisions related to arranging for you to help adults learn is the combination of mission and resources of the parent organization with which your provider is associated. In addition, your understanding of such organizational goals, priorities, trends, resources, and constraints can enable you to anticipate likely constraints and to emphasize topics and arrangements likely to win support and assistance. For example, from several alternative units of a program, you can choose the one that best fits organizational directions, facilities, materials, and staff assistance.

Usually books and articles are available that can help you understand and harness some of the distinctive contextual influences of your organizational setting to the benefit of your program. For example, employers' human resource development programs are greatly affected by supervisors' attitudes and practices. Writings on training and development in business and industry emphasize the importance of corporate goals and including supervisors as partners in the training process (Bishop, 1976; Craig, 1976; Laird, 1978; Michalak and Yager, 1979). Staff development in health care institutions is subject to similar influences, along with attention to patients as active beneficiaries, relations among the health professions, and the impact of new knowledge and procedures (Brown and Uhl, 1970; Cooper and Hornback, 1973; Green, Grosswald, Suter, and Walthall, 1984; Redman, 1980; Stritter and Flair, 1980). In penal institutions, conflicts between security and rehabilitation greatly affect educational efforts (MacNeil, 1980; Wagner, 1976). In libraries and museums, the centrality of collections of materials and exhibits shapes related educational activities (Burge, 1983; Collins, 1981). Continuing professional education programs are affected by trends and issues in each professional field (Green, Grosswald, Suter, and Walthall, 1984; Houle, 1980; Kaslow and Associates, 1977). Continuing higher education and extension programs provided by a land-grant university are affected by institutional resources and issues (Boyle, 1981). When an urban university helps local citizens examine local issues, the resulting program is affected by influences from both the metropolitan and the institutional settings (Johnson, 1965).

Even in work-related programs, there may be influences related to nonoccupational aspects of the participants' lives. In contrast with the early part of life, with its emphasis on dealing with external reality, during adulthood many people seek greater unification of ideas and outlook. For many adults, this entails developing a balance between one's work identity and one's social identity (Lippitt, 1980). Societal changes place a premium on lifelong growth. Responsiveness to opportunities for growth results from adaptability and openness to changes in activity and location, along with life and career planning. Striving to achieve human potential includes physical, emotional, social, intellectual, esthetic, and spiritual aspects.

Lippitt (1980) suggests five ways that adults can achieve greater personal and career integration. He urges adults to inventory their lives; engage in mind, body, and spirit stretching; take charge of their lives; develop an action plan; and arrange for support, review, and evaluation. Such aspirations suggest ways in which teachers of adults can contribute to a humanistic and developmental process. Such an approach requires that we also consider the broader societal context, which influences both the educational program and the setting in which adults apply what they learn.

An approach to context analysis to enhance teaching of adults is illustrated by the experience of Vernon Jackson, a land-grant university professor of creative writing with a special interest in working with older rural adults. Reminiscence as a developmental feature of later maturity, combined with the professor's special interest and the successful publication of works by older novice writers in several urban areas, made a creative writing workshop for older rural adults a desirable project. Unfamiliarity with similar projects made Vernon uncertain how to proceed.

Conversations with people familiar with similar workshops in urban areas in other states, along with people familiar with rural areas of the state, contributed greatly to Vernon's workshop planning. The increasing numbers of well-educated older adults whose families no longer lived nearby and the examples of older adults who began writing for publication were sources of encouragement. Media coverage of such success stories of older writers helped overcome negative attitudes by friends as well as older people themselves about their ability to write for publication. The university seemed to be the only institution offering an educational program on creative writing for older adults in a rural area.

To encourage initial participation and to provide follow-up assistance for the long process of beginning to write for publication (until success is achieved), Vernon decided to cosponsor the workshop with local schools, religious institutions, community colleges, and interested community groups. In each county where a workshop was held, interested local continuing education practitioners formed an advisory committee of representatives of cosponsors. One provided facilities, others contributed staff assistance, and all helped to identify older residents who might be interested and sent personal letters of invitation. Such cosponsorship helped keep costs down, so that only a nominal fee was charged. Vernon conducted three afternoon workshop sessions two weeks apart for older participants, with assistance from local writers who agreed to provide follow-up assistance.

Vernon Jackson's experience illustrates only some of the

situational influences that might be considered. Has this section suggested any new ideas that you might use to analyze the context in which your programs occur?

Objective Setting

Needs assessment and context analysis can be major sources of information in setting program objectives, but there are other sources as well. Where do objectives for your program come from? Who is involved in the process? How is the final set of objectives selected?

Most instructors have a fairly good idea of what they want to teach. Deliberate attention to setting educational objectives can strengthen the process by clarifying reasons for using formal procedures, by providing an understanding of procedures that could be used, and by identifying ongoing ways to improve the objective-setting process.

Formalizing objective setting for the sessions you conduct can help you and others emphasize and help achieve *important* outcomes. Conclusions from needs assessment, context analysis, and criteria for judging desirable performance usually produce many more potential objectives than your program can address. You, the learners, and often other people (such as resource persons and continuing education coordinators) want to agree on learning objectives and activities that are productive, satisfying, and efficient. Formalizing the objective-setting process—through writing objectives, using a planning committee, or devoting program time to the process—enables participants to contribute to it. Benefits to participants of clarifying particular educational objectives for and with them include increasing their understanding of and commitment to achieving the objectives, helping them understand relations between current and desired proficiencies, preceding answers with questions, and helping them learn how to learn beyond your program (Houle, 1972; Knowles, 1980; Knox, 1980b; Knox and Associates, 1980; Smith, 1982).

You can use important, clear, and agreed-on objectives in several ways. Explicit objectives help you select materials, outline content, decide on methods of teaching and learning, and prepare evaluation procedures. When other people (such as resource persons and coordinators) help plan and conduct a continuing education course or workshop, agreement on clear and realistic objectives contributes to coordination and effective working relationships.

Program objectives typically evolve, mainly during planning but throughout implementation as well. In best practice, the process is interactive, with successive approximations from preliminary objectives to stated major objectives that participants are expected to achieve to modified objectives as the program unfolds to implications for objectives when the program is next offered. Formalizing the process beyond the implicit choices you might otherwise make helps increase the understanding and commitment of learners and others who must help achieve the objectives.

Once you have explored the main sources of potential objectives, there are several criteria for selecting those of high priority from the unmanageably long list that typically results. One criterion is desirability given pertinent information about learners, content, and provider. Another criterion is feasibility given pertinent information about learning and resources.

The most useful objectives briefly and clearly specify intended learner proficiencies expected as a result of the program. Such specific statements of intended learner outcomes may focus on knowledge (for example, understanding, recalling, contrasting), skill (for example, manipulation of equipment), or attitudes (indicators of feelings or beliefs). However, a set of actual program objectives typically includes a combination of knowledge, attitudes, and often skills that constitute desired proficiencies, such as the capability to engage in problem solving.

Clearly stated specific objectives are based on understanding the learners, their current proficiencies, and the conditions under which they are expected to demonstrate the extent to which they achieved desired proficiencies. The wording of learning objectives should emphasize such terms as *write, solve, list,* and *compare,* which are specific enough so that you, the learners, and others can use them as standards to aim toward and to assess progress in achieving minimal or optimal proficiency. It is also helpful to indicate how achievement of objectives will be achieved (Mager, 1962). Such clearly stated objectives can pertain to any educational outcomes, including appreciation, and not just performance.

Ways to achieve agreement on objectives include planning committees, nominal group process, examples of successful practice to highlight intended outcomes, devoting program time and emphasis to agreement on objectives, and starting with an existing group of adults who have goals and developing a facilitative educational program with them (Delbecq, Van de Ven, and Gustafson, 1975).

Effective continuing education instructors think about objective setting in some additional ways. They realize that they can emphasize important topics and issues and avoid trivial ones. Decisions about what is important can include attention to likely consequences and the participants' commitment to apply what they learn. Special attention can also be given to higher-level objectives, such as analysis, evaluation, unexpected outcomes, and problem finding as well as problem solving. This is especially important for topics such as interpersonal relations (Marlowe, 1985; Argyris, 1982). The findings from program evaluation can also be used to refine objectives as the program progresses. Different instructors' approaches to objective setting vary greatly. Some approaches emphasize scientific design of instruction to accomplish prespecified objectives (Carkhuff and Fisher, 1984); others emphasize humanistic assistance to adults as they discover and clarify objectives important to them (Rogers, 1969).

Sometimes learners take at least some responsibility for educational objective setting, even though they are encouraged to take major responsibility for their own development. An example is learner-controlled instruction (LCI) in work settings (Feeney, 1981). This approach assumes that specification of desired proficiencies for a complex and unfamiliar job requires learner understanding and commitment as well as the perspective of supervisors, experts, and education specialists.

The major steps for an instructor who uses an LCI approach begin with analysis of the new job assignment, with attention both to the component tasks and to how the job fits into the larger organizational structure. The specification of each component task includes both performance standards and necessary human and material resources. This is followed by a list of questions the learner should ask to know about and perform each task. The next step is to prepare a learning-task sheet that describes learning activities and resources that enable the learner to achieve desired proficiencies, along with information about how the learner will be evaluated and by whom.

With this preparation, the person selected for a new job assignment meets with the immediate supervisor (or someone else who will serve as tutor) to assess the learner's current proficiencies. The learner and tutor then jointly prepare a learning contract, which specifies the desirable learning outcomes (based on discrepancies between the learner's current proficiencies and the desired proficiencies that were specified). The lists of questions and resources that were prepared then help the learner to prepare a highly individualized educational plan for acquiring the desired proficiencies. Implementation of the plan should enable the learner both to perform well and to be better able to engage in future self-directed learning activities (Knowles, 1986).

The tutor helps to schedule and monitor progress through a useful sequence of learning activities, provides assistance, identifies resources, and evaluates progress until full proficiency has been achieved. In this learning-by-objectives approach, the learner pursues a self-paced individualized action learning project, and technical experts in the organization certify that proficiency standards are achieved. It is important that there be positive career advancement consequences of the effort for the learner. An LCI approach depends on supervisory time and support.

A special aspect of objective setting is attention to creative growth and innovation. This applies to your approach to teaching as well as the learners' approach to applying what they learn. Odiorne (1979, 1984) suggests useful guidelines for creative goal setting. Some guidelines emphasize being curious about new ideas and developments that could be adapted and used, especially for innovation. This entails being open to and obtaining a basic understanding of the new idea, exploring the feasibility of the new idea in a particular situation, and introducing desirable changes. Suggestions for successfully making changes include the following: Make sure a change is important, fit new ideas into familiar patterns, reinforce progress, allow varied methods of application, and start small, evaluate, modify, and expand. Are you helping learners to consider such objectives? Are you enhancing your own creativity as an instructor?

The remaining guidelines are for looking within an activity group or an organization to analyze past results in order to achieve future improvements. This is aided by openness of communication and lack of defensiveness in an atmosphere that encourages creativity. Ways to create such an innovative atmosphere include emphasizing expectations, examples, assistance, and incentives for innovation; obtaining commitment from individuals and teams; having leaders who are dissatisfied with the status quo; providing favorable consequences for people who innovate; and supporting people who can encourage and assist the person who should be more innovative. Additional suggestions include involving other people in goal setting, including outside suggestions; focusing on a manageable number of desirable, feasible, and challenging objectives; providing guidelines for action; and setting intermediate targets to assess progress.

Most important of all, you can use the objective-setting process to achieve consensus on what outcomes you, participants, and other people associated with your educational program are committed to help achieve. Your special contribution is to help assure that the objectives are feasible as well as desirable.

In what ways might you modify your objective-setting procedures so that they better serve the participants and the program? After you have considered the ideas in this section and information from various sources, your personal judgments are likely to be very important.

Conclusion

This chapter reviewed three components of program planning that may suggest modifications in your procedures for needs assessment, context analysis, and objective setting. Formal needs assessment procedures can help you identify important discrepancies between participants' current and desired proficiencies as perceived by themselves and others. The extent and type of needs assessment that seem warranted in a particular instance depend in large part on what additional information about participant needs and expectations would be useful for planning.

In parallel to needs assessment, your context analysis considers major influences such as societal trends and issues, opportunities from other providers, and the mission and resources of your own provider organization. You can then consider information about both needs and context as you seek agreement between yourself and the potential participants on desirable and feasible learning objectives.

The next chapter reviews additional planning components regarding activities and arrangements. Planning for program evaluation is covered in the first part of Chapter Nine.

FIVE

Choosing and Implementing Effective Learning Activities

This chapter continues our overview of program planning. Decisions about needs, context, and objectives, covered in Chapter Four, result in intended program outcomes. This chapter covers the plans for how to accomplish those outcomes by selecting and organizing learning activities and by making supportive arrangements, such as for attracting participants, providing counseling assistance, choosing educational materials, and arranging for placement for those who complete the program.

How do you typically plan activities and arrangements? How are content and methods decisions related? Who else helps with the planning? Why? How satisfactory is the process? Is there any way in which you would like to strengthen these aspects of planning? This chapter contains many suggestions about available options. Look especially for new ideas that might enhance your instructional planning.

A remaining and crucial component of program planning is evaluation, which is also integral to program implementation. Therefore, Chapter Nine is devoted entirely to evaluation. The first part of that chapter deals with planning evaluation, which entails feedback and input for planning of all the other components of program development.

Learning Activities

How do you decide which learning and teaching activities to include in each program you conduct? Most instructors use only a few methods with which they happen to be familiar. This

77

section covers criteria you might consider, the variety of available methods, and guidelines for organizing those you select.

The most familiar decision when planning to instruct adults is the selection of activities in which participants learn and you assist them. At the planning stage, it is helpful to have a rationale for considering learner characteristics, program objectives, and your perspective when choosing and sequencing learning activities. Later chapters deal with selection and preparation of educational materials and with decisions you make about learning activities while the program is progressing. This chapter suggests some basic concepts for your rationale for selecting and organizing learning activities, describes major features of various types of learning activities that you might consider, and explores ways to organize learning activities to increase their impact on performance (Bergevin, Morris, and Smith, 1963; Davis and McCallon, 1974; Gage, 1977; Gagné and Briggs, 1970; Houle, 1972; Kalamas, 1986b; Knowles, 1980, 1986; Knox, 1980b; Laird, 1978; Lindquist, 1978a; Loughary and Hopson, 1979; Sork, 1984).

If you have clearly stated some important and realistic objectives (based on conclusions from needs assessment and context analysis), it is relatively straightforward to design the educational program to achieve those objectives and draft your plan for conducting the sessions. (If you lack stated objectives for a program you have conducted before, it might be helpful to extract the objectives that are implicit in the activities, for the benefit of the participants as well as your planning.) The resulting instructional plan typically specifies objectives, content, and activities by participants as well as yourself. The details of the plan will vary depending on whether you will provide individual assistance or work with a group of learners and depending on whether the focus is on instruction (in which you share your expertise with those who lack it), inquiry (in which you and participants jointly seek new insights or solutions), or performance (in which actual performance is a major vehicle for enhancing proficiencies) (Houle, 1980). Also remember that educational activities are both the ways that participants learn and the ways in which you assist them.

Selection Criteria. Three general considerations in planning learning activities are program objectives, learner characteristics, and your perspective. In each instance, pertinent information can help you plan more responsive and effective learning activities.

Continuing education programs that extend beyond a session or two, whether designed for individuals, groups, or organizations, are typically divided into units or parts. Objectives for early units tend to emphasize learners' familiarity with educational objectives and procedures and the relations between current and desired proficiencies. Objectives for middle units emphasize practice and enhancing proficiencies. Objectives for late units emphasize application.

Educational objectives that include both the subject matter content to be learned and what participants should be able to do with that content provide a useful basis for selecting learning activities likely to enable learners to achieve those objectives. This emphasis on desired proficiencies is fundamental to competence-based learning, in which participants master what they need to be able to do to achieve the objectives. Your commitment to helping adult learners acquire the attitudes and abilities to continue related learning activities beyond your program is a strong reason for having some objectives that pertain to active learner involvement in decisions about the process of learning (Oddi, 1986; Smith, 1982).

The differential effectiveness of learning and teaching methods in relation to learner characteristics and outcomes is a strong reason for using a variety of methods. Such variety can increase learner interest as well as enhance various aspects of desired proficiencies (Ludwig and Menendez, 1985; Marshak, 1983). When program objectives emphasize knowledge acquisition, it is helpful to select methods that help learners relate important new concepts to their current understandings and put new ideas in their own words. When objectives emphasize skill building, one might select methods that demonstrate the skills and help learners practice until mastery is achieved (Erdman, 1984; Slaninka, 1983). When objectives emphasize modification of attitudes, one should select methods that help learners consider different attitudes as well as influences on their current and modified attitudes (Grossman, 1984; Hill, 1960; Mouton and Blake, 1984a).

Chris Starovich considered the relation of methods to objectives and to learner characteristics as she planned a noncredit evening ceramics course for adults offered through the local community colleges' arts and humanities division. Her course had three broad goals. Most participants enrolled to acquire specific skills such as use of the potter's wheel, mixing and applying glaze, and firing. A few learners already had these skills but wanted access to the wheel and kiln. These more experienced potters helped Chris demonstrate techniques and answer questions for the novice class members. During most of each weekly session, Chris went from wheel to wheel, observing, answering questions, praising progress, making suggestions, and sometimes demonstrating. She knew that skill building revolved around head and hand working together with the clay.

A second goal pertained to knowing why as well as how. Because of the long waiting list, college policy restricted the number of times a person could take the course. So Chris was especially interested in helping participants understand about clay consistency for throwing pots on the wheel and about firing temperatures for various glazes, so they could make these decisions later when working on their own. The division director valued the knowledge base that was acquired, and many participants commented on how much they appreciated the explanations, checklists, and suggested readings that Chris provided as they helped her with tasks such as mixing or firing.

However, Chris's main goal was esthetic. . Ceramics provided a tangible way to enhance peo-

ple's appreciation of shape, color, and texture.
Chris encouraged participants to view and discuss
examples and illustrations for the benefit of their
pottery and their lives. For adults who seemed interested, she encouraged reading an interesting little book on centering that explored the ideas as
applied to centering clay on a potter's wheel but
also to centering in esthetics and in life.

In selecting learning activities likely to be most effective
in achieving the main program objectives, it may be helpful to
consider how other practitioners rank method effectiveness in
relation to program purposes. In two surveys about a decade
apart, coordinators of educational programs that employers provide for their employees ranked methods similarly in relation to
objectives (Neider, 1981). For example, for knowledge acquisition and retention, the preferred methods were programmed instruction, case study, and conference discussion, whereas for
changing attitudes and interpersonal relations, the preferred
methods were role playing, sensitivity training, conference discussion, and case study. For problem solving and application of
new learnings to improved performance, the preferred methods
were case study, simulation games, and conference discussion.
Methods rated low for all purposes included presentations in
person or on film or video.

Chapter Two reviewed the types of information about
participants that are useful for decisions about instruction generally. Several aspects of adults as learners are especially pertinent to planning decisions about learning activities. The most
important aspect (which should have been identified as a result
of needs assessment activities) is the learner's current proficiencies related to program objectives (Ausubel and Novack, 1978).
Current proficiencies affect how new ideas and practices are
perceived, and they are often reconstructed as a result of new
learnings (Bandura, 1982). Your understanding of the learners'
current proficiencies enables you to introduce intermediate
models that allow participants to relate current proficiencies,
program objectives, and intended applications (Knox, 1985).

Eric Boyd even discussed intermediate systems models as he planned a series of briefing sessions and field trips for adults entitled "Reading
the Landscape," provided by a natural history museum. The purpose of the program was to help the
public understand interactions among weather,
soil, and vegetation in natural areas. Participants
typically recognize familiar species of trees and
plants, along with distinctions between well-drained
sandy or rocky soil at higher elevations compared
with wet soil along creek bottoms and ponds. Eric
wanted them to understand the model of ecologi-
cal succession to help explain why a particular mix
of trees and plants evolves when a change occurs in
a given location. On a field trip to a climax beech
and maple forest with little undergrowth, he
pointed out how shallow topsoil and exposure to
prevailing winds had contributed to an area of
blowdown of large trees during a period of heavy
rains and winds. The new growth of shrubs, black
cherry, box elder, and yellow birch in the clearing
that resulted was quite different from the surrounding climax forest that remained. As participants walked back from that location, they appreciated the balance of nature with a new richness.

A closely related aspect is participants' preferred learning
styles. Information about typical learning styles allows you to
plan activities that fit and broaden such preferences. Another
aspect is the adult roles and settings from which educational
needs arise and in which enhanced proficiencies are to be applied. The foregoing aspects, and some aspects of personality as
well, contribute to participants' willingness to devote their time
and effort to learning activities until objectives are achieved.
Your understanding of this aspect lets you know how strongly
motivated they are and how much and what type of encouragement and support you should give (Landerholm, 1984; Reid,
1985).

There are several sources of information about learners' characteristics to be considered when selecting learning activities. Experienced instructors accumulate general impressions of the typical distribution of learners' backgrounds, goals, and preferred learning styles. Conscientious instructors acquire more detailed information from the participants at the outset of each program. For most instructors, the question is not desirability but feasibility of how much information to collect. How can such information be collected and used efficiently so that the results are worth the effort by instructor and participants? Pertinent information about background and goals can be obtained as part of registration and introduction procedures. Information about preferred learning style typically requires more formal procedures.

Various learning-style inventories have been used in educational programs for adults, especially in those that last more than a few days (DeNovellis, 1984, 1985; Ihlanfeldt, 1981; Kolb, 1984; Myers and Myers, 1980; Smith, 1982). When used diagnostically, such inventories can help identify potential learning problems, match participants to activities, and reduce attrition. With some inventories, a computer is used for scoring and for generating a report for each learner with suggestions for using strengths to advantage and both strengthening and compensating for weaknesses in learning style. You can help learners interpret the report for their decision making as well as use summary information for your own decisions about types of learning activities to emphasize.

Alice Leland distributed copies of a standard learning-style inventory, along with instructions for completion, self-scoring, interpretation, and preparation of an anonymous summary sheet, to the well-educated participants at the end of the second session of her continuing education course. She collected and tabulated the summary sheets and compared the tabulation with that for previous years and with her course plan. The strong and widespread preferences for collaborative learning and the math anxiety expressed by a vocal minority resulted in a few modifications, but her main use of the summary sheets was for planning the next course. She discussed the profiles and interpretation with some participants who hadn't considered preferred learning style before and wanted to talk about implications for their choices of learning activities. Alice's main use of this information was to make sure each participant had learning activities available that were responsive to his or her preferences and aspirations. Summary information allowed Alice to plan effectively so that the options were available from which the participants could choose.

In addition to information about objectives and learners, your plans for learning activities should reflect your perspective. Your abilities, interests, and past experiences helping adults learn contribute to your teaching style. When alternative learning activities are equally appropriate for the objectives and learners, it seems desirable to select those that use your distinctive abilities and contributions. As you plan programs that call for types of teaching methods you haven't used before, you have an opportunity to broaden your repertoire. It is likely that responsive educational programs that take objectives, learners, and your unique perspective into account will be individualized to some extent and will allow learners to be actively engaged in the process (Daloz, 1986; Eble, 1983; Kalamas, 1986b; Wlodkowski, 1985a).

Types of Learning Activities. Continuing education instructors usually select methods with which they are sufficiently familiar to feel confident using. Such familiarity includes understanding the distinctive features (given the objectives and learners) so that the method is used to advantage. The following listing shows the distinctive characteristics and typical uses of various instructional methods. They are grouped by individual, temporary group, organizational, and community formats. The description of each method includes a definition, examples, and features of effectiveness.

The foregoing selection criteria should suggest ways to review the following list of activities. Familiar activities can remind you of some to consider when planning an upcoming program. This introduction to unfamiliar activities can encourage you to discuss and read about those that seem promising.

a. *Individual.* Each participant interacts with instructor and materials but not with other learners. Emphasis is on individualization and self-directedness.

1. *Coaching. An experienced person demonstrates in an actual setting. The learner gradually masters roles by practice and feedback.* Examples include apprenticeship, on-the-job-training, supervisory orientation, and explanation of an organizational role. This method depends on a competent and patient coach who divides the new role into a helpful sequence of tasks that are clearly demonstrated, followed by sufficient practice and constructive feedback. Its effectiveness is also related to learning in an actual setting, which helps the learner in the application of new learning but may hinder its transferability.

2. *Computer-assisted instruction (CAI). The learner interacts with an elaborate computer program, which may present information to master, problems to solve, or simulations to explain complex relationships.* Examples include drill and practice, simulations, monitoring, and feedback. CAI depends on access to equipment, enough users so that development and use of the program are cost-effective, and a well-designed interactive program. Effective programs present important concepts, use small steps, explore complex relationships difficult to understand through other methods, maintain interest for practice, and provide constructive feedback.

3. *Correspondence. Syllabus, text, and other materials such as recordings are sent to learners at a distance, who complete lessons and return assignments and tests by mail to an instructor who evaluates them and provides feedback throughout.* Examples include corre-

spondence, home study, external degrees, and other types of teaching at a distance that typically use some form of correspondence or guided individual study. There may be some telephone contact. The method depends on effective, interesting, and up-to-date materials, a sufficient number of independent learners to be cost-effective, and able and supportive instructors. It allows participants to select preferred time, place, and pacing and to receive individualized feedback but requires highly motivated learners. Materials may include options for further individualization. This method is more effective for mastery of knowledge than for acquiring skills or changing attitudes.

4. *Reading. Learner mainly uses printed materials, with some guidance by self, tutor, or coach or from a set of guidelines.* Examples include homework reading assignments, how-to books or pamphlets, prior readings, focused and systematic study, or a specific library project. This method depends on good reading ability and interest, focus, and the availability of appropriate materials. It allows the learner to select the time, place, and pace.

5. *Project. The participant uses some combination of observation, experience, demonstration, interviews, trial, reading, and conversation to plan and conduct a supervised individual or field learning project.* Examples include contract learning, fieldwork, action learning, internship, or a pilot project with evaluation. This method depends on access to an appropriate setting, learner self-directedness, and a tutor or coach who supervises the study aspects of the project. It can be effective when the study and action aspects are combined.

6. *Television course. The learner views a series of television programs, completes readings, and writes a paper or takes a test.* This method may be combined with a correspondence course or a discussion group. Examples include a televised standard course and a noncredit supplement to a series. The method depends on an in-

teresting and informative series (either planned as a course or adapted for the purpose) and providers willing to use this format. It allows convenient location for viewing but requires set times and pacing, unless the learner has a videocassette recorder.

7. *Tutoring. The learner receives help in planning and conducting a learning project, similar to coaching, except that the tutor is not associated with learners' performance setting.* The tutor may be a content specialist, such as a professor or other expert, or may be process-oriented, such as a counselor or an external degree mentor. The distinctive features may be similar to those of coaching except that the tutor seldom demonstrates task performance but instead helps learners plan, analyze, and evaluate performance in other settings.

b. *Large group.* Emphasis is on presentation of ideas to temporary groups of almost any size. Presentation may be live or may use media. These methods are often combined with discussion groups or readings. The first three are forms of presentation, and the remaining two are ways of following up to provide for audience interaction.

1. *Lecture. Expert presents participants with an organized in-depth presentation, often accompanied by audiovisuals and questions and answers.* Examples include lecture series, lecturette, lecture forum, and presentation with or without reaction panels or listening teams. This method depends on an interested audience and an important, organized, and interesting message. It is usually most effective when combined with other methods.

2. *Panel. Two or more speakers make presentations on different aspects of an issue, otherwise similar to a lecture.* Examples include panel, panel forum, symposium, and colloquy. This method is similar to the lecture, except that advocates can present differing points of view. This feature can help avoid a lecture's narrowness or blandness and a debate's overemphasis on winning.

This method depends on well-selected topics and panelists and a moderator who orients panelists and audience and who keeps to the time schedule to assure opportunity for interaction among panelists and the audience.

3. *Debate. Similar to a lecture or panel, but two or four debaters argue two sides of an important issue to clarify differences and related reasoning.* Each side may be represented by one debater or by a team dialogue. This method depends on the importance of two sides of the issue, the ability of debaters and moderator, and a general commitment to enlightenment instead of winning.

4. *Subgroup discussion. Audience divides into small subgroups for discussion of ideas presented, questions for speakers, implications.* Examples include huddle group, buzz groups, and concurrent sessions. This method depends on provocative discussion questions, well-selected and oriented discussion leaders, and agreed-on timing and arrangements. It is especially effective in helping participants relate new ideas to their situation and in encouraging application.

5. *Forum. Participants question and discuss the presentation as a total group.* Examples include question period, film forum, screening panel, and chain reaction forum. A major feature is interaction with an audience without subgroups. This method depends on an effective moderator.

c. *Small group.* Emphasis is on discussion and analysis of ideas among a temporary group of about fifteen but no more than thirty participants. It may or may not be preceded by readings or presentations, but participants should have shared background and interest.

1. *Discussion. Participants exchange ideas face to face on a topic of shared interest in a group typically between six and twenty for about an hour, depending on topic and group size.* Examples include brainstorming, sensitivity group, training group, round table, and diagnostic session. This method depends on shared interest

and effective group leadership, which may be widely shared. This is one of the most widespread and effective continuing education methods, in part because participants become resources for one another's learning.

2. *Seminar. Discussion focused on expertise and project reports of participants.* Examples include colloquium and clinic. This method depends on participants' interest and expertise in both content and process.

3. *Case analysis. Discussion of a prepared case situation, which helps participants understand and practice problem-solving and decision-making procedures.* Examples include critical incident and minicase. This method depends on well-prepared cases, experienced participants, and an effective discussion leader who uses questions well.

4. *Simulation. Imitation of interpersonal or other dynamics, often using materials and roles, to help participants feel as well as understand the dynamics of a complex situation.* Examples include in-basket exercises, computer simulation, role play, educational games, and role reversal. Effectiveness depends on the realism of the simulation and having as much time to discuss the experience as to engage in the simulation.

5. *Demonstration. Demonstrators and sometimes equipment show how a procedure is performed and typical results.* Examples include demonstration with practice by learner, show and tell, rehearsal, drills, skills practice lab, and presentation with video feedback. Effectiveness depends on clear and credible demonstration and on opportunity for practice and feedback.

d. *Organizational.* Members of an ongoing organization participate in educational activities related to organizational functioning in which organizational dynamics influence all aspects of program development, especially needs and application. The emphasis is on organizational health and productivity.

1. *Self-study. Members organize and conduct a study of*

*all or part of the organization's past, current, and fu-
ture goals and activities, with an emphasis on recommendations to strengthen organizational functioning.*
This method is sometimes combined with an external
review by a team or consultant. Examples include self-
study groups and meetings where members discuss recommendations by a consultant. This method depends
on members' commitment to improve aspects of organizational functioning such as consensus on goals,
productivity, communications, conflict resolution, and
team building. It also depends on support from organizational leadership and process guidance by an OD
consultant.

2.   *Work-team sessions. Members who work closely together meet to review past experience and agree on
ways to improve interpersonal relations through team-
building activities.* Examples include problem-solving
sessions, quality circles, and committees to discuss proposed organizational changes. This method depends on
members' willingness to improve the organizational
unit, the OD facilitator, and responsiveness of leadership structure to recommendations for improvements.

3.   *Action learning. One or more members plan and implement a project in which learning and action interact to
produce individual growth and organizational improvement* (action research). This method depends on a feasible project, organizational cooperation, and assistance
with planning and evaluation.

e.   *Community.* This is similar to organizational, except that
members of two or more segments of a community cooperate to strengthen one or more aspects of the community
for which such cooperation is important. A community development (CD) specialist serves in a process role similar to
that of the organization development specialist. As with organization development, community development activities
include individual and group learning, but the focus is on
community problem solving.

1.   *Community survey. A CD specialist and a representa-*

tive committee assemble data and opinions about the problem area, resources, and goals. An example is a community study group. This method depends on a manageable local problem, citizen interest in solving it, and assistance by a CD specialist.

2. *Field trip. Citizens associated with a CD effort visit people and examples associated with the types of improvements they want to make in their own community, to understand the results that were achieved in similar settings and the influences and procedures that contributed to the results.* Examples include result demonstration and technical briefing. This method depends on availability of useful examples and citizens' interest in learning from them.

3. *Community problem-solving project. Local citizens interested in solving a particular problem engage in learning activities as a part of doing so.* The action project is a vehicle for learning, and informal educational activities contribute to understanding of the current situation, consensus on goals, and procedures for problem solving and leadership. The method is similar to action learning and field projects in organizational and temporary group formats. It depends on sufficient expertise and resources to deal with the selected problem and assistance with procedures for problem solving.

Organizing Learning Activities. The foregoing methods for teaching and learning constitute building blocks available to you when you design a continuing education program. How many of them have you used? Only a few would be used in a single instance. A continuing education course by an educational institution, a staff development program by an employer, a workshop by an association, or a conference by a community group would be composed of multiple units and various methods. Effective program planning entails selection of methods that you believe fit the objectives and participants (Keller, 1979; Klevins, 1978; Rosenberg, 1982; Tallmadge and Shearer, 1969).

How do you handle this process of selecting and organizing learning activities in your program planning? For most instructors, such decisions tend to be informal and intuitive. How satisfactory is your planning of learning activities?

Effective use of most of these methods depends on planning. This is so whether your approach is competence-based, with an emphasis on established objectives for expected learner outcome behaviors, or whether your approach includes the participants in decisions about goals and methods. In the latter approach, planning includes estimating learner characteristics so that materials, equipment, and procedures are available to be responsive to the participants.

Your success in using any method of teaching and learning will reflect various influences, including content, objectives, learner characteristics, group size, and available time, equipment, facilities, and budget (Randall, 1978a). For example, an especially useful and effective method is problem case discussion (Boyd, 1980; Stenzel and Feeney, 1970). Effective case discussion should enable participants to practice and enhance problem-solving procedures. The discussion case that you select or develop should be realistic for the learners, involve decision and action choices, suggest underlying problems that are not evident, and include discussion questions to guide inquiry. However, even with such case materials, effectiveness depends in part on participants' having sufficient background and interest, along with your use of other instructional methods to complement case discussion.

For repeated programs that emphasize application, simulation materials can enhance program efficiency and effectiveness. Simulations have proven utility for helping adults learn, and guidelines are available for their selection and development (Abt, 1970; Horn, 1977; Olivas and Newstrom, 1981; Parry, 1980). Simulations are especially beneficial for developing analytical thinking, insight, and sensitivity and for providing practice working with people and tasks. They emphasize the process of discovery and application, not just knowledge acquisition. Simulations enable learners to be active, learn from experience without the price of wrong decisions, compress real-life events into short time periods, receive rapid feedback, engage in realistic discussion, obtain a more comprehensive perspective, become more receptive to new ideas and viewpoints by virtue of personal involvement, and develop human relations skills. Effective simulation materials should entail preparation, enable participants to learn by experiencing the consequences of their actions, and encourage postsimulation discussion of strategies, rationale, and feelings with other participants.

Simulations are attractive and effective vehicles for learning. They don't have to be complex and expensive like computer simulations or the use of simulated patients and videotapes for medical education, described in Chapter Three (Barrows and Tamblyn, 1980). Many simulation games are available for educational purposes, many of which require only paper and pencil and simple instructions (Abt, 1970). The materials for an in-basket simulation for administrators consist mainly of a packet of correspondence and phone messages such as might accumulate in the basket for incoming mail during several days' absence. The administrator is given a few hours to decide which items to respond to and then make decisions and draft replies. His or her implicit decision-making approach can be compared with choices and rationales by experts and then discussed with other participants. Such simulations do not deal with right answers so much as reveal rationales for decision-making strategies. Case-study role plays to explore interpersonal dynamics, such as organizational power structure or the process of an interview, can serve similar purposes. You can select prepared cases or role plays, if satisfactory ones can be located, or develop your own, perhaps with help from participants.

Bob Cahill's preparations for his program illustrate a planning timetable.

Months before his program, Bob studied the clientele by means of a basic needs assessment, reviewed general program goals, and made early decisions about timing, facilities, and other resource persons. With the competence-based approach he was using, he prepared competence statements and arranged to have them validated in actual settings by several advisory committee members using basic task analysis. Then a month or two ahead he prepared the final program plan, prepared and ordered materials, arranged for remaining resource persons, and discussed with his coordinator such arrangements as publicity, facilities, and equipment. Just before the program started, he checked on other arrangements, such as enrollments, resource persons, facilities, equipment, registration, hospitality, and parking.

The planning process covers not only the decisions in preparation for the program but also the plans for what should occur during and after the program. Whether the program occurs in a day or extends over many months, one type of planning decision is what should be emphasized early, middle, and late in the sequence of sessions. (Most meetings, courses, and workshops are composed of multiple sessions, units, or segments.) For example, early units should clarify and respond to the actual participants' initial apprehension, their interest in relevant questions and problems, and their current proficiencies. This will enable you to help them feel welcome and achieve early success. Middle units should help participants relate current proficiencies to new concepts and procedures that enable them to achieve desirable outcomes and should provide varied practice to achieve desired mastery. Late units should encourage and help participants to continue to learn and apply what they learn beyond the program.

Following are some additional suggestions for sequencing units or topics within units.

- Begin with topics of interest or concern to learners and sequence remaining topics to make sense to the learners.
- Provide an overview early to enable learners to recall or acquire a cognitive map or structure into which to fit the details.
- Emphasize early essential proficiencies for learners to achieve objectives or perform desired tasks.

- See that learners spend most of their time on activities pertinent to the objectives.
- Schedule frequently used proficiencies early so that they can be practiced and refined, after which less frequently used proficiencies can be added.
- Emphasize continuity from topic to topic and unit to unit.
- Sequence to allow practice of entire tasks as they would be applied.
- Enable participants to acquire usable proficiencies even if they are unable to continue to the end of the program.
- Include learning activities that can actually be implemented with available time, personnel, materials, and facilities.

Some of these suggestions pertain to sequencing of subject matter content to reflect participants' current proficiencies as well as the nature of the content and objectives. Some pertain to sequencing of methods and procedures for learning and teaching to reflect preferred learning styles. Both are important. An important consideration in method selection is encouraging learners to persist and to apply what is learned. Adults are more likely to persist to mastery if methods are satisfactory. Although there is little relation between various methods and typical achievement test results, methods do influence persistence and application. Learning-style inventories can help learners recognize their preferred learning styles and use that insight both to select satisfactory methods and to broaden learning style for greater flexibility and effectiveness.

Sequencing of learning activities depends in part on the general program rationale regarding goals and contributions by participants, concurrent experience, and you and others who help adults learn. Learning methods have been grouped in three modes: *instruction, inquiry,* and *performance.*

Instruction involves learning from didactic presentations by experts to learners who lack understanding. An example is demonstration and explanation for an inexperienced new employee as a part of on-the-job training. Sequencing might entail demonstration and explanation followed by practice and feedback for each component task until sufficient mastery is achieved.

Inquiry methods come closer to problem solving, as participants (and resource persons as well) seek to discover answers, instead of receiving them from an organized presentation. An example might be a seminar for experienced managers or engineers, organized around an actual problem to be solved. Sequencing might entail clarification of organizational objectives and details of the problem situation, followed by brainstorming to explore unusual solutions, case analysis to understand pertinent organizational dynamics, and task forces to learn about and propose solutions to aspects of the problem.

Performance-oriented methods involve learning closely associated with actual performance. Examples include learning from experience in on-the-job training and action learning projects for administrators, as well as internships and practicums provided by educational institutions. Sequencing of learning activities would be organized around the tasks, problems, opportunities, and questions that people confront in practice settings. Networking and locating relevant ideas are part of the praxis that occurs as participants alternate between learning and action (Argyris, 1982; Keeton and Associates, 1976; Knox, 1974; McNulty, 1979; Mouton and Blake, 1984b; Odiorne, 1984; Rinke, 1982).

Another useful way to plan learning activities pertains to the match between learners' needs and the instructors' contributions. Responsive instructional approaches include attention to desired outcomes and perspective on adult development. Planning entails selection and orientation of resource persons likely to be responsive to the educational needs of individual learners. For example, adults who feel incompetent might appreciate a developmental approach in which they gain both the ability to perform and an enhanced sense of proficiency. By contrast, adults who feel ignorant might appreciate a rational approach in which they gain knowledge. Likewise, those who feel conflicted might appreciate a therapeutic approach in which they gain insight; those who feel diffuse might appreciate a humanistic approach in which they gain a more positive sense of self.

In each instance the instructional approach is responsive to the backgrounds and concerns of the particular participants. Recognizing which type of alliance seems most appropriate in a given instance can suggest useful educational objectives and developmental perspectives to emphasize and methods, materials, and resource persons to select (Epperson, 1974).

Another consideration when planning learning activities is the extent and type of attention to application. Sometimes adults seek personal outcomes (such as art appreciation or understanding public issues) in which they assume the responsibility for application. At other times, however, especially in work-related educational programs in which other people have a stake in the learners' subsequent performance, there are several ways in which your planning can encourage application. Included are interesting practice opportunities, attention to likely influences on subsequent performance, inclusion of teams of learners who can be supportive about application (for example, in quality circles), and emphasis on the benefits of improved performance for learners and others.

Guidelines for organizing learning activities vary among settings. For example, technical education provided in work settings tends to emphasize improved performance (Feeney, 1980). Early steps include analysis of standards and actual performance. Desirable performance standards emphasize the outputs of performance, including the economic and other benefits associated with achieving the standards. Such standards can guide baseline assessment of current performance to decide how closely it meets the standards and to serve later as a reference point to evaluate how much educational activities contributed to improvements in performance. Assessment of performance can be based on records, reports, and observations. Such performance improvement analysis can also identify performance problems whose reduction would yield the highest benefits.

In his behaviorist procedures for technical training, Feeney urges a systems approach to "cause analysis" to identify internal and external influences such as specific and realistic standards, satisfactory feedback systems, and benefits to employees for improved performance. Observation of actual performance can help educators and supervisors understand causes of performance problems and provide the basis for understanding employees' rationales for their actions.

Group instruction may not be the most effective way to

improve performance. One alternative is a performance feedback system that enables employees to compare their actual performance with standards and make adjustments. Other techniques include positive employee consequences for excellent performance (such as praise, public recognition, financial rewards, and career advancement) and the use of job aids that clearly show standard procedures.

Evaluation can document performance improvements and the proficiencies aided by educational activities that contributed to those improvements. Such feedback can assist employees in guiding their own occupational growth and can be used in summary form to justify the educational effort.

Organizing learning activities reduces complexity for the instructor and increases efficiency and interest for the learner. Ways to do so vary with the type of program.

For example, job instruction methods are widely used in work settings to enable supervisors with limited teaching experience to devote time to training and thus avoid having to spend much more time on problems that training could have reduced (Gold, 1981; Sullivan and Miklas, 1985). Four basic components of job instruction are to make preparations that enhance learner motivation, to present the procedures clearly to assure learner understanding, to have the learner try out the procedure to allow active participation, and to provide followup to achieve application to ongoing performance. If you plan to assist supervisors in providing job instruction, consider the following procedures.

Preparing for instruction begins with breaking down the job to be learned through a written task analysis (usually accomplished by a specialist), with an emphasis on helping an employee who is unfamiliar with the job learn how to do it safely and well. Then prepare an instruction plan designed for the particular employee that takes his or her background into account. It is also important to put the learner at ease and stimulate motivation by emphasizing the benefits and feasibility of training and by providing support and encouragement.

A clear presentation of the procedures to be learned is aided by four activities—tell, show, demonstrate, and explain.

When the supervisor tells the main steps of the entire job, the employee gains an overview that aids subsequent learning of the detailed procedure. When the supervisor also uses visuals and brief demonstrations of the main procedures, the employee learns what is involved, by means of seeing as well as hearing. As the supervisor slowly demonstrates the detailed procedures, beginning with major tasks that can be readily mastered, it is helpful to progress from the simple to the complex or from the known to the unknown, to aid the employee's progress and confidence. Explaining why procedures are done in a recommended way contributes to meaning, mastery, self-reliance, and adaptability.

The employee's active participation in trying out the job to be mastered while receiving helpful feedback from the supervisor is the heart of the job instruction method. The main steps are to have the employee talk through the job, then explain to the supervisor how the job is done, and then do the job. During this time, it is important that the supervisor provide both positive and negative feedback. Early mistakes are part of learning, and so the supervisor should avoid overcorrecting. Positive feedback is valuable because practice makes perfect only when it is oriented toward standards and progress.

Follow-up after the main training period contributes to application and satisfactory performance, when the supervisor reviews progress frequently at first, expresses genuine interest in the employee's progress, continues to provide feedback, lets the employee know where to go for help when the supervisor is unavailable, and then tapers off progress checks.

Benefits of effective job instruction methods include rapid and sound learning of a new job, higher productivity, less turnover, and less supervisory time devoted to problems associated with incompetent employees (Gold, 1981).

Sometimes the organization of learning activities is highly individualized, as in the case of developmental dialogues between managers and first-level supervisors (Mahler and McLean, 1980). Newly appointed supervisors confront many adjustments, such as making sure employees do their work well, introducing new procedures, dealing with human relations problems, and developing self-confidence in the role. The needs of each new supervisor are much affected by background, turnover, and type of employees supervised.

Accordingly, a manager can provide a folder of information about a supervisor's situation and the employees who are supervised. The manager also provides the supervisor with a series of instructional units on fundamental supervisory topics such as role, planning, delegation, development, and styles. After supervisors review the information from the folder about the local situation pertaining to the topic and read the instructional materials, they complete a work-related exercise or assignment and discuss all this with their supervisors. Each such developmental dialogue enables the manager to clarify concepts and review and perhaps modify action plans before they are implemented.

The effectiveness of developmental dialogues depends on basic self-study materials based on fundamental supervisory concepts and practices that are broadly applicable and do not soon become obsolete. The materials are combined with action learning projects, developmental dialogues with the manager, and a motivational assist by the manager-once-removed designed to facilitate specific application in the organizational setting. The manager receives a guidebook with step-by-step help with the process of conducting effective developmental dialogues. For a typical topic, the self-study takes two hours, the exercise another hour, and the dialogue from half an hour to several hours. In addition to your own use of procedures such as job instruction training or developmental dialogues, there may be times when you want to orient and assist supervisors who use those procedures in behalf of participants in a program that you conduct.

Another decision in organizing learning activities is when to use self-paced materials. Smith (1980) provides guidelines for choosing between self-paced (individualized) and group-paced instruction, after making six other instructional design decisions he considers even more important: relevance, learner motivation, practice opportunity, encouragement to apply, program evaluation, and instructor proficiency. He also provides a brief questionnaire to help you decide whether to devote time and money to self-paced instruction in a particular instance, depending on such influences as content, learner characteristics, other instructional design considerations, development constraints, and other administrative considerations. Group-paced instruction may be more individualized in ways other than pacing, such as accommodation of varied backgrounds and interests. The questionnaire addresses the following questions.

1. What types of proficiencies are to be developed? Self-pacing is especially useful for learning standardized tasks by large numbers of adults with widely varying backgrounds and needs for practice. Group pacing is especially helpful when there is no one right answer or procedure, so that discussion of various viewpoints and approaches is especially valuable.

2. How many learners are to be served? The development costs for self-paced instruction are more readily recovered with large numbers of learners, and once the materials are developed, they are useful when there are small numbers and short notice.

3. What are the participants' backgrounds? When learners' current proficiencies vary greatly, self-paced materials (such as learning modules and programmed instruction) allow individuals to set their own pace and to concentrate their practice and review on parts they want to master. Group-paced activities may be preferable for individualizing for purposes other than pacing, such as appreciating viewpoints of other participants.

4. Are interpersonal relations or teamwork to be improved? If so, group pacing is usually preferable.

5. How standardized and predictable are the tasks to be mastered? Group-paced methods, such as discussion and case analysis, are especially useful when there are great variations in the procedures and circumstances associated with performing the tasks to be learned, because the instructor and other participants can suggest adaptations to the varied circumstances.

6. Is attitude change important? If so, group pacing and group interaction are preferred.

7. How serious are the consequences if learners fail to achieve mastery? When the consequences are serious, self-pacing contributes to practice and self-assessment that enable partici-

pants to achieve standards. Group-paced activities may contribute to peer pressure and other influences on application of enhanced proficiencies.

8. Will extensive practice be required? The more extensive the practice, the greater the difference between the fastest and slowest learners, and self-pacing accommodates different learning rates better than group pacing.

9. How can feedback to learners be provided? If feedback is by printed materials (including self-scoring), self-pacing works well, as it does if the instructor must provide extensive individualized feedback. If other participants can provide feedback, this can be handled through group pacing.

10. Especially for self-paced activities, would most learners find the method boring? If so, add entertaining features and perhaps combine contrasting methods.

11. Does the provider or the learner have facilities available for self-paced instruction? If so, attractive and quiet study areas encourage persistence.

12. Can educational facilities and instructors accommodate participants when they want to begin? If not, self-paced instruction may be more accessible.

13. Will instruction be provided by a supervisor? If so, one-to-one self-paced may be easier for both learner and instructor.

14. Is it important to control administrative costs and include the expense of participants' salaries while they are engaged in educational activities? If so, self-paced instruction can be organized so that it takes less employee time away from work. This benefit can be offset if group pacing stimulates more rapid educational progress.

15. How quickly are the course materials likely to become obsolete? Self-paced instruction typically takes more time and money to prepare than group-paced instruction, and the expense is less justified when materials must be updated frequently.

16. What is the lead time? Self-paced courses take longer to develop.

17. Is it important to control course development costs? Self-paced courses cost more to develop.

18. Is the person who will do the course development experienced? Self-paced courses are difficult to design because of the heavy emphasis on materials preparation. In group-paced courses, the instructor can supplement the materials provided by the course developer much more easily than in self-paced instruction.

These questions reflect a distinct point of view about the desirability of programmed instruction. How well does it fit your program objectives and preferred teaching style? If it fits your style, perhaps the questionnaire can be useful as you decide when and how to use self-paced activities. If not, in what ways do you want to individualize group-paced instruction? On what basis might you decide?

This section on learning activities has suggested many options, only a few of which would be included in a particular program. This overview can help you select and organize the combination of activities that seems best as you plan an upcoming program. Planning program evaluation activities, another important component of planning, is described at the beginning of Chapter Nine. Evaluation results can be used when making planning decisions about each of the other components.

Arrangements

In addition to planning for needs, content, objectives, activities, and evaluation as five essential components of the educational program, it is important to arrange for additional resources and assistance required to have a successful program. Neglect of supportive arrangements can diminish educational impact. Although some instructors make all their own arrangements, usually other people assist. Many of the arrangements entail establishing and maintaining cooperation with other people. More detailed suggestions for arranging for program support are provided in Chapter Eleven.

For purposes of planning, it is helpful to recognize that decisions about each of the arrangements occur at various points throughout the process of planning, implementing, and follow up. Planning consists in deciding *who* should do *what*, *when.* This is illustrated by the following planning checklist. Within each aspect of planning (participants, resource persons, finances, materials, facilities, records, coordination), questions to be answered in the planning process are listed in chronological order.

Planning Checklist

A.   Participants
1. What characteristics of potential participants are most important to consider for planning purposes?
2. What program-related topics or issues are most likely to interest them?
3. What channels of communication are most likely to encourage their participation, and what is the best timing for publicizing your program?
4. How should persistence and application be encouraged?
B.   Resource persons
1. Who should help plan and conduct the program?
2. What commitments should be made to whom so that the program as a whole is well planned and conducted?
3. How can orientation and assistance be provided before and during the program so that it is well coordinated?
C.   Finances
1. What amounts and sources of finances are expected for support of the program?
2. What budget is desirable to support the program and feasible given probable income?
3. As the start of the program approaches, what budget adjustments should be made?
D.   Materials for learners
1. What type and amount of print and electronic materials are desirable for the program?
2. Who should do what to ensure that learners have access to appropriate materials?
3. Are materials prepared to support the instructional program?
E.   Educational facilities, equipment, and materials
1. What facilities, equipment, and materials are desirable for the program?

    2.   Which of these are available, and who will arrange for them?

    3.   Who should do what to ensure that arrangements are made and confirmed just before the program for any additional facilities and equipment?

F.   Records

    1.   Who will respond to requests, confirm mail registrations, and maintain program records?

    2.   Who will handle the process as participants enter the program, such as providing identification and orientation information and collecting information on registration and payment of fees?

    3.   Who will provide reports, such as for enrollments, attendance, fees collected, materials distributed, and achievement?

G.   Coordination

    1.   Who will assist with coordination of the program?

    2.   What will those persons' roles be?

Which of these aspects of planning for supportive arrangements are pertinent to your program? For those aspects that are pertinent, which do you handle? Who takes care of the remainder? How satisfactory are the arrangements? What might be done to improve planning of supportive arrangements?

Conclusion

Program planning can entail many interdependent decisions. In practice, you typically know how you want to conduct many aspects of your educational program. The foregoing overview can help you identify aspects that you want to modify. Criteria for selection of learning activities include objectives, learner characteristics, and your perspective. Considering the distinctive features of individual, group, and organizational activities can help you select and organize a sequence of activities likely to encourage participants to persist until their objectives have been achieved. Activities may be related to instruction, inquiry, or performance and may be individual- or group-paced. Program success can be harmed by unsatisfactory planning for supportive arrangements regarding participants, resource persons, finances, materials, facilities, records, and coordination.

The main components of program planning are reviewed in this chapter, on activities and arrangements, together with Chapters Four (needs, context, and objectives), Six (materials), and Nine (evaluation). The combination of these seven planning components may be overwhelming. To avoid the inertia that could result, use this overview of options to identify a few aspects of your typical program planning that you would like to strengthen. For each aspect selected, note what you would like to improve and then decide on some specific steps you can take to do so. Useful ideas may come from pertinent subsections of these planning chapters, cited readings, and conversations with effective instructors.

SIX

Selecting and Preparing
Useful Instructional Materials

Selection, development, and sequencing of educational materials are important parts of planning. Select from existing materials if they suit your purposes, content, and learners. When
satisfactory materials are not available (or when you or the
learners want to create them), it may be desirable to develop or
modify materials. Guidelines for doing so can increase quality
and decrease wasted effort. Similarly, criteria for planning the
sequence of materials can help ensure that they are an integral
part of the program and not an add-on.

There are hazards related to educational materials. Slav-
ish dependence on prepared materials, such as a set of readings
or a textbook, can make a program unresponsive to learner
needs and your distinctive contribution. Insufficient materials
can prevent participants from receiving essential orientation,
ideas, practice, and feedback. Irrelevant materials can distract
participants from the main messages.

What types and extent of educational materials do you
use in your program? Where do they come from? How satisfactory are they? How might you improve them? This chapter provides many guidelines for selecting and developing materials.
Use the guidelines to decide on a few improvements to make in
your materials.

Selecting Materials

Planning and conducting educational activities for adults
usually entails selecting and using educational materials—for

example, selecting a text for a course, slides for a presentation, a discussion case for a workshop, an audiotape for correspondence study, or a checklist for on-the-job training. The materials selection process is most effective when you are aware of various types of applicable print, visual, and electronic materials; when you use pertinent criteria to evaluate and select materials that fit the purposes, content, and learners; and when you include materials selection as an integral part of program planning (Anderson, 1979, 1983; Davies, 1981, 1984; Hortin, 1982; Wedemeyer, 1981).

Types of Educational Materials. The following examples of materials are grouped by the senses that are used to obtain information and by how remote or close they are to providing firsthand experience (listed from most vicarious to most direct). As you read through the examples in each category, note those that you typically use and those you might be interested in adding.

> *Print.* Includes all types of publications, whether originally intended for educational purposes or not. Examples include books, magazines, newspapers, pamphlets, reprints of articles, study guides, summaries, annotated bibliographies, programmed texts, outlines, checklists, and workbooks.
>
> *Audio.* Includes all types of mass and personal audio media, such as radio, records, and audiotapes.
>
> *Visual.* Includes all types of electronic and other ways to provide still or moving visual images (without sound), such as slides; filmstrips; projected pictures, charts, or diagrams; chalkboards, corkboards, flannel boards, flip charts; printed images, drawings, maps, charts, posters, and photographs.
>
> *Audiovisual.* Includes all combinations of sight and sound media, such as films, slide tapes, television, videotapes, computer software, and plays (including skits and puppet shows).
>
> *Simulations.* Includes all types of paper-and-pencil, mechanical, and computerized simulations, such as case

studies, critical incident cases, discussion guides, role
playing, in-basket exercises, decision-making games,
and patient management problems. Computer simulations are especially promising (Gueulette, 1982; Meierhenry, 1982; Reynolds, 1983).

Examples. Includes all types of found or fabricated objects, such as specimens, collections, dioramas, equipment demonstrations, working models, and mock-ups.

Selection Criteria. For any particular educational session
or series of sessions (with specified objectives and clientele),
many of the foregoing materials could be used, some would be
especially effective, and only a few would be used to a major
extent during a single session. But on what basis should the selection be made? Four bases are suggested: educational purposes, materials assessment, specific criteria, and user satisfaction.

A useful starting point for materials selection is the set of
program purposes and especially the main contribution to be
made by materials. The following list suggests some of the variety of purposes that materials might serve.

To help learners become more independent in future
learning projects.

To facilitate interaction among participants around a
common theme and guidelines.

To present a clear explanation of a complex set of relationships.

To provide an overview of an unfamiliar topic, which
may also serve as a checklist for subsequent review.

To facilitate review and encourage application with, for
example, handouts.

To help learners visualize.

To allow individualization and self-pacing, especially for
learners who need remedial help or want to progress
faster in special directions.

To present memorable examples from outside the learning setting.

You can focus on the types of materials likely to serve whatever purpose or combination of purposes is important in your program. Such a focus results in a more manageable number of materials to be evaluated as a basis for selecting those that appear most promising. The following guidelines suggest how you might make that selection from available materials.

Content. How much will the materials help learners master content pertinent to important program objectives?

Organization. To what extent are the materials organized to help learners interact with them during and after the program?

Background. How appropriate are the materials for the learners: is the readability level appropriate, do materials minimize vision or hearing problems, are they challenging but not overwhelming at learners' current level of proficiency?

Interest. How responsive are the materials to the learners' personality characteristics (such as motivation, confidence, preferred structure)?

Materials that meet the educational purposes of the program and are evaluated as the most satisfactory can then be judged by the following criteria to select those most likely to be effective for the learners in each session.

Beneficiary. Who is the main beneficiary of the program—the learner, an organizational group, or the community? If a group or community, the materials should encourage appropriate interaction and application.

Prerequisites. Are the materials at the right level given the learners' abilities and prerequisites? If not, alternative or modified materials should be provided.

Dialogue. Do the materials foster an active dialogue with the learners? Effective materials serve as tools or resources to enable active questioning or problem solving during and after the program.

Personalizability. Do the materials help participants feel a part of the program and the people connected with it? Humor, information about learners and resource persons, and an informal or familiar style can personalize forbidding materials.

Internalizability. Do varied materials encourage practice or rehearsal and help participants internalize new concepts or procedures and achieve mastery? If not, alternative or modified or more varied materials should be provided.

Plan. Are the materials part of the total instructional plan, not an addition? If not, start with the program objectives and rationale to locate or develop materials that fit.

If more materials remain after the foregoing screening than are required for the program, the final selection screen is the satisfaction of the participants and resource persons. This (very subjective) basis for selection asks: Which combination and sequence of materials is most likely to generate and sustain interest and growth for both learners and resource persons?

After reviewing the foregoing types of materials and selection criteria, how satisfied are you with your materials? If you would like to improve the process, what initial steps might you take?

Developing Materials

Most materials used to help adults learn are selected from those already available. They may be prepared commercially or by other instructors or earlier by the present instructor. Why, then, do you decide to develop new materials? Perhaps a satisfactory item to serve an important program purpose is lacking, or you or the participants feel an urge to create some educational materials in part as a challenging and growthful activity. Practitioners recognize that writing materials and developing audiovisuals are important proficiencies for helping adults learn.

General Design Guidelines. How can you develop educational materials effectively? The following broad guidelines for design of any educational materials provide a general overview of the process. They are based on concepts and procedures for design of learning activities generally and for selection of materials. However, they emphasize the development of materials that are integral to the process of teaching and learning and the application of instructional design concepts to development of effective materials. The general guidelines are followed by more detailed suggestions for preparing sets of slides or transparencies for presentations, printed materials, cases for discussion, videotapes with participants, and study guides for independent learning projects.

Rationale. Effective materials work well because, in addition to being well done technically and artistically, they fit the instructional *context* for their use. To design such materials, in addition to program purposes, content, and clientele, it is important to clarify your own rationale about the purposes of education and the process of learning.

Relevance. For many uses of educational materials, it is important that they contain interesting new content that is relevant to the learners' current proficiencies. This aim is aided by highlighting questions, paradoxes, problems, or opportunities likely to be interesting and relevant to participants, combined with familiar examples that establish connections with current proficiencies.

Responsiveness. Information about pertinent learner characteristics can help you design materials that are intelligible, challenging, and responsive to learners' backgrounds and preferred learning styles.

Focus. Materials can simplify complex content by emphasizing the most important aspects early, dividing the content into major parts, and then explaining interrelationships.

Interest. Effective materials attract and retain the learners' attention to encourage participants to persist until objectives are achieved. Such materials are varied, are realistic and concrete, relate the known to the unknown, stimulate emotional involvement, are persuasive because they are credible, and are clear and attractive.

Channels. Materials that use multiple communication channels reinforce content (by allowing learners to see, hear, and touch) and allow learners to compensate for inadequate ability to see or hear by using the other sense.

Repetition. Because learning and change result from repeated exposure, practice, or rehearsal, effective materials use varied repetition.

Resources. It is cost-effective to use existing resources (such as materials and people) where they can contribute to the finished product.

Flexibility. Materials should be applicable to various learners and circumstances, both to accommodate individual differences and to encourage learner directedness.

Action. Learners should be able to actively interact with materials. Participants should be encouraged to plan, select, produce, question, analyze, and discuss.

Feedback. Effective materials enable learners to compare their proficiencies against standards and thus receive feedback that aids learning. The feedback may be separate and formal (as in a quiz following a chapter) or integral and informal (as in performance evaluation in a computer simulation).

Modification. An advantage of prepared materials, in contrast with an oral method such as discussion, is that they lend themselves to pilot testing, formative evaluation, modification, and refinement so that they can be improved over time.

The following brief sections describe distinctive design and development considerations for five types of materials. These sections illustrate ways to adapt and elaborate general guidelines for specific types of materials.

Slide Sets. Sometimes for an important presentation it is desirable to select or produce a set of slides to help learners understand or visualize major concepts or procedures. Slides are usually used as part of a larger instructional effort that includes an accompanying oral presentation or audiotape or a subsequent discussion session or tour. (The following guidelines also apply generally to series of transparencies or opaque projections, filmstrips, or excerpts from motion picture film or videotapes.) Slide sets (and similar visual aids) have been shown to increase the effectiveness of presentations.

1. *Purpose.* Slides should be used when they are the best way to achieve an educational objective, by helping learners understand or *visualize* the main idea or an object or procedure. This can be done with magnification, time lapse, photographs from places where the learners are unlikely to go, or artwork that clarifies the essence of a concept or the relations of technical procedures. The visual should distinctively supplement the oral message.

2. *Rationale.* Begin with a rationale about your message and your audience, and then prepare a set of slides that helps to communicate that message. Specify educational objectives that reflect both the learner proficiencies to be enhanced and the major influences on acquisition and use of those proficiencies. Then write or outline a conversational script that relates the content to learner concerns. Either prepare production cards or note in the script the types of slides to help communicate the main ideas to be visualized. For example, select line graphs to show trends but pie charts to show proportions. Next, evaluate and select from available slides (or plan new ones) so that each one fits the commentary and achieves an important objective by presenting a major idea or legible title with a minimum of nonessential information.

3. *Sequence.* Arrange the commentary and slides in a sequence that early engages the learner's attention, memorably presents the main ideas to promote understanding and appreciation, and encourages reflection, questions, discussion, or action. Blank slides between sections and at the end provide transitions and avoid the harsh flash of bright light on the screen. Effective

slide or slide/tape presentations are typically shorter than ten minutes. Carefully prepared handouts can summarize the main points, leave space for notes, and suggest next steps. Often a next step is for the learners to do something with the ideas presented, such as questions and answers, subgroup discussion, or engaging in a procedure, preparing a project, or undertaking an action plan.

4. *Logistics.* Effective slide presentations evolve from planning, trial, revision, and follow-up. In addition to the importance of the content and the interest of the learners, attention should be given to refining the logistics. For example, to ensure that all can see, make sure ahead of time that the room can be sufficiently darkened and that the width of the screen is about one sixth of the distance from the screen to the back row. To ensure a smooth presentation, check out and practice with the projector and other equipment, including such small items as knowing where a replacement bulb is.

Printed Materials. Guidelines for developing print or visual materials are similar to the foregoing ones for preparation of slide sets. Clear and interesting educational materials of any type can help prepare for, enhance, and extend program impact. Included are prior readings, visuals, handouts, and suggestions for implementation. Effective materials should help achieve the educational objectives by being relevant, clear, well organized, nonoffensive, neat, friendly, and dignified. Following are some suggestions for development of any such materials (Anderson, 1983; Brockett, 1984; Joseph, 1981).

It is helpful to include an overview that lets the learner know the objectives, why they are important, and how the materials are organized. Such an overview helps participants relate the new ideas to past experience and to future applications and to use the materials in self-directed ways. You can also use this overview to interpret your efforts to administrators and policy makers.

Print materials are best when they reflect basic principles of clear writing. Choose clear and familiar words, keep sentences short and simple, use active-voice verbs, and include people in the writing by addressing the reader directly and by describing what people have done or should do. Attention to headings, short and varied paragraphs, white space, and layout will make each page more readable.

Visuals and graphics used with audio or text should fit and serve the objectives. Visuals should be relevant, interesting, clear, and realistic, should complement the other forms of communication, and should avoid being punishing, objectionable, or excessively redundant. It is also important that visuals be legible: be sure a visual contains a satisfactory amount of material and is sufficiently large-scale to be read, and pay attention to contrast, glare, and color.

Cases. In contrast to slide sets or printed materials, which facilitate a presentation to learners, case materials should facilitate interaction among learners. Each case should enable participants to achieve an educational objective, usually to better understand and be able to deal with some aspects of interpersonal relations in which a problem is to be solved or a decision made. Participants should have enough background and interest in the topic to be able to deal actively with the issues and relationships as realistic and important. You, as the instructor, should ensure that there are facilities, materials, and time for presentation and discussion of the case. You should also emphasize the process of inquiry by the learners more than the presentation of content by yourself. The case materials that you prepare or select should promote inquiry, discussion, and practice with problem solving.

The following guidelines for writing a discussion case can also be used to select or revise a case (Boyd, 1980; Stenzel and Feeney, 1970).

1. *Concepts.* Begin with the concepts or relationships that the learners should better understand or be better able to deal with. Most discussion cases involve some aspects of interpersonal relations that should help learners develop or modify strategies to interact with other people and achieve goals. Such aspects include recognizing problems, using procedures, winning cooperation, resolving conflicts, and considering implications. As the instructor, help the participants understand the objectives they are to achieve and select or develop cases to do so.

2. *Situation.* Select or develop a case situation that focuses on the concepts or relationships that learners should become more proficient with. Although a case analysis is only an approximation of actual practice, the discussion case should be as realistic as possible, dealing with positive and negative symptoms of concrete problems and specific concerns with which the learners can identify. Develop the characters who realistically portray the central actors in your little drama and the main people with whom they interact. If the symptoms pertain to a decision to be made, a problem to be solved, or an opportunity to be pursued, the other characters usually can influence the central characters or are affected by them. Select interesting names that make it easy to remember each character during the discussion. Also give characters organizational roles, personal attitudes, and styles of interacting that constitute portrayals of believable people with positive and negative characteristics. Write the case in narrative style with a minimum of unnecessary detail. Describe the situation, characters, symptoms, and attitudes that reflect the problems or decisions related to the concepts to be better understood.

3. *Influences.* Human relations problems do not occur in isolation. Provide background information about major influences on people and events. Examples include social, economic, or organizational trends; past encounters or precedents; and new policies or procedures. The case presentation should neither include a solution nor suggest an obvious solution. Instead, it should contain enough information about symptoms, people, relationships, and influences that those who discuss it can add compatible information such as they would have available in a real-life problem-solving situation.

4. *Questions.* It is helpful to include some basic discussion questions at the end to guide analysis and exploration of the case situation. These questions are not to obtain factual information but to assist learners to clarify and explore important and discussable issues—for example, to recognize major influences, to discover basic problems or opportunities, to analyze relations among facts, to consider alternative solutions or courses of action, to propose effective strategies, or to antici-

pate likely results. Questions to be used early in the discussion should help learners acquire a feel for the situation, middle questions should help clarify problems and solutions, and concluding questions should help explore actions and implications.

5. *Draft and revision.* A first draft of a new case description or a revision of an existing one should present the foregoing information simply and clearly. It can be as brief as a page or can contain much technical information from which participants can select what is relevant. A written case can be supplemented with audiotapes or visual aids. The revision and refinement process can include several procedures designed to produce a case description that is clear, plausible, and interesting, such as having experienced instructors suggest revisions and using the draft with adult learners. Such reactions can help you remove irrelevancies, add missing but necessary information, clarify the presentation, and add humor and other touches for interest.

Videotapes. In contrast to the instructor's preparation of slide presentations or case discussion materials, the participants can prepare educational materials in which both process and product are vehicles for learning. In addition to learner-prepared slides or cases, examples range from language experience procedures (in which illiterate adults dictate stories that they then learn how to read) to action learning projects (in which administrators work with other people to prepare reports and plans for both learning and action).

An innovative example is an interactive media approach in which less advantaged adults are helped to produce videotapes about neighborhood problems that they would like to have solved. In addition to using the completed videotapes (by themselves or with discussions with local residents) to communicate the problems to people who should help solve them, the process helps empower the less advantaged adults to help solve community problems (as a result of identifying symptoms and problems, producing the videotapes, and using them to communicate with decision makers). The basic interactive media approach can also use photographs or murals for clarifying problems and exploring solutions. In another approach, microteaching, people trying to improve their teaching performance use videotapes to gain feedback. They, peers, or experts view the videotape of a brief teaching session, identify aspects of performance to be improved, and then try it again.

Videotapes have many applications. During the past decade, continuing education practitioners have acquired sufficient experience with the development and selection of videotapes that some helpful guidelines for their use are emerging (Chamberlain, 1980; Rhodes and Azbell, 1985; Solsbury and Harris, 1978; Wilkins, 1977). Basic concepts include responsiveness to learner characteristics and integration with other aspects of the total instructional effort. The guidelines are for when to select videotapes.

Effective videotapes are responsive to pertinent learner characteristics, including needs for enhanced proficiencies that should be reflected in instructional objectives, experience on which to build program relevance and interest, and learners' search for meaning that the content and images of videotapes should facilitate.

Videotapes can be both alternatives to other media and components of a total instructional effort. A videotape is preferable to a printed booklet when it. is desirable to help the learner to visualize a process or situation and to comprehend complex relationships with the benefit of video techniques and ability to replay for review purposes. A videotape is preferable to a film because of lower cost, ease of videotaping real-world situations where filming might be difficult, and ease of showing a videotape. Most instructional uses of videotapes are as components of a total instructional effort that may also include printed worksheets and group discussion. Usually, instructors contribute through planning, preparation, individualization, and follow-up to encourage application.

Especially when a videotape serves specific instructional objectives, it can be very cost-effective. For example, tapes for sales training can contain memorable presentations that aid retention of factual information, can be used for repetition for mastery of skills, and can dramatize for attitude change. Videotapes can facilitate problem solving and stimulate use of related learning activities. They can be inexpensively shipped to remote locations for use by individuals and groups and can also be used by sales personnel with the customers when produced for that purpose (thus serving as a work aid as well as a training aid).

Study Guides. Study guides, syllabi, and observation checklists can help adult learners organize learning activities at times and locations that they prefer. Like other types of materials, effective study guides help learners focus on what's important, which means that the instructor needs to build this into the study guide.

You can do so by beginning with the outcomes that you hope the learners will achieve as a result of reading, observation, experience, interviewing, or trying something new. Such intended outcomes are enhanced proficiencies such as new insights, useful concepts, or mastery of procedures. If you want participants to discover certain concepts for themselves as a result of an inquiry process, it is not necessary or desirable to present the concepts in the materials, but you should have them clearly in mind so that the study guide helps the learners discover them. Before preparing the study guide, you should also review the resources and activities that learners can use to enhance their proficiencies. Many effective study guides contain the following sections.

1. *Purposes.* It is helpful to provide even a brief indication of what the learner should achieve and how the study guide should help.
2. *Resources.* This section lists available materials, equipment, and people to help learners achieve their objectives. Examples include attached materials to read, a bibliography for further readings, and suggestions for objects or activities to observe, types of people to interview, equipment to try out, or activities from which to learn.
3. *Procedures.* Learners appreciate suggestions about how they can use the resources to achieve their objectives: study questions to use when reading materials, a list of relationships to look for when viewing a film, an interview guide with spaces to record responses when asking people about

their experiences and views, a checklist when observing equipment being operated or a procedure being demonstrated, a planning form for preparing menus for nutritious meals, or suggestions for preparing a report.

4. *Outcomes.* This section suggests typical outcomes of such study projects along with standards and procedures for evaluating how satisfactory the results are. Illustrative outcomes are adoption of a procedure, achievement of a goal, or preparation of a report. Evaluation procedures might include self-assessment inventories, external reviews, taking a test, or critique by an expert.

An important consideration when preparing a study guide is that it be responsive to learner characteristics, such as interest level, reading ability, prior experience, intended application, and preferred extent of self-directedness. To prepare such a study guide, you need greater content mastery and understanding of learners than if you were to use more directive instructional procedures.

Study guides are especially valuable to guide participants through great amounts of detailed information or to assist learners who are at some distance from you. The following two examples illustrate these uses of study guides.

Special problems are associated with the organization of educational activities and materials when there is an enormous amount of detail to be mastered and learners have limited verbal abilities. An example is staff development for manufacturing operators and maintenance personnel (Holden, 1980). Holden reports a two-step procedure that entails detailed task analysis followed by simplification of the information to be presented by use of job performance aids and audiovisual modules.

The main purpose of the task analysis is to select critical and frequent tasks on which to focus educational activities and materials. If critical tasks are not performed properly, injury or financial loss is likely. If frequent tasks are performed well, the aggregate cost/benefits are great. Job performance aids include checklists, simplified diagrams, suggested strategies, and performance standards that help people learn and perform a complex task well. The educational activity, then, helps the employee understand why the job performance aid should be followed and helps supervisors provide such assistance.

Teaching at a distance has become increasingly familiar in recent decades as higher education institutions and other providers of correspondence study have used television and other technology to enable adults to pursue an individually paced course of study away from the institution (Chamberlain, 1980; Wedemeyer, 1981). Similar concepts and procedures are also used in teaching-at-a-distance programs that employers provide for employees at decentralized locations (Kearsley, 1981). Cost-effective and motivational features of technology have contributed to the expansion of teaching at a distance. Such features also influence your decisions about study guides and other materials and equipment when you teach at a distance.

Effective teaching at a distance requires special attention to developing materials and monitoring learner performance. In contrast with group instruction, which depends heavily on the instructor's face-to-face interaction with learners, instructional design is especially important when learners study individually at remote locations. Any instruction benefits from interesting materials, provocative questions, helpful examples, and periodic practice and feedback (Erickson, 1984; Gage, 1978; Keller, 1979; Weingand, 1982). Instructional design decisions seek to ensure that the educational materials you provide for distance learners have these desirable characteristics.

If you teach at a distance, it is important both to know about the learners' backgrounds, interests, and circumstances so as to establish rapport and to allow them to know about you so as to personalize the instructional process (Loewenthal, Blackwelder, and Broomall, 1980). Many distance education programs are team efforts in which several specialists contribute to a high-quality educational program. Without peer interaction to encourage persistence, it is especially important to follow guidelines such as these: emphasize the main ideas, let learners know why these ideas are important, provide active learning, divide the content into manageable parts, pilot-test materials, provide an outline or overview of parts, assure readability, include useful examples, provide for interaction, reinforce the main ideas, and emphasize application.

The initial segments (lessons, sessions) are crucial to clarify objectives, increase attention, and minimize threat. The highest attrition usually occurs at this stage. Asking learners why they are participating helps them to establish an appropriate mind set and to recall pertinent prerequisite learnings. Here as throughout the program, it is important to emphasize relevance and interest. One way to do so is to encourage transfer and application. Alternative materials enable participants to select and adapt to fit their preferred learning style. Because distance learners typically have more responsibility for educational decisions than sometimes occurs in group settings, it is important to help them learn how to learn if they are inexperienced with distance learning procedures.

It is helpful to encourage distance learners to develop a schedule and for the instructor to monitor it and provide gentle reminders. Monitoring progress can be combined with reinforcement and evaluation of main ideas, self-assessments, guidance, and recognition for progress. You can use information about learners' progress to revise materials. If feasible, arranging for contact among learners can be useful and can maintain commitment and interest. Some decentralization at locations where there are several participants can be helpful, but program staff must let them know about one another.

Do you prepare any of the materials for your programs? If so, does any of the foregoing guidelines suggest ways to improve the process? If not, and there are materials you would like to use that seem not to be available, you might consider adapting or developing a few items and refining them through use. In addition to the evident benefits for participants, some instructors gain satisfaction from the creative process. Exchanging materials with other instructors can be additionally enriching for all concerned, and in some parts of the field there are attractive publication opportunities with royalties as one reward.

Planning Use of Materials

In addition to selecting and developing effective materials, you should consider what materials to include at each *stage* of the program. Learners are unable to attend to everything at once, so consider a helpful *sequence* for materials as you prepare a study guide or syllabus for participants or even a plan for your own use. The following planning guidelines can help in sequencing materials.

1. *Start with objectives.* Materials are most effective when you begin with specific objectives for each session or unit and then (using your familiarity with learners, content, and materials) select or develop those materials likely to best serve the educational purposes. Such materials will be part of the program design or redesign and not just an add-on.

2. *Consider learner preferences.* Many adults with little formal education depend heavily on listening and observing; those with more education make more use of reading; those with learning disabilities may compensate by using the abilities they have. Varied educational materials allow learners to use their preferred modes of information seeking and to broaden the ways they learn.

3. *Provide choice.* Alternative materials that differ in emphasis and complexity result in program flexibility and responsiveness to learners. Participants can then select materials that are relevant and challenging to them, set their own pace, and maintain interest through variety.

4. *Present relevant content.* Learner persistence is increased by interesting materials that are not too difficult. Examples of such materials from participants' lives include procedural guides, repair manuals, job application or tax forms, newspapers, magazines, and cookbooks. Such materials can be provided or suggested by participants themselves and by people in various related roles.

5. *Focus on basics.* Many potential materials contain too much confusing detail. You can increase learning efficiency by reducing the overload of unnecessary detail and excessive categories, by helping learners process new information by clarify-

ing what they already know about the topic, and by establishing a useful mind set based on fundamental concepts and procedures on which they can add details.

6. *Provide opportunities for review.* Throughout a program, materials can be used for varied repetition and easy review, combined with immediate and anonymous feedback. Such review promotes both learning and learning how to learn.

7. *Include questions.* Materials can pose questions that encourage learners to process ideas—by raising study questions to guide inquiry, by presenting content to be questioned, and by suggesting questions about how new concepts or procedures might be applied or used in practice. A question-and-answer format is useful for many educational materials, as it parallels the dialogue that many adults use in informal learning projects that entail conversations, observations, and even silent dialogues in which many people engage when reading a book or listening to a talk.

8. *Encourage application.* Materials can help adults use what they learn by providing something new to apply, by providing opportunities to practice doing so soon after acquisition, by clarifying expectations about use of content, and by encouraging application by use of suggestions and guidelines.

As you sequence materials in your programs, do you use any of the foregoing guidelines? Might any guidelines that you do not use improve your planning of materials?

Conclusion

This chapter contained planning guidelines for selecting, developing, and sequencing educational materials. The main criterion for *selection* of materials is the educational purposes they should serve. More specific criteria pertain to learner backgrounds and interests and to program content and organization.

Similar criteria apply in *developing* your own educational materials. Clarify your rationale for the contribution the materials should make so there is a focus on important matters. Responsive materials are interesting and relevant to the variety of participants. Use of existing resources and multiple channels can contribute to active and flexible use and repetition for practice and mastery. Feedback can enable participants to compare their current proficiencies with desirable standards and can enable you to modify and refine the materials.

There are also guidelines to help you plan the *sequence* of materials to use at each stage of the program, including specific program objectives at each stage, learner decisions about selection and pace of materials, early focus on fundamental concepts and procedures, relevance to encourage practice review and persistence, and use of questions and inquiry to facilitate learning and application.

As you use these guidelines to review your planning and use of materials, consider not only their contribution to program objectives but also the other messages that materials can convey. The extent of attention given in the materials to some ideas and exclusion of others, compared with your intended scope of program content, can imply relative importance. The ways the materials characterize various types of people and organizations can convey implicit stereotypes that may or may not be consistent with your intent. Your critique of program materials can help you make modifications so that they serve program purposes.

The first half of the book has emphasized planning. The remainder deals with implementation.

SEVEN

Building Supportive and Active Learning Environments

First impressions are very important. One reason for program planning is to enable you to initiate the program in ways that build on and enhance participants' commitment and interest. Early program sessions are crucial because the highest attrition typically occurs at this stage. At the outset, participants can clarify what they can expect from the program, and instructors can decide what they hope to accomplish. It is therefore helpful to fine-tune your understanding of participants' needs and expectations, establish a supportive and challenging climate for learning, and obtain agreement on specific objectives. This chapter explores those three early tasks as you guide the teaching/learning transaction.

This focus on early tasks and procedures to actively engage the learner in the program builds on ideas in Chapter Two about adults as learners that suggested characteristics to consider throughout program planning and implementation. What do you do during early program sessions to engage the participants in your program? How satisfactory are those procedures? If there are ways in which you might strengthen the process, look for useful ideas in this chapter about how and why to do so.

Motivation and Responsiveness

Even though the main influences on motivation and learning are within the participants themselves, there are many ways you can help adults become engaged in and persist in learning activities. Your effective use of procedures for engaging adult learners depends on how well you understand their motives for participation and how well you use information about their unmet educational needs (Ausubel and Novack, 1978; Bandura, 1982; Bigge, 1982; Brundage and Mackeracker, 1980; Chickering and Associates, 1981; Merriam, 1984).

For each adult who is engaged in an educational program you conduct, there are many similar adults who are not sufficiently motivated to do so. Motivation is important not only for initial participation but for learning and application as well. Motivation depends on multiple influences, some personal and some situational (Fitzgerald, 1984; Knox, 1985; Whaples and Booth, 1982). Examples of personal, or internal, influences include aspiration and confidence. Examples of situational, or external, influences include opportunities and expectations of other people. The combination of multiple personal and situational influences usually results in a temporary equilibrium, as a person will enact but a few of the many changes that could be made. Selective perception and rationalization help to maintain the equilibrium. When an adult initiates or reacts to a major change, that event tends to precipitate learning activities to facilitate adjustments and a shift in outlook that helps the anticipated change seem more desirable (which disrupts the equilibrium and adds to the momentum for change). These are the dynamics discussed in Chapter Two (Apps, 1981; Aslanian and Brickell, 1980).

But you know that you have little direct influence on such motives. One useful source of information is a needs assessment such as those described in Chapter Four. Building on such general understandings of motivation and educational needs, this section suggests some *procedures* you can use with particular learners to try to achieve and maintain an optimal level of motivation and involvement in learning activities that they perceive as beneficial (Wlodkowski, 1985a, 1985b). Your conclusions about these participants will enable you to better individualize learning activities that are responsive to their backgrounds and interests and to select topics, materials, examples, and activities that contribute to persistence, learning, and application. Most of all, such conclusions should help you get the learners started on the right foot.

Assumptions. Your readings and experience regarding adult learners and their educational needs contribute to your assumptions about the incoming participants in a particular program (Knox, 1977). A major source is experience and evaluation findings from previous similar programs. But just how can you test those assumptions? If the participants seem to have sufficient experience and education, you might have them rate their degree of interest in a list of educational needs you assume they have (or to do so implicitly by reacting to a draft of program objectives and session topics and methods). If the participants lack experience and education and are unlikely to question your list by written responses, you might ask them to talk about what they want to accomplish and compare a summary of their responses with your list (Anderson and Niemi, 1969; Bacon, 1983; Darkenwald and Larson, 1980; Grotelueschen, Gooler, and Knox, 1976). Such procedures can be used early to ensure that early sessions are responsive. As you come to know the participants better informally, such procedures can be reserved for upcoming units when you are uncertain about relevance. When you discover that your assumptions about participant needs seem unwarranted, you will have sufficient lead time to modify topics, examples, and materials or to arrange for greater individualization or subgrouping.

Depth. Another use of your preliminary assessment of the participants' unmet needs is to decide how much further needs assessment is warranted. If you have substantial past experience with similar participants and your assumptions about the needs of incoming learners seem to be confirmed by their interest, satisfaction, and initial achievement, then little in-depth needs assessment may be justified beyond informal monitoring for responsiveness as the program progresses. If, however, you decide that more detailed needs assessment is worth the effort, the following procedures might be used during initial sessions with a minimum of your time and program disruption.

Procedures. Needs assessment is a form of evaluation for planning, focused on learners, that compares current with desired proficiencies. Recognizing discrepancies between the two can help you decide where to start as well as select content and methods likely to close the gap, and it can help participants reduce complacency and increase motivation to achieve relevant objectives. In addition, involvement in needs assessment enables participants to use such procedures in future self-directed learning activities.

Sometimes a self-assessment inventory, test, or self-scoring quiz is available or can be developed that provides a satisfactory estimate of proficiency early in the educational activity. It is helpful to you and the learners if items or sections are selected that are pertinent to likely program topics. Examples of prepared assessment inventories include the self-assessment inventories prepared by some professional associations, the pretests for parts of the General Educational Development (GED) exam for high school equivalency, and various course tests and licensing exams. The evaluation items may be multiple-choice or simulation in format. Satisfactory interpretation of scores depends on evidence that items discriminate among learners according to level of proficiency and on profiles of test performance by adults at various levels of proficiency.

An easy procedure with a small group of adults who can discuss their needs and concerns is agenda building. The agenda can be used to guide discussion and brief presentations during the remainder of the session or in future sessions. To build an agenda, ask the participants to think of their own unmet educational needs related to the content area to be covered, taking into account their current proficiencies (based on reading and experience) and the proficiencies to which they aspire. Then have them name particular topics or questions they would like to explore, and write each on a board or flip chart for all to see. Leave space as you list them, so that you can write similar points next to each other, and encourage participants to add points missed earlier. You can add topics also. When a fairly representative list has accumulated, review it once to remind people and ask them to select a few in which they are most interested. Then read the list a second time, and write down the number of people who raise their hands for each topic. Given the number of topics on the list, the number for which more than half the group voted, and the time available for discussion, you can assign letters to selected topics to propose a useful sequence (so that discussion of early topics prepares for later ones), and the amount of time spent discussing a topic should be based on the proportion of the group interested in doing so. If the general topic area is understood and the group is not too large, in a short time participants can express their needs and interests. More specific objectives can be established at the outset of discussing each topic. A similar procedure could be used with only one learner: Both of you would compile a list of topics, and then the learner would select those of highest priority.

Another form of needs assessment is to have the learners demonstrate their current proficiency through actual or simulated performance. For performance-oriented learning tasks, such as using tools, skiing, typing, or playing a musical instrument, participants can show how well they can currently perform. You and they can then compare that performance with desired proficiencies and decide which discrepancies to address first. Task analysis and competency models can be used to specify desired proficiencies. Using evaluation criteria and procedures is often helpful. For some tasks, participants can use observation guides or other evaluation tools to analyze an object or a procedure or to solve a problem. For cognitive tasks, participants can explain a process, analyze a relationship, or propose a course of action and indicate the concepts that constitute the rationale. This occurs in discussion of supervisory cases. For affective tasks, participants can express feelings and explore what may have contributed to those feelings. This occurs in sensitivity training and encounter groups. In each instance, you and the learners specify discrepancies between current and desired proficiencies that are important to narrow, which can be the focus of relevant educational activities.

Sometimes learners' enthusiasm is very high because the program content pertains to a strong interest in occupational advancement, a leisure interest, or solution of an organizational or community problem. If not, it is especially important that you be stimulating in order to maintain attention, build interest, and develop involvement. Wlodkowski (1985b) suggests many ways to do so, including the following: Relate the topic to participants' interests, provide frequent opportunities to all learners for active participation, use questions to stimulate interest, vary instructional methods, use examples and metaphors creatively, use humor frequently, clarify uses of new learnings, and include challenges.

In what ways are you responsive early to participants' needs and motives? How satisfactory are the procedures you use? What might you do to strengthen them?

Setting and Climate

In addition to being responsive to learner needs, effective interpersonal settings for continuing education are both supportive and challenging. A supportive physical and interpersonal setting in which participants feel secure and welcome is especially important for adults with little formal education or without recent educational experience. Adults with little interest in further education and training tend not to recognize opportunities and influences related to either learning settings or the settings where new learning is applied. A challenging setting is problem-centered, is neither boring nor threatening, promotes worthwhile educational achievement, and helps participants understand the problem situation, as well as the problem, and strategies for formulating effective solutions (Barrows and Tamblyn, 1980; Lindquist, 1978b; Mouton and Blake, 1984a; National Center for Research in Vocational Education, 1986; Renner, 1983; Squyres, 1980; Stritter and Hain, 1977). In such a climate, participants are expected to be actively involved in learning and problem solving. However, some adults resist such an active role because they are apprehensive about its excessive effort, responsibility, and risk.

Following are some ways to create such a supportive and challenging setting, especially for the first session.

1. *Choose attractive facilities.* Select facilities that participants are likely to find hospitable and encouraging of sharing. Educational facilities influence learning (Finkel, 1980, 1984;

Vosko, 1984). Such facilities include not only rooms for total-group or subgroup meetings but also the areas that conference centers should have for recreation, eating, sleeping, and informal conversation. Facility design can increase active participation and reduce fatigue and distraction, thus increasing listening, concentration, contemplation, and openness to new ideas. Concrete measures include comfortable chairs, arrangements of chairs and tables that encourage interaction, decor that reduces distractions and fatigue and increases concentration and learning, tables for six to eight persons to encourage discussion, attractive areas for informal interaction and for individual study, recreational facilities for tension reduction, and an electronic audience response system to give session leaders instant feedback about participants' understanding and preference.

2. *Help participants get acquainted.* Arrive early so you can welcome participants as they arrive, talking informally with as many as you can individually. Reviewing registration information about participants just beforehand can help, and providing them with name cards and encouraging them to get to know one another are also important. Refreshments can also help. Subgroups can help participants become acquainted if many are strangers, as at a conference (Bell and Margolis, 1985).

3. *Present yourself as a person.* It is also important to introduce yourself and to be informal enough that participants can come to know you as a person. Your words and actions should indicate your teaching style and your respect for them as varied adults who have the main responsibility for learning and for applying what they learn. Be yourself; your enthusiasm for what you teach and your concern for participants should reassure them of both your qualifications and your approachability.

4. *Reduce apprehension.* Providing some informal activities can reduce apprehension for yourself as well as the participants. Using warm-up activities, icebreakers, problem-solving games, and puzzles in ways that reflect your empathy and confidence can encourage the participants to relax and focus on important learning tasks (Brue, 1985).

5. *Encourage active participation.* Encourage participants to become involved early by introducing themselves—name, lo-

cale, background, and expectations of the program. This encourages sharing, helps you refine your estimate of group needs, exposes participants to role models, and encourages them to reflect on their own educational needs. Even a break in the session can be used to encourage interaction.

6. *Provide an overview.* Provide an introduction and overview of challenging and rewarding content that promises early success, responsive methods of facilitating learning, and basic procedures and logistic rules. Use what you know about participants, content, and methods to provide some brief and memorable demonstrations, examples, or presentations and some opportunities for discussion and raising questions. There can be a "coming attractions" quality to this initial encounter, similar to the lead paragraph of a news story or the first scene of a television drama.

7. *Obtain feedback.* Obtain some indication, however informal, of participants' initial reactions to help you decide what adjustments would improve subsequent sessions.

8. *Encourage return.* Summarize major points covered, review achievements, and indicate features of the next session, as ways of encouraging persistence. The greatest attrition tends to occur right after the first session. Telephoning or writing to inquire about those who are absent from the second session can also reduce attrition.

9. *Be available.* Being around for informal conversation between sessions (in person or by phone) can have multiple benefits parallel to many discussed earlier as desirable outcomes for the first session.

10. *Review for planning.* Soon after the initial session, review what happened and explore implications for the next sessions. Discussing the first session with someone who attended it can be especially helpful.

Crucial as the foregoing considerations are during the initial session, they continue to be important throughout the entire program. Planning can help ensure that facilities and equipment will be available and will contribute to program success. Participants' expertise can be shared by asking them to provide presentations, examples, demonstrations, and reports of experience. Resource persons can be identified who can enrich individual sessions. Such support and encouragement are important for both learning settings and the action settings where adults are to apply what they learn.

How do you handle initial sessions to provide a supportive and challenging climate? Do you find out from participants how satisfactory this process is for them? If you would like to strengthen it, do any of these ten procedures seem promising?

Agreement on Objectives

In addition to being responsive to learners' needs and providing a supportive and challenging setting, effectively engaging participants depends on agreement on objectives. The section on objective setting in Chapter Four emphasized concepts and procedures you can use to establish preliminary objectives in preparation for the initial session. Some of these concepts are also important as you interact with participants in setting objectives. They include the evolving nature of objectives, which are modified as program planning and implementation progress; the emphasis in most adult programs on enhancing proficiencies, which constitute capabilities to perform effectively; the importance of emphasizing higher-level objectives such as analysis, application of principles, problem solving, and evaluation; and the various ways you can use clear, realistic, and important educational objectives such as outlining content, selecting materials, deciding on methods, and preparing evaluation procedures.

As the program begins and you interact with participants, there are several ways you can review the preliminary objectives that resulted from the planning process and decide whether any shifts in emphasis or priority are desirable and feasible. As you review and perhaps revise objectives as the program begins, it is helpful to consider information about learners' needs and characteristics, contextual influences such as resources and constraints, and your own outlook on content and methods.

As the program progresses, ask yourself two questions: (1) What information, if any, do you have about the needs, abilities, expertise, connections, and other characteristics of individ-

ual participants (as from registration forms, introductions, informal conversations, or early sessions) which indicates that preliminary objectives should be modified? (2) What modifications
of objectives are implied, and how feasible and desirable are
such revisions given contextual influences and your own outlook?

Once the program has begun, there are several questions
you might consider about contextual influences (such as demands, constraints, resources, and opportunities) that might
lead to modification of objectives to be responsive to the actual
participants: (1) What resources or opportunities in the parent
organization of your provider agency (such as resource persons,
special projects, materials, and equipment) were not considered
when you prepared the preliminary objectives and program plan
but seem very pertinent now that you know more about the
learners and the program? (2) What similar resources or opportunities from the larger community or service area should you
now consider, and what do they imply for revising the objectives? (3) What demands and constraints in learners' expected application settings (such as policies, procedures, and supervisory
attitudes in an employment setting; habits and attitudes of family members for a nutrition education program for homemakers;
job market for a retraining program; or recreational opportunities for a leisure education program for older adults) have implications for objectives to be emphasized? (4) Which proposed
modifications of objectives based on contextual influences are
compatible with what you now know about learners' needs and
characteristics?

As you are reviewing and perhaps revising preliminary objectives in light of new information about learners and context,
you can also consider some questions about desirability and
feasibility, relying on your content mastery and experience in
helping adults learn: (1) Are concepts and procedures available
to implement the proposed objectives? (2) How compatible are
the modified objectives with what you know about adult development and learning? (3) What adjustments should be made to
ensure that the modified objectives are realistic in relation to
available time and resources? (4) What major content ideas are

so basic that if participants do not appreciate their importance and propose to omit them, you have an obligation to use your content mastery to be persuasive about why they are important? (5) What are your personal preferences, considering the distinctive contributions you can make to program planning and implementation?

The general reason for learners to participate in the objective-setting process is that it increases their understanding of and commitment to achieving the objectives. Having learners help to formulate and agree on objectives also has more specific advantages. Doing so increases their motivation to receive the expected benefits of achieving the objectives, enables them to use the objectives to guide their own learning efforts, allows various activities to achieve the objectives, and allows learners to assess their own progress. All these benefits together enable you to work with learners to provide learning activities that are responsive and effective.

You can use some of the following procedures to gain learner agreement on important educational objectives.

1. Use a learning contract as a formal arrangement for individual learners to work out with you the educational objectives they want to emphasize, how those objectives fit with the total program, and how they plan to achieve the objectives and evaluate their progress (Clark, 1978; Knowles, 1975; Sanders and Yanouzas, 1983). An early section of such an agreement is a list of objectives the learner expects to achieve.

2. Even when there are many participants in your program, in an early session use subgroups as small as three persons to discuss and critique the preliminary objectives. Subgroup recommendations can be combined and program objectives modified was warranted. Efficient use of this procedure can be educationally beneficial to the participants, in addition to any program improvements that result.

3. A planning committee (composed of representative participants, yourself, and perhaps others) can work with you to explore options and recommend courses of action, including formulating or revising objectives. This procedure is especially valuable and effective when you are working with an ongoing

group to draw out objectives that are important to them (in contrast with starting with the objectives and content and then recruiting interested people) and when there is sufficient latent consensus that a planning committee is likely to propose objectives that the participants will agree to, perhaps with modification.

4. The nominal group process is a structured technique for generating program objectives and then assigning them priorities. The entire process can take up to an hour. It works best for groups of five to fifteen; larger groups can be subdivided so that subgroups can work concurrently and then compare results (Delbecq, Van de Ven, and Gustafson, 1975). The basic steps are as follows:

- Participants list proposed objectives individually. (You and resource persons can contribute.)
- Each participant in turn contributes one new objective, which is written on a master list on a flip chart or chalkboard. Participants cross off items on their lists as other people mention them, and the process continues around the group until all items are on the master list.
- The items on the master list are then clarified and further combinations made, but the importance of the objectives is not discussed, nor should efforts to persuade occur.
- Without discussion, each participant individually selects five objectives that he or she considered most important and then assigns value points (from 5 for the most important through 1 for the least important).
- The value points assigned by each participant are recorded for each item on the master list and are then added. The objectives that receive the most points receive the most emphasis in the subsequent program sessions. Participants whose high-priority objectives receive low priority in the group can then make individual arrangements to achieve them.

5. Examples of effective performance can be presented to clarify desirable outcomes to which participants aspire. The presentations can be in the form of actual or videotaped demonstrations or written or oral descriptions. Participants can then

try to emulate or critique the examples. Participants who want to achieve desired proficiencies can then specify the implicit objectives and ways to achieve them.

6. One use of program evaluation (especially participants' reactions to the relative importance of program objectives and influences) is to modify objectives and procedures as the program progresses.

Agreement on educational objectives can raise participants' motivation to achieve the objectives and their understanding of how the objectives can serve as evaluation criteria. Gaining agreement can clarify connections between program content and participants' concerns and values, as well as the rationale for requirements if there are any. Almost by definition, the process creates some disequilibrium, but it is desirable that pursuit of initial objectives results in positive experiences. It is also desirable that initial objectives provide attractive challenges and opportunities for exploration and that they confirm learners' responsibility for their own achievement (Wlodkowski, 1985a).

Engaging the learner can occur on a one-to-one basis in a work setting.

As a manager, Mark Rosenblum met periodically with each supervisor who reported to him to review performance and growth goals. The first time a new supervisor met with him for this purpose was usually a bit tense, but later sessions tended to be very constructive. Performance review results and supervisors' aspirations typically yielded more educational needs that the supervisor recognized as desirable than were feasible. Consideration of organizational demands and constraints helped to reduce the list and identify potential support. Mark involved each supervisor in the process of actively reviewing current and desired proficiencies and the why and how of learning activities. A supervisor's professional development priorities were negotiated after options were actively explored. Mark was convinced that the resulting understanding and commitment to learning projects enabled and encouraged each supervisor to learn and apply in ways that were beneficial to the individual and the organization.

Conclusion

There are various ways you can help participants become committed to the program: understanding the needs and expectations of the actual participants, establishing a supportive and challenging climate for learning, and obtaining agreement on objectives. Because learners may have many reasons for participating in your program, it is important to test your assumptions about their needs and expectations. Doing so will help you decide on the extent and types of further needs assessment procedures to use with the participants, such as self-assessments, agenda building, and performance review.

Ways to establish a supportive and challenging climate for learning, especially during early sessions, include selecting conducive facilities, arranging for you and participants to get to know each other, providing warm-up activities, and having early sharing of information about backgrounds and expectations. Other ways include providing an overview of the program, periodically obtaining participants' reactions, and encouraging persistence.

The specific ways in which you obtain agreement on objectives and use the ones agreed on will vary from program to program. Typically, you use information about participants and context obtained near the start of the program to modify objectives, while considering both desirability and feasibility. Procedures for gaining agreement on objectives include learning contracts, group discussion, planning committees, nominal group process, examples of effective performance, and evaluative feedback.

Do any of the foregoing ideas about ways to engage the learner, during early sessions especially, suggest changes you might make in your instructional approach? If so, try one or two in your next program.

EIGHT

How to Provide Challenging Teaching-Learning Interactions

The essence of helping adults learn occurs in the teaching/learning transaction. Your understanding of adult learners, planning of activities and materials, and efforts to provide a supportive and challenging learning climate culminate in the learning activities that occur in the program sessions. Without educational achievement in those sessions, concerns about application and program support are empty. The satisfaction that you and the participants gain from the program experience depends on such procedures as use of questions and examples, provision of practice opportunities, sequence of activities for progression, satisfactory pacing, positive reinforcement, and program evaluation that provides useful feedback to participants and to you. Both activities and evaluation are integral parts of the teaching/learning transaction. (Evaluation is covered in Chapter Nine.)

As the program sessions unfold, what typically occurs? What are your usual roles and those of the participants? How do those roles vary with the size and type of group? How do you use questions and examples? What amount and type of practice occurs? How are learning activities sequenced? How do you handle pacing and reinforcement? What has gone poorly that you would like to improve? These aspects of the ongoing teaching/learning transaction occur in some fashion, if only by default. As you review this chapter, use the ideas in each section to reflect on your usual practice and your rationale for it. A useful result would be a few new ideas to try out in your next program.

As in sales, athletics, and the performing arts, it is the quality of performance in actual teaching and learning activities that justifies all the preparation and assistance. Although what participants learn and apply is the main criterion for judging the success of the effort, how you perform your role as you interact with participants is usually the single most powerful external influence on learner activity and accomplishment.

Instructional Modes

There are many ways of effectively helping adults learn. They vary with content, learner characteristics, teaching style, and mode of teaching. As indicated in the previous chapter, it is important to engage the learner through responsiveness to learner needs and motives, a challenging and supportive setting, and agreement on objectives. However, this can be done in various ways, depending on circumstances. The same applies to learning activities (Davis and McCallon, 1974; Gage, 1978; Joyce and Weil, 1972; Knowles, 1980; Knox, 1980b; Laird, 1978; Michalak and Yager, 1979; Mouton and Blake, 1984b; National Center for Research in Vocational Education, 1986; Redman, 1980; Robinson, 1979; Rogers, 1971; Smith, 1982; Sork, 1984; Wlodkowski, 1985a).

Three general modes of helping adults learn are instruction, inquiry, and performance. Emphasis on the three modes will vary with teaching style, and each will be effective for its general purpose if the mix of learning activities is effective enough to achieve the objectives, familiar enough to overcome apprehension, and varied enough to sustain interest. However, each mode has its own purpose and rationale (Epperson, 1974; Houle, 1980). An instructor can use any combination of modes.

As indicated in Chapter Five, the most familiar mode of teaching is instruction, in which one or more experts who have mastered content or procedures transmit them to participants who have not. Usually the problem is ignorance, the goal is mastery of knowledge, and the process is didactic instruction. The teacher's expertise is a major resource and provides an entree to other pertinent resources, such as readings and specialists. Typically teachers provide rules and standards that learners follow and emulate.

Instructional programs for adults are widespread. Many introductory and updating courses provided by educational institutions are in this mode. Examples include public school GED courses for high school equivalency, community college evening courses to provide an introduction to accounting or a foreign language, and university workshops or off-campus courses on computer programming or social stratification. Many education and training programs that employers provide for employees on technical procedures are also in the instructional mode, such as training for nurses in a new clinical procedure or for factory workers in use of new equipment.

A contrasting mode of teaching is *inquiry*, in which instructors and participants work together to solve problems that neither has completely mastered. Usually the emphasis is on the process of problem solving, the educational goal is mastery of inquiry procedures so that participants can discover and formulate the most satisfactory solutions, and the process is practice in doing so in ways that lead to inductively derived generalizations. The instructor's contribution emphasizes helping participants use inquiry procedures so that they learn how to learn. Typically instructors help learners discover major rules and concepts.

Some educational programs in the inquiry mode focus on problem solving in organizational settings. Examples provided by employers occur within the context of organization development, such as quality circles or efforts to improve communications. Some inquiry programs emphasize personal development— the "grid seminar" to strengthen managerial style, provided by the employer or by a consulting firm; the encounter group to help adults deal with personal feelings, difficult adjustments, and interpersonal relations, provided by voluntary associations and self-help groups.

A third mode of teaching uses *performance* as a vehicle for learning. The goal is to achieve a high standard of performance and to learn how to do so in such a way that it can be repeated in the future. The instructor's contribution is to match learners with practical experience that will be growthful and successful. Usually a work supervisor or a coach demonstrates desirable performance, which the learner can imitate and practice in order to improve. The instructor, who may also be the supervisor, emphasizes standards, feedback, rationale, and, in general, the "why" of performance. Examples among programs provided by employers include on-the-job training, rotating assignments as orientation for new managers, and action learning projects. Examples among programs provided by educational institutions include internships, practicums, cooperative education, and preceptorships. The benefit of learning through performance depends on the learner's doing real work (in contrast with observing) and devoting time to reflecting on why (usually through interaction with some combination of teacher, supervisor, and peers).

In each of these teaching modes (and in some others associated with counseling and social action) there are distinctive teaching/learning alliances as reflected in sources of learner discontent, pertinent resources, and perspectives on adult development. However, there are also some common themes, concepts, and procedures to be used in any mode to strengthen the teaching/learning transaction and increase participants' progress toward their educational objectives. The themes pertain to questions, practice, sequence, pacing, and reinforcement.

Questions and Examples

Especially early in an educational program (course, workshop, encounter group, action learning project, internship) and in individual sessions, it is helpful to raise questions, problems, issues, or concerns. The procedures discussed in Chapter Seven on engaging the learner should have identified some relevant problems and concerns of the learners for which you can pose provocative questions and issues.

There are several reasons for emphasizing questions and examples early. The fundamental reason is that it helps learners recognize questions before answers, problems before solutions, and reasons before information. The questions, problems, or reasons will not be complete, just illustrative. As participants master the answers, solutions, and information, they will, you hope, discover new questions, problems, and reasons. Your task is to arrange for provocative questions and challenging examples that are important to achieve the program objectives, are relevant for the participants, and provide a useful starting point because they simplify a complex learning task that could otherwise be confusing or overwhelming. Initial questions and examples encourage participants to clarify and use their current proficiencies and allow you to introduce concepts and procedures that serve as advance organizers (fundamental ideas or actions around which learners can organize subsidiary knowledge, attitudes, or skills).

Using Examples. There are many types of examples that you can introduce, depending on the content, the objectives, and the learners' background. They may be actual examples or recorded on film or videotape. Possibilities include equipment to be demonstrated, operated, or repaired; specimens or artifacts; performance (as in athletics, sales, teaching, counseling, or performing arts); and interpersonal relations. Analyzing and critiquing examples enables learners to recognize and apply their current proficiencies, as well as to focus on what they want to learn in order to achieve more desirable standards of proficiency. In some settings, you or a supervisor or a resource person or another participant may serve as a model by demonstrating a practice or procedure, having learners emulate your example, and providing feedback so they can improve.

Using Questions. The question is one of the most powerful and flexible teaching tools you can use. You can ask questions to guide group discussion, provide written questions to help learners with study and review, and encourage participants to use questions to organize their own learning activities. Following are some of the purposes for using questions to facilitate learning:

- To *diagnose* learners' current proficiencies (knowledge of facts, understanding of concepts, attitudes toward content, mastery of skills) so that you and they can build on useful proficiencies and modify misunderstandings and undesirable habits.
- To guide efforts to *master* the content by focusing on impor-

tant concepts, relationships, or procedures around which to organize the details.

- To facilitate *exchange* of ideas and viewpoints so that learners can benefit from the outlooks of other participants.
- To formulate action *strategies* for problem solving, which at each step take into account the results of earlier steps.
- To understand the *meaning* of the content by exploring "why" questions about assumptions, values, interpretations, and implications.
- To evaluate the *application* of the content to the learners' situation, life, beliefs, and plans.

Questions are especially valuable when used interactively in the flow of a session with a group of participants or an individual learner. The most familiar application is group discussion (Flynn and LaFaso, 1972; Knowles, 1980; Wlodkowski, 1985a). The following guidelines indicate how questions can be used interactively to guide inquiry and discussion.

- Ensure that learners feel enough *rapport* and familiarity with you and among themselves that they are prepared to interact and deal with the questions. Encourage all to participate.
  Have *materials* available (paper, chalkboard, handouts) to facilitate inquiry and discussion by listing topics, questions, and answers to enable participants to review, remember, select, and use them as needed.
- Carefully *prepare* questions to be used, especially at the outset, that establish connections between participants' backgrounds and interests and important content and objectives.
- Follow the flow of participants' thinking, and use questions most likely to help them *progress.* At a given point, questions may deal with assumptions, influences, facts, interpretations, relationships, reasons, procedures, applications, or implications. (This is the highest art of teaching, and doing it well depends on great understanding of both content and learners. The outstanding teachers of history have asked thought-provoking and insight-producing questions.)
- Use questions to guide the *process* as well as the content of

learning. Questions can be used to draw out the reticent learner, broaden the discussion beyond the most vocal participants, explore varying viewpoints, keep the discussion on track, and summarize progress.

Effective questions can serve similar purposes in training programs as well. Randall (1978b) lists arousing interest, getting attention, stimulating discussion, encouraging sharing, guiding thinking, and assessing understanding. For such purposes, effective questions typically have the following characteristics: they have a specific purpose that is pertinent to the content and fits the flow of the session; they are brief and clear and pertain to one main idea; and they require thinking (not just yes or no) but can be answered by the participants. Your questions should be friendly and sincere so participants realize you are trying to be helpful. Useful questions include: How do you view this problem? Would you give an example? Describe how you . . . . How did you work out your solution? What might a first step be? Tell us why . . . ? What are your reasons . . . ? How else might this be viewed?

Give participants time to respond. It may seem longer to you until someone breaks the silence than it actually is. Acknowledge responses to reinforce valuable comments and to use further questions for responses that seem unclear or incorrect. Also use questions for discussion and sharing among participants.

Although questions are valuable tools for anyone who helps adults learn, they are especially so for reading-based small-group discussion, such as Great Books and other volunteer-led discussion groups provided by libraries, community organizations, and religious institutions. A typical ground rule is that all participants must have read selected materials on which the discussion is focused. Questions are sometimes classified as knowledge, analytical, and evaluative.

Sawyers (1972) describes techniques leaders can use for sustaining a line of inquiry in a discussion. Examples are: pause after a question to allow time for thought and response; to encourage careful listening, don't repeat your question or the participant's response; and redirect questions to or seek clarification from other participants to encourage interaction and explore various points of view. Discussion leadership depends on preparation. Suggestions for preparation include: study the material to be discussed; list the discussable issues or problems (such as meaning or belief) that are raised; decide on the main issues for the session; formulate session objectives; and prepare a sequence of questions for each issue. In the flow of discussion, questions will be selected and rephrased, and new questions will be formulated. In general, however, early questions help participants to interpret readings, challenge other participants' interpretations, and revise their own interpretations on the basis of new insights. Later in the discussion, questions can help participants explore their reactions to ideas and express their own convictions.

Lynn Heissner made imaginative use of both examples and questions in a workshop session co-sponsored by a university and an association of sales managers. He unobtrusively audiotape-recorded conversations between customers and sales personnel in the type of business in which the sales managers worked (but not in their particular firms). At the outset of the workshop session, Lynn played several anonymous and brief but fairly complete conversations; one conversation ended in a sale and one did not. He then asked some questions, guided the discussion, played several more taped conversations, and repeated the process several times.

Illustrative questions included: How effective was the salesperson? Why? If you overheard this conversation and afterward the salesperson asked you for comments, what would you say? In responding to the questions, the experienced sales managers sometimes differed dramatically in their evaluations and rationales. The discussion progressed toward the "how" and "why" of effective sales, differing styles, and contributions of sales managers. The questions helped the participants proceed inductively from the examples toward powerful insights and generalizations.

Practice

In your programs, is it important for participants to practice, rehearse, or review in order to achieve mastery? If so, how well does this work? What do you do that influences practice by participants? This section explains why and how you can encourage and help participants to keep practicing until desirable levels of mastery are achieved.

Most learning, growth, and change depends on repeated interaction. The interaction is with the content to be learned, which may be in the form of printed materials, visual aids, demonstrations by resource persons, discussion with participants, or observation of objects or situations. This active process is called "practice." When you seek to gain mastery of an area of performance (typing, acting, playing a musical instrument, speaking a foreign language, writing a computer program, playing tennis), it is apparent that practice is essential to progress. However, even to enhance proficiencies that emphasize knowledge or attitudes, if mastery, retention, and application are to occur, there must be sufficient practice, rehearsal, or review. This is similar to the repetition that produces gradual changes in knowledge, skills, and attitudes in the natural flow of our daily lives.

However, practice alone does not make perfect. Mindless practice results in boredom and attrition. For progress to occur, practice should be combined with feedback about discrepancies between current and desired proficiencies, which contributes to both focus for efforts and motivation to persist. The section on learning activities in Chapter Five contains a list of types of learning activities for use in individual, large- and small-group, organizational, and community settings. That list includes most of the available opportunities for practice and feedback. The present section suggests ways to combine various types of activities to achieve sufficient interest and interaction so that persistence and progress result. The next section suggests how you can sequence activities for maximum progress. The following guidelines for practice and persistence pertain to realism, contiguity, and variety.

Realism. The more realistic your practice activities are, the more likely the learner is to persist and to apply what is learned. The main constraint on helping adults learn in the actual situation in which they intend to use what they learn is cost—the cost (in time and money) to you and the provider of using an actual situation and the cost (psychological as well as physical and monetary) to the learner that attends failure in the actual situation. (This is the reason for the Link Trainer to educate airline pilots and the simulated working model to educate power-plant operators.)

Practice exercises can be sequenced in descending order from realistic to abstract. Such a continuum might be: an organizational effort to improve team building, a supervised action learning project, a role-playing exercise to learn interviewing, a computer simulation, a case discussion, and a film followed by diagnostic questioning. At each stage of the program, try to provide as realistic activities as you can consistent with learner success, and try to move toward more realistic activities as the program proceeds.

Practice is also essential for skill mastery, as in educational programs to help industrial electricians engage in troubleshooting to diagnose the precise cause of malfunctions (Mallory, 1981). An effective method is simulation based on videotapes, workbooks, and computer practice exercises. Such an individualized and self-paced approach can include many conditions conducive to adult learning. The individualized format reduces excessive concern about making a mistake and about peer pressure and thus reduces the resulting defensiveness, and it allows sufficient presentations, practice, and feedback.

A combination of workbook units and brief videotaped demonstrations can ensure that each unit deals with a coherent procedure, preceded by an overview, so that the complexity of the total process is not overwhelming to the learner at the outset. If the simulation and related materials are accurately based on task analysis, the learner should obtain a clear understanding of a desirable sequence of tasks to be performed along with a rationale essential for meaningful practice.

Videotaped demonstrations have the advantage that they can be revised and improved through pretesting and formative evaluation. Workbooks or computer simulations can provide practice and feedback that reinforces sound problem-solving strategies and pinpoints needed improvement. For example, as the learner uses the computer to simulate identification of symptoms and then possible causes of malfunction, the computer records and analyzes the learner's problem-solving strategy, which is compared with the optimal strategy and solution stored in the computer. As a result, the learner can compare points of departure between actual and optimal strategies, along with the rationale for the recommended steps. Learners report positive reactions associated with individualization, low pressure, relevance of the simulation, high motivation, mastery learning, and short learning time.

Contiguity. Opportunities to practice or apply what is learned should be available as soon after presentation as possible. In the instructional mode of a didactic course, concepts presented in readings can be used in brief written exercises that follow, and concepts presented in a film can be used next in case discussion. In the inquiry mode, learners can use the generalizations they discover inductively to solve a simulated problem, and the inquiry procedures they master in a basic problem can be applied to a more complex one. In the performance mode, observation, demonstration, trial, feedback, and trial again can occur in quick succession for individual tasks before the learner is expected to assemble multiple tasks to perform a complex activity.

Variety. Some idea of standards of desirable proficiency helps learners understand the difference between change and progress, and feedback helps them realize the progress they are making and focus on important next steps. In addition, however, there should be enough variety that learners will persist until mastery. A variety of opportunities for practice allows participants to select those that most interest them, thus being responsive to individual differences. Varied activities also help maintain interest over time for each learner. It is desirable to intersperse active and passive segments, difficult and easier ones, those that present new concepts or procedures and those that explore how to use them in various situations.

The general idea that should undergird the realism, contiguity, and variety of practice is that it should be interspersed with attention to standards and feedback so that learners can benefit from the focus and motivation that can result from recognizing discrepancies between current and desired proficiencies. It is this concern for sequencing learning activities that the next section addresses.

Sequence of Learning Activities

Although varying the sequence of learning activities can increase learners' interest and persistence, the main reason for carefully planning and modifying the sequence of activities is to help participants progress in the achievement of their educational objectives. Time limits prevent achievement of all that is desired. The section on learning activities in Chapter Five includes a list of suggestions on planning the sequence of the entire educational program, many of which apply to individual sessions. The current section deals with ways to improve the sequence of activities as the program proceeds.

In introducing a new topic, procedure, or session, consider what you know about the content and learners so you can select activities and content likely to seem interesting and logical to participants. Emphasize content that enables learners to have early success experiences and provides useful prerequisites for subsequent topics. It is sometimes reassuring to participants to combine unfamiliar content with familiar methods or unfamiliar methods with familiar content.

It is also reassuring and helpful to provide an overview of a topic, unit, or session before proceeding with details. Such an overview helps participants recognize and build on their current proficiencies that pertain to what they are about to learn. It is also helpful to introduce early the subtopics that are especially important or will be frequently used in the session or unit or can be readily applied by the participants. Such an overview can be provided by a demonstration, brief tour, or film. For example, before analyzing a piece of music, play it through once. Before teaching individual tasks that constitute a complex procedure, demonstrate the entire procedure. Then demonstrate the subtasks and allow the participants to practice them until a sufficient level of mastery is achieved (Richardson and Harbour, 1982). Provide feedback at each stage. Finally, have learners assemble all the parts and practice using them together. This method has been shown to be especially effective for adults with limited learning abilities who had experienced difficulty with less organized methods. Careful attention to subdividing and sequencing learning tasks reduces difficulties due to information overload. When dealing with subtopics, it is important to maintain continuity so that learners understand relations among the parts.

It is usually helpful for difficulty to increase from the beginning to the end of a unit or program. As much as possible, participants should find learning activities challenging and objectives achievable, avoiding both being bored and being overwhelmed. However, keeping early activities easier will contribute to both mastery and confidence. There are several ways to keep difficulty level manageable at the outset. One is to begin with the simple and move toward the more complex. In the instruction mode, emphasizing deductive reasoning, this means beginning with simple concepts that are easy to grasp and have few exceptions and using them to explain or solve examples to which they readily apply. In the inquiry mode, emphasizing inductive reasoning, it means beginning with examples from which the generalization or procedure can be readily discovered.

Another way to keep difficulty manageable is to begin with the basic and to move toward the specialized. The general and basic ideas or procedures that are first introduced can help learners consolidate and apply their current proficiency, serving as a solid structure on which to build the details in an organized way. This structure contributes to both acquisition of enhanced proficiency and later recall, because by beginning with the fundamental ideas, the learner can reconstruct much detail that might be difficult to remember if acquired in isolation.

A third way to keep difficulty manageable is to begin with basic "how to" questions and defer detailed consideration of questions about "why" and "unusual applications" and "next steps" until basic tasks have become somewhat routine.

By contrast, sometimes you want to help learners deal with higher levels of difficulty and understanding. Following is a progression of increasingly higher levels of understanding that can be used to diagnose the underlying mental processes that participants currently use, to help them select learning activities at the next higher level, to enable them to master a more powerful learning approach, and to assess the extent of their achievement in doing so (Bloom and others, 1956; Flavel, 1976; Ford, 1981; Kirschenbaum and Perri, 1982; Krathwohl and others, 1964; Morrill, 1980; Richards and Perri, 1978; Rothwell, 1983).

1. *Fragmentary understanding.* Learner processes facts and details superficially, without central concepts or broad integrating themes, and considers or describes only one side of a problem or issue with little attention to similarities, differences, and gradations.
2. *Comprehension.* Learner deals with central concepts or integrating themes to recognize similarities but without relation to supporting facts and details that help to distinguish differences. Opposing views are perceived as compartmentalized or negative.
3. *Understanding of relationships.* Learner integrates concepts and themes with facts and details, by identification of both similarities and differences and deep multiple processing, within the context of information presented.
4. *Inclusive understanding.* Learner uses deep processing of integrating themes to go beyond the context of information presented, using personal experience and additional knowledge to provide reasons for similarities and differences and to explore relations among alternative views, which contributes to better retrieval and new insights.

Groups of participants typically include learners at various abilities and levels of understanding. It is therefore desirable to individualize the educational materials (such as with self-assessments, alternative readings, and differentiated subgroup activities) to provide feedback, options, and guidance to enable each participant to progress toward the next higher level of difficulty and understanding.

Progression can be facilitated through attention to process as well as content. Analyses of group behavior distinguish three types of contributions made by participants and instructors. One is task behavior, which deals with content, achievement, and accomplishing objectives. A second is maintenance behavior, which contributes to communication and cooperation. A third is self-serving behavior—nonfunctional activities that satisfy personal needs at the expense of others in the group. In the flow of a program, your understanding of these three types of behaviors can enable you to decide how much attention to give to each.

Following are major *task* behaviors:

- *Initiating* new ideas, perspectives, or activities.
- *Giving information,* facts, opinion, or beliefs pertinent to a group task.
- *Clarifying* or elaborating on a topic being considered, sometimes by restatement or giving examples.
- *Seeking information* from others or initiating such search.
- *Synthesizing,* or showing relationships among ideas or suggestions.
- *Reviewing* progress toward objectives, questioning the direction of the discussion, asking whether an action should be taken.

Following are major *maintenance* behaviors:

- *Encouraging* and praising others and their ideas by being friendly, responsive, and accepting of their contributions.
- *Setting standards* for the group by proposing content, procedures, or rules.

- *Directing* members' contributions by encouraging reticent members and limiting the most talkative so others have a chance.
- *Mediating* and harmonizing differences, including arranging compromises when needed.
- *Following*—listening and using the ideas of others.
- *Relieving tension* and reducing disruptive negative feelings through humor or conciliatory efforts.

Following are major *self-serving* behaviors:

- *Dominating* or manipulating the group or members by interrupting, giving orders, or trying to assert authority.
- *Aggression,* or seemingly unprovoked hostility toward the group or members, as reflected in criticizing, blaming, deflating, or attacking others' motives.
- *Blocking* and interfering with group progress by tangents, irrelevancies, rejection, or returning to issues already resolved by the group.
- *Seeking recognition* and attention through boasting, excessive talking, or extreme ideas.
- *Special pleading* beyond reason for pet ideas, with exaggerated claims.
- *Withdrawing,* or disengaging from the group, as reflected in indifference, passivity, whispering to others, or excessive formality.

It is not sufficient to recognize such behaviors in yourself and in other group members. To use such insights to help adults learn, it is important to be alert to how beneficial a current or potential behavior is likely to be in the flow of an actual session. This can help you decide whether to give more or less attention to task or maintenance behavior, recognizing that there are sometimes trade-offs between content and process. For example, you may restrain your impulse to give information because it seems more important to draw out reticent members and set standards of learner-guided inquiry behavior. It is desirable for participants to understand and deal with all three types of behaviors. By precept, example, and positive reinforcement, you can encourage their group leadership behaviors that seem beneficial and, in extreme instances, discourage disruptive behaviors (Fetteroll, 1985). With shared leadership, other participants can also make constructive contributions to reducing the problem.

> Vicki Alvarez was especially effective with disruptive participants. With the overly talkative, she gave recognition for their valuable contributions; tried to seat them to the side, avoided eye contact, and used body language to discourage excessive comments; interrupted after the basic point had been made to relate it to the current topic or asked how other participants felt about the idea; and, in extreme cases, talked with the disruptive participant in private about the problem.

Your contribution to sequencing can extend beyond guiding large- and small-group learning activities. For example, it can include preparatory activities by learners before group sessions, such as reading, self-assessment, and analysis of their situation or problem to which what they learn is to be applied. Other types of activities to be sequenced include consultation, self-directed study, and intermittent solitude.

Pacing

Closely related to sequencing for progression is attention to pacing. This includes how fast the learners proceed through educational activities and materials (whether presentation and practice activities are concentrated or distributed over time) and allowance for individualization. The fundamental guideline regarding pacing is simple: Let learners proceed at their preferred pace. There is great variation in learning style and in preferred pace. Most adults learn most tasks best when they set their own pace. Their opportunities to do so depend on your planning and flexibility.

Ways to provide such opportunities include adjusting total-group demonstrations and presentations, with the aid of feedback, so they are most satisfactory for most participants; using fast, medium, and slow subgroups; and using self-paced materials such as audio- and videotapes, readings, and computer simulations.

Pacing is also affected by scheduling of sessions. Sessions should be long enough to allow introduction of new experiences, concepts, insights, or procedures; practice, rehearsal, or review of the new content; and feedback on mastery or application. However, sessions should not be so long that fatigue or boredom results. Optimal session length before a break or change of activity varies greatly with content and learners but seldom exceeds an hour or two. For stressful content and participants with limited education, an optimal session may be fifteen minutes.

For some content—for example, athletics, performing arts, and typing—it is usually desirable to distribute brief practice sessions over a long period. Distributed practice builds stamina, reduces resistance due to fatigue, allows consolidation and informal rehearsal between sessions, and reduces development of bad habits that have to be unlearned.

By contrast, some content, such as sensitivity training or learning to speak a foreign language, benefits from concentrated attention through extended immersion. Concentrated practice helps screen out the habits and influences of daily life that resist new ways of thinking, feeling, and doing. It takes a while, on entering an educational setting, to put aside external concerns and concentrate on the content, especially if the concerns entail strong feelings. With short, distributed sessions, progress can be just starting when it's time to end. Weekend marriage encounter retreats, two-week sensitivity training programs in a residential setting, or month-long intensive language institutes provide time to clarify current proficiencies, present models of desired proficiencies, allow for practice and feedback, and repeat the process in a supportive setting so that the learner experiences both progress and confidence. Concentrated scheduling can allow greater attention to the interplay of knowledge, skills, and attitudes as they relate to performance.

Some aspects of individualization you can plan for, such as alternative content, methods, materials, and subgroups that participants can choose. However, some aspects of individualization depend on self-directedness by participants. You can help them by providing role models, self-assessment inventories, and guides to materials and resources. But usually individualizing pacing also entails helping participants learn how to learn as well as what to learn. Adults who think of themselves as dependent learners will appreciate your patience, support, and assistance as they become more able to guide their own personal growth.

Sometimes external circumstances such as a deadline, exam, or directive seem to dictate unreasonable coverage within set time limits that make standard pacing unworkable. Possible solutions include increased time in or out of program sessions, use of concurrent groups (perhaps with volunteer assistance), focus on high-priority content, and frequent change of pace and even relaxation exercises to reduce stress.

Reinforcement

Feedback and reinforcement have been referred to throughout this chapter, but it might be useful to focus on how you can use such concepts and procedures to help adults learn. (Chapter Nine deals with your use of evaluation to strengthen the total teaching/learning transaction.) The current section deals with three interrelated concepts—feedback, reinforcement, and unlearning.

Feedback. Feedback includes all ways by which learners obtain information about how their learning activities are progressing. It includes self-assessments as well as reactions by the instructor, peers, and other people. The feedback can be oral, written, or directed observation of an example. Feedback is important to learners because knowledge about the progress they are achieving and what affects it aids their decisions about persisting and adjusting their efforts. There are several ways you can contribute to useful feedback.

1. *Receptivity.* If participants help plan or select feedback procedures and understand the rationale for their use and

the usefulness of the conclusions, they are likely to be receptive to the feedback and to minimize defensiveness, distortion, and denial.

2. *Organization.* It takes some planning and expertise to have evaluation instruments that are valid and efficient, to make judgments based on the evidence, and to report conclusions in useful ways. The most effective instruments and procedures for evaluation and feedback to adult learners result from use and refinement.

3. *Judgments.* Evaluative feedback about educational efforts entails explicit or implicit judgments. Learners should understand the basis on which such judgments are made, regardless of who is making them. The most useful judgments interpret learner progress in relation to stated objectives, expectations, standards, or desired proficiencies. Feedback about discrepancies with the standards that learners want to achieve (even if the conclusion is poor initial performance) can be used diagnostically. This depends on clear objectives or expectations and criterion-referenced instruments or forms that allow learners to compare their achievement with their expectations. By contrast, learners can do much less with judgments that result from comparisons of educational achievement with that of other participants or with unstated standards.

4. *Quality.* The amount and quality of feedback should be sufficient and timely so that learners have something to work with. A list of strengths and weaknesses of a trial performance is far more useful than a summary critique such as "satisfactory" or "unsatisfactory." Receiving a critique right after some of the trials so the conclusions can be applied to the next trial is far more useful than receiving a critique a week later when no more trials are scheduled.

5. *Use.* It is helpful to suggest to learners specific uses they can make of evaluative feedback and to provide opportunities for them to do so. In a series of sessions for new supervisors on conducting meetings, each participant might have several turns to lead brief sessions. After each session, critique forms might be completed by the session leader, other participants, and the instructor. The leader would then indicate what went well and what changes could be made to improve. The instruc-

tor and other participants would then offer constructive criticism by commenting on both strengths and weaknesses, and the discussion of that session would conclude with the leader suggesting changes to try the next time. The leader would also be able to review the critique forms in preparation for conducting a session the next time. Such detailed and timely feedback focused on improvement reduces defensiveness by the learner and emphasizes constructive change.

Reinforcement. Positive feedback is a form of reinforcement. People change gradually in response to multiple influences, and it is as important to reinforce what is done well as to criticize what could be improved. Rewards and praise are other forms of reinforcement. Recognition can range from a simple "Very good" from a respected peer or instructor to an award by distinguished judges for "world class" performance.

Many adults receive reinforcement for satisfactory performance and feedback on suggested improvements from exposure to role models and standards of best practice. They can compare their own practice with the standards and both derive satisfaction from what they are already doing well and focus motivation to make improvements. Memorable encounters with role models or standards of excellence can leave especially lasting impressions. However, it is important that the standards not be so far beyond the learner's current proficiencies that the learner becomes intimidated and discouraged. Self-assessment inventories can provide detailed and useful reinforcement and feedback. It is also important to minimize negative conditions that discourage learning.

One of the most influential forms of reinforcement is successful use of what is learned. Although reinforcement from the actual performance setting beyond the educational program may be the most powerful, it may also be accompanied by undesirable side effects such as defensiveness by the learner, dysfunctional influences by other people, and even an element of danger. Consequently, simulations such as computerized patient management problems for physicians or Link Trainers for airline pilots may sometimes be more satisfactory sources of feedback and reinforcement.

In general, it is desirable to provide feedback and external reinforcement only some of the time and on an irregular schedule. This encourages a more self-directing and self-correcting approach by the learner and discourages undesirable dependency.

Unlearning. Sometimes "unlearning" is called for, to clear up misunderstandings, reorganize confused concepts, extinguish minor fears, or correct bad habits (Newstrom, 1983). In each instance, obsolete or dysfunctional prior learnings interfere with efforts to acquire new proficiencies. You can help learners recognize this potential interference and promote "unlearning" by noting differences between the new and the old, reinforcing aspects common to the old and the new proficiency, and then proceeding to extinguish the unwanted aspects of the old proficiency and replace them with the preferred aspects of the new proficiency.

How can you use the foregoing ideas about feedback, reinforcement, and unlearning as you help adults learn? A useful starting point is to review your current teaching practice. Where do learners obtain standards and objectives against which to assess their progress? How specific and useful are those standards and objectives? How do you and the learners discover points at which "unlearning" may be desirable? What more might be done? How well does your teaching provide for the five aspects of feedback (receptivity, organization, judgments, quality, use)? If a preliminary review suggests that your reinforcement procedures might be strengthened, you can use the concepts and procedures suggested in Chapter Nine to analyze this aspect of your teaching and obtain detailed recommendations for improvement.

Which modes (instruction, inquiry, performance) do you typically include in your instruction? How familiar were the five themes (questions, practice, sequence, pacing, reinforcement) as you reflected on your instructional procedures? Are there any aspects of the teaching/learning transaction in your program that you would like to strengthen? If so, select a few pertinent ideas from this chapter that seem most promising and use them.

Conclusion

Participant learning and application depend on both engaging in growthful learning activities and receiving constructive feedback. The teaching/learning transaction thus includes both activities and evaluation. Your resulting interaction with participants in program sessions can be the most challenging and satisfying part of helping adults learn.

Three modes of learning are from instruction, inquiry, and performance. There are five themes common to these three modes. One is the valuable contribution of questions and examples as tools by which you can guide learning. A second is the importance of providing practice opportunities characterized by realism, contiguity, and variety. A third includes various ways to sequence learning activities for progression. You can begin with an overview of fundamentals and help participants progress toward higher levels of understanding. Attention to sequence can also include process concerns (such as participant behaviors that serve task, maintenance, or self-serving purposes). A fourth theme is pacing, including ways to help participants set their preferred pace and to schedule distributed or concentrated activities depending on the circumstances. A fifth theme is reinforcement, which includes attention to participant receptivity, refinement of procedures, comparing proficiency with standards, and suggesting improvements and applications. Reinforcement tends to be most effective when it is irregular.

Which of these modes (instruction, inquiry, performance) do you emphasize? Of the five themes (questions and examples, practice, sequence, pacing, and reinforcement), are there any aspects of the teaching/learning transaction that you would like to strengthen in your programs? If so, what steps might you take to do so?

NINE

Using Program Evaluation Information Effectively

How is your program evaluated? Who evaluates it? On what basis? Who does what with the results? How do you feel about the process? Few aspects of helping adults learn generate more concern and less action than program evaluation. Though discussed in this chapter, it should relate as much to program planning as to implementation. Effective evaluation should be part of each component of planning and of all aspects of the teaching/learning transaction.

In best practice, program evaluation provides feedback to you, participants, and decision makers to guide program decisions. It can be as much a political process as an educational one. Implicit conflicts can surface as a result of evaluation activities. This chapter emphasizes your use of evaluation concepts and procedures as part of program planning and implementation.

Planning Program Evaluation

Educational programs for adults are continually evaluated informally—when learners judge the usefulness of their educational activity and decide whether to persist, when instructors judge the effectiveness of educational materials and decide whether to change them, and when program administrators judge instructors' performance and decide whether to have them teach next time. In each instance, people associated with the program make judgments about a program's worth and effectiveness.

There are three main reasons for *formalizing* program evaluation as a part of the program-planning process. First, you are more likely to accurately describe influences, performance, and expectations. Second, you are more likely to make sound judgments clearly based on pertinent evidence. Third, you are more likely to use an evaluation process that communicates findings in ways that encourage people associated with the program to use those findings for decisions on program planning, improvement, and justification (Grotelueschen, 1980; Grotelueschen, Gooler, and Knox, 1976; Kopp, 1986b). This can help strengthen your program, in part by enabling you to protect it from inadequate judgments by other people that might be at least partly offset by your evaluation findings.

Focusing Your Evaluation: Addressing Audiences and Issues. Many aspects of the program could be evaluated, and many evaluation procedures could be used. It is important to be selective when you plan evaluation so that the benefits from evaluation exceed the time and money spent. For example, program evaluation could focus on educational objectives to be achieved, program designs, effectiveness of implementation, or outcomes achieved. Evaluation plans can also be selective about the main purpose to be achieved. When the purpose is planning, the evaluation activity is needs assessment or market research, as discussed at the beginning of Chapter Four. Sometimes the main purpose is program improvement, as when people closely associated with the program use formative evaluation procedures to assess its effectiveness in order to make changes to strengthen it. Sometimes the main purpose is program justification, as when people outside the program help to assess impact for purposes of accountability.

Perhaps the most important question to consider when planning evaluation is: Who are the main audiences for the evaluation report, and what issues concern them that your evaluation could address? Clarifying the audiences for your evaluation report helps you specify not only the general purposes and scale of the evaluation effort but also specific objectives and criteria. For example, you as the instructor might evaluate for your own use changes in learner satisfaction and achievement associated with use of different instructional methods. By contrast, findings from an evaluation of educational materials might be used by yourself and the learners as you try to help them become more self-directed in materials selection. Or findings from a follow-up study of past participants might be for the benefit of yourself, the administrator of your program area, and several policy makers interested in program impact and in whether the resources they allocate for your program are justified.

Clarifying the purposes, audiences, and issues of evaluation helps to decide not only what extent of evaluation is warranted but also when data collection should occur and reports be made. For example, if the issue is an unacceptably high attrition rate, it may be necessary to collect data each time people enroll or drop out. If you plan to introduce a new program for a new clientele, you may conduct a special evaluation project for initial planning and improvement and phase it out as soon as the new program is proceeding well. By definition, a follow-up evaluation should occur around the time when former participants are likely to apply what they learned. Over the years, in various types of provider agencies, follow-up studies have shown that well-designed continuing education programs can have a major positive impact on subsequent performance (Knox, 1979c). However, policy makers usually want to know, in a particular instance, both the extent of impact and the changes that might be made to improve results. An evaluation plan should therefore include the purposes, audiences, scale, and timing of the evaluation effort.

Constraints of Feasibility. These early steps in drafting an evaluation plan indicate what is desirable. It is also important to consider what is feasible given the available money, commitment, time, and expertise. Commitment and expertise are especially important, because willingness to devote the necessary time by people who together have the requisite evaluation expertise can usually attract the necessary money and other resources. Similarly, the availability of money for evaluation can be used to arrange for sufficient time of people with the expertise to plan and conduct the evaluation.

Feasibility is partly a matter of the intended scope of the evaluation effort. Practitioners seldom conduct a thorough and comprehensive evaluation of either their course or total agency offerings. To do so would typically cost more than to provide the program. One way to reduce the scope is to emphasize planning or improvement or justification as the main purpose of the evaluation. Another is to address the issues of importance to the main audiences for the evaluation report. In addition, the four previously mentioned program perspectives to review (goals, designs, implementation, outcomes) can be combined in a grid with four program elements (participants, instructors, topics, contexts) to produce sixteen cells, each of which is a potential aspect on which to focus evaluation (Grotelueschen, 1980). This technique can be useful to focus the evaluation of a single course or workshop.

Phases of Evaluation. When the evaluation extends beyond a straightforward review of one or two program aspects, it is usually desirable to conduct the evaluation in two stages. The first stage (usually using less than one quarter of the time and resources) is a pilot study to identify the issues to assess in greater depth and to refine the approach and procedures. The second phase is to conduct the main evaluation study. The scope, purpose, and approach of the evaluation are also related to who coordinates the evaluation and who else is involved.

Two considerations entering into who is to contribute to an evaluation effort are commitment and expertise. It is especially important that people in crucial positions to use the findings be involved in planning and conducting the evaluation effort, both to benefit from their suggestions and to encourage their use of findings. Knowing about basic ingredients for program evaluation can enable you to recognize when you and others associated with the program to be evaluated lack essential expertise, so that you can arrange for supplementary assistance.

Data Collection and Analysis. The core of an evaluation plan is the design and the procedures for data collection and analysis. Typically, quantitative and qualitative data are collected from representative samples of participants, instructors, administrators, and records in ways that minimize disruption of the ongoing program and encourage use of findings. Someone with evaluation expertise can help design data collection so that essential categories of valid data are efficiently collected. Typical sources of data include standardized and local tests, observation checklists, questionnaires, interview guides, organizational records, and sometimes evaluation committees. Pretesting of questions and forms can clarify wording and increase validity. Multiple sources and types of data are valuable for key variables. Comparison groups are important in follow-up studies to allow conclusions about the program's probable contribution to the changes found.

A frequent flaw in evaluation studies is inadequate planning of data-analysis procedures. The unhappy result is an inability to draw useful conclusions and implications because data were not collected for key variables or were not collected in a form required for the most appropriate data-analysis procedures. If you are not familiar with the design of research and evaluation studies, it is usually a good investment at the planning stage to consult someone who is. People with such expertise may be higher education research or evaluation specialists or may be engaged in evaluation or market research in a business or a community agency. Evaluation can be conducted on any scale and depth, but the validity and usefulness of findings usually depend on a soundly designed plan for data collection and analysis (Cook and Reichard, 1979; Merriam and Simpson, 1984).

An early part of data analysis is summarizing data within each category. For example, when evaluating discrepancies between your and participants' expectations of what they should learn and their actual achievement and satisfaction, you might prepare the following summaries:

- A list of the proficiencies that you believe participants should acquire in the program.
- A list of the proficiencies that the participants hope to achieve.
- A tabulation of scores showing how well each participant mastered the learning tasks and achieved the educational objectives.
- A summary of participants' responses to questionnaire items

on their satisfaction with their learning process and outcomes.

Such descriptive summaries for early units of a course
allow you to make judgments about program effectiveness, with
implications for modifying your approach to later units. The
data analysis includes comparing descriptive summaries to answer the following types of questions:

- Did you and the participants generally agree on the proficiencies to be achieved? If not, how could greater consensus
  be achieved?
- To what extent did achievement meet or exceed expectations? Were there unexpected outcomes?
- Did variations in participants' satisfaction with the learning
  process and outcomes parallel variations in their achievement? What are the implications for instructional procedures?

These questions address the instructional decisions you
can make. In addition, each participant can review the data on
his or her expectations, achievement, and satisfaction as a basis
for evaluative judgments to use in making decisions about his
or her ongoing educational activities.

Use of Findings. The purpose of program evaluation is to
make judgments for planning, improvement, or justification.
This entails encouraging use of findings for decision making. An
evaluation plan that specifies purposes, audiences, and issues has
many implications for reporting. A sound evaluation plan
should also indicate effective ways to report pertinent findings
to each of the audiences and ways to encourage actual use of
findings. As an instructor, you are one of the main users of evaluation findings. Perhaps other people also make instructional
contributions. What type of evaluation report (detail, format,
implications) would be most useful for making instructional
decisions? How can you include participants in the process of
planning and conducting evaluation activities so that data are
valid, findings are relevant, and suggestions are used? Such feed-

back to learners is important to reinforce achievement and encourage persistence, as well as to modify plans and facilitate
self-directedness. How can you include administrators and policy makers in the evaluation process as appropriate so that they
develop sufficient commitment to understand and use the findings to maintain or adjust the support they can provide? Constructive use of written and oral evaluation reports is more
likely if you organize them around the issues and questions of
concern to the recipients.

Planning for evaluation also includes thinking about the
roles to be performed in planning and implementing an evaluation and using the findings. The basic role occurs when you as
an instructor or one of the participants engages in a self-assessment. Roles become somewhat more complex and interrelated
when two or more persons cooperate in planning and conducting an evaluation. For example, both instructors and participants have a stake in, and contribute to the success of, the
teaching/learning transaction. Frequent reciprocal feedback is
important but requires planning and coordination. Another reason planning is important is that someone should provide continuity in collection and summary of comparable data from
needs assessments, formative evaluation, and summative evaluation. When program evaluation covers many courses or workshops, even more planning and coordination are required.

When those associated with an evaluation have enough
experience, background, and expertise, planning can be informal. However, as an evaluation becomes more complex, it is
important to give deliberate attention to both formal planning
and available expertise. Evaluation experts can be especially
helpful for developing new forms to collect evaluation data,
for follow-up studies, for external summative evaluation, for
evaluating the evaluation process, and for suggesting materials
and resources that could contribute to evaluation.

Conducting Evaluation

Having planned your evaluation, how can you conduct
that evaluation to judge the worth and effectiveness of the
teaching/learning transaction and to use the judgments to im-

prove that transaction while it is occurring? The emphasis in this section is on doing evaluation for program improvement, for which you would be the main user of findings. Learners and coordinators would be secondary users of findings. You can use formative evaluation to improve each of the aspects of conducting learning activities described in Chapter Eight—questions and examples, practice, sequence, pacing, and reinforcement. Realistically, you must be selective. The benefits from program improvements should warrant the time, money, and effort expended on the evaluation. You should also consider the likely dissatisfaction among participants, supervisor, and yourself if enough attention is *not* given to evaluation.

The examples in this section are grouped by whether they are mainly summative evaluation, for judging whether a particular type of activity is valuable enough to repeat, or mainly formative evaluation of process, for purposes of improvement. It is desirable to include both summative evaluation to find out the results you produce and formative evaluation to find out how to improve them (Brinkerhoff, 1981, 1983; Bunker and Cohen, 1978; Deshler, 1984; Fink and Kosecoff, 1978; Guba and Lincoln, 1981; House, 1983; Kopp, 1986b; Miles, 1965; Neider, 1981; Swierczek and Carmichael, 1985; Tyson and Birnbrauer, 1985).

The potential scope of program evaluation is so great, and the limits on the time, money, and expertise available for an evaluation project are so severe, that it is helpful to have a general framework to help focus the effort (Grotelueschen, 1980; Brethower and Rummler, 1979). Evaluation could help you judge the worth or effectiveness of any or all aspects of helping adults learn, such as these:

- Numbers, backgrounds, and expectations of the participants who enter your program.
- Teaching and learning activities, including content, methods, and materials.
- What the participants learn as a result of the program.
- Importance and achievement of program goals and objectives.
- Contributions of people in various roles who help participants learn.

- The settings and expectations where participants are likely to apply what they learn in the program, which affect their success in doing so.
- Impact of the program in the form of application and benefits.
- Feedback about any of these aspects (including evaluation) to enable you or others to make adjustments for program improvement.

Because participants usually want to use what they learn from your program by applying it in their life roles such as work or family, in your program evaluation it is helpful to consider the broad social system that includes such settings, as well as your educational program. However, you can seldom evaluate all these aspects, and so the reason for such a broad view is to select those aspects that are most important to include in a particular instance.

For example, if you are evaluating an educational program to help employees in an organization improve their performance, your main evaluation purpose may be to assess program impact on participants' subsequent performance. Thus, you may give much less attention to evaluation for detailed program improvement or for planning future programs. By focusing on evaluating connections between program implementation, improved performance, and organizational benefits, you are likely to give much less attention to evaluating other contexts; your teaching style; program goals, content, and design; and the participants' expectations, satisfaction, and learning gain. To increase the feasibility of such an evaluation activity, conduct the simplest evaluation possible that will answer the questions that you want to have answered, sample and use existing data where you can, and recognize that real-world evaluations should contribute information and commitment for decision making, in contrast to typical research projects aimed at more precise explanations. Although conclusions-oriented research may yield generalizations, instruments, and procedures, the focus in this chapter is on decision-oriented evaluation to judge worth and effectiveness.

Summative Evaluation. Summative evaluation of program outcomes has several uses, including assessment of impact on learner performance and benefits to others. Such uses of summative evaluation include justifying whether it is worthwhile to offer the program or use the activity or procedure again and being confident about the results that you and the learners can expect from the activity (Belasco and Trice, 1969; Cervero, Rottet, and Dimmock, 1986; Rosenheim, 1977). In the context of this section, the main use is to guide your decisions about how beneficial your program and its components are.

A prime example of summative evaluation is the set of studies of the relative effectiveness of alternative instructional methods. Guidelines that include typical outcomes to expect from various activities to help adults learn are sometimes based on judgments of anticipated impact. Similar informal evaluation occurs when you compare the results of new methods or materials and those you typically use. The usual procedure is to compare the actual outcomes with objectives or expectations.

If you want to refine the general impressions and guidelines about the relative impact of instructional methods in order to choose the best learning activities for your content, participants, and circumstances, consider the following procedures.

1. Review your own experience with (and past feedback on) the relevant alternative methods of teaching and learning, listing the main learner outcomes you would like to produce with any of them, and then compare and contrast the methods, including process, outcomes, and your satisfaction with them. This preliminary review can clarify your rationale so as to guide both evaluation and use of findings.

2. Locate summaries of research and evaluation studies that have compared these methods, perhaps with different content and learners. Outline the main findings on use of methods and relative effectiveness and also the procedures that were used to collect and analyze data about process and outcomes.

3. Reflect on what you have found so far and clarify the main questions, issues, or reasons that you want to evaluate and improve the effectiveness of the methods you use. Compare your experience and rationale with the generalizations you ob-

tained from research and evaluation studies. If this process enables you to answer the questions that arose from your earlier disssatisfaction or aspirations, set aside the remainder of these suggested procedures for summative evaluation and instead use your new insights to modify your teaching activities, using formative evaluation procedures to refine the activities. Return to summative evaluation when you conclude that major attention to outcomes is warranted.

4. If at any stage you decide to conduct a summative evaluation, specify the major desirable and feasible outcomes you want to achieve regardless of method. Include indicators that the educational experiences produce changes in participants' performance as they apply what they learn, as well as benefits that their changed performance is likely to bring to other people in their family, work, or community settings. Specifying likely impacts enables you to state a rationale for the connection between one or more educational methods and intended outcomes. Without such anticipated objectives, it is hard to design a satisfactory summative evaluation study.

5. Briefly describe the main similar and different features of the methods you want to compare. Consider characteristics such as types of activities, related materials, your contribution, and time and expense required. This description helps both to select data to collect and to interpret findings and suggest implications of them.

6. Briefly describe pertinent characteristics of the content and learners with which the methods will be used, along with major influences on the program or on participants' efforts to apply what they learn.

7. Design the most basic and efficient impact study you can that is likely to answer satisfactorily your main questions about outcomes (Knox, 1979c). If you have limited background for conducting research and evaluation studies, this is one of the points at which specialized assistance may be very worthwhile. Designing the study is when your earlier efforts regarding questions, outcomes, methods, content, learners, and influences will be very useful. A summative evaluation of instructional methods typically compares the impacts of two or more methods on common outcomes, given similar inputs and situational influ-

ences. This entails studying a system with all of its complex interrelationships, which usually is not feasible. Therefore, you should vary only the method used and try to keep everything else as similar as possible—context, content, and instructor. To make the study feasible, select the *minimum number* of variables for which to collect data to answer your *basic question* about relative impact. If you lack the interest, expertise, time, and resources to plan and conduct this basic scaled-down study, now is the time to recognize that and proceed accordingly. If such a basic study *is* feasible, consider what you might add so that the ratio between the costs and benefits of the evaluation is even more favorable.

8. Consider the data you require or could use for the study that are already available (or that you have collected in the past). Using existing data or procedures minimizes needless duplication and increases the likelihood that the data will be well collected and used.

9. Plan and conduct the study as one of a series of approximations. The explanation of relative impact of methods based on your experience (and that of other people whose reports you reviewed) constitutes a first approximation. A pilot study to refine data-collection and data-analysis procedures, along with the rationale and variables included, constitutes a second approximation. The actual study is a third. Using the findings to improve your teaching methods is a fourth, especially if you use formative evaluation to guide the improvement process. Further approximations occur as you repeat summative evaluation studies as major questions arise.

10. Collect the remaining data required, giving special attention to one or more valid indicators of impact. Use or modify existing instruments (such as questionnaires, interview guides, observation checklists, or tests) to save yourself the work of developing satisfactory ones from scratch. In the pilot test, make sure that the instruments assess what they are supposed to and that the form of the data will be satisfactory for data analysis. Use data-collection procedures that minimize disruption to the program (give attention here to length and complexity of instruments).

11. Data analysis consists mainly in summarizing the

data in each category (outcomes, processes) for the participants who used each method and then comparing the results achieved with each method. Understanding of the basic concepts and procedures of probability helps set confidence levels, to decide how large a difference has to be before it *makes* a difference.

12. Draw implications for improvement. All the preceding steps can enable you to draw sound implications. This final procedure includes both interpreting the findings and suggesting ways to improve your teaching.

The foregoing example of summative evaluation procedures to compare the impact of instructional methods deals with only one aspect of the teaching/learning transaction. To conduct such a study would require that you arrange to teach the same content and similar participants using different methods and that you collect data during and after the program. However, most of the work of planning and conducting the study would be done outside program sessions. Furthermore, following the foregoing guidelines, you might conclude that one method was better than others but not discover what features of that method contributed to its effectiveness.

By contrast, the following two brief examples of summative evaluation follow the same basic concepts, but most of the effort would occur during session time and the participants would learn more about the evaluation process. One example deals with individualization and the other with feedback.

A learning contract is a way to individualize learning activities, and evaluation is part of such a contract. After participants draft their proposed learning contracts, you (perhaps with a committee of participants) might review them to find similar outcomes. If there are some, you might invite the participants who prepared learning contracts that proposed similar outcomes to participate in a small comparative study. Those who volunteer would help plan and implement the following modest evaluation study designed to help them learn how to assess their learning projects as well as help you guide future learning contracts.

Suppose that several learning contracts propose as an outcome identifying and introducing an improvement in work procedures that affects co-workers, which they agree to help implement. You might operationalize a generic measure of that outcome that would fit the selected learning contracts, such as a set of rating scales on extent of acceptance and implementation to include in interview guides or questionnaires to collect data from participants, co-workers, and supervisors.

If participants include these common rating scales in their plans for evaluating the impact of their learning contracts, they can analyze relations between these data on the common outcome and the individualized data they collect about the process of conducting their learning project and their satisfaction in doing so. By completing learning projects before the end of your program, the participants who collaborate on conducting parallel evaluations can share their findings and then discuss variations in project success and what seemed to contribute to it. You will gain a more detailed idea of the results of the learning contracts and some idea of the arrangements associated with the more effective projects. In addition to evaluating the success of this program, you can use the findings to guide participants in similar future programs as they plan and conduct learning projects.

An example of an even easier summative evaluation is on feedback and reinforcement. Assume that you frequently teach a course or workshop for similar groups of adults. Participants' end-of-program reaction-form ratings on evaluation and feedback have been low, and you share their opinion that feedback procedures should be improved. You have concluded that participants will vary in the extent and type of feedback on progress which they prefer and from which they are likely to benefit.

Prepare a brief description of feedback procedures, using your syllabus statement and materials on feedback, past participant reaction-form ratings and comments, and your own familiarity with the feedback procedures you have used. Use that description and suggestions from readings on evaluation and from other people interested in evaluation to identify some likely ways to improve feedback, including procedures to do so. Early in the next program, ask each participant to rate each procedure on a list that describes ways of providing feedback that you are prepared to use. Examples might include brief rating forms that you could complete for participants' presentations, reports, and projects; self-scoring review forms on readings; self-assessment inventories that participants could score themselves; and critique forms to be completed by peers, supervisors, or others who can observe application of what participants learn. Participants would then use the feedback procedures they select, and both you and they would see the results.

At the end of the program, each participant's pattern of extent and type of feedback received would be compared with level of achievement in the program, ratings on feedback on the end-of-program reaction form, and response to a new open-ended question on the participants' perception of connections between feedback procedures and his or her program achievement and satisfaction. The individual participants would benefit from the content of the feedback they received. The conclusions that you drew from analysis of the data would help you strengthen the evaluation process. If participants' achievement or satisfaction with feedback procedures increased and if they recognized that relationship, the results would be valuable to all concerned. If not, at least you could provide useful feedback procedures for future programs and suggest some ways of using them and likely benefits.

Your conclusions about improvements would depend on the comparability of the program characteristics other than feedback procedures (content, participants, methods) between the experimental program and previous programs with which it was compared on achievement and satisfaction with feedback. The main reasons for using more formal evaluation procedures are greater validity of data-collection procedures and greater confidence in attributing improvements to the changes you made. The trade-off is that the more formal evaluation procedures take more time, money, and expertise. In addition, the heavy emphasis on outcomes may result in firm conclusions about extent of impact but too little attention to what influences the outcomes. A contrasting emphasis on process and its modification is the focus of the last section of this chapter, which deals with formative evaluation.

The next two examples focus on impact and application. When you want to evaluate the impact of your educational program, sometimes circumstances call for a multiple-baseline approach (Knox, 1979c; Brown, 1980). For example, in work or other organizational settings where you will be teaching a series of similar groups of employees or members in separate sites, baseline information about performance can be collected from all employees or members at times when you are completing one round of programs and beginning another. If there is little overlap of participants among the various programs, misattribution to your program of effects that likely resulted from informal interaction with participants from other programs is minimized. You can then do a time-series comparison of comparable multiple-baseline data for each of the participants. For each group of participants, a relatively stable performance trend before participation, followed by major improvements during and directly after participation, followed by a more constant and higher performance trend, provides relatively convincing evidence of educational impact. If similar findings emerge from replications across locations and time periods, the results are even more conclusive. If participants report using program ideas to make changes similar to those that appear in the multiple-baseline trends, your evaluation conclusions are even more powerful and useful. Such estimates of improvements can be further refined by including in the self-assessments an estimate after the program of performance and outlook before the program, which can take into account a broadened frame of reference that may have resulted from participation (Mezoff, 1981).

The final example deals with follow-up studies. Even in a diffuse program such as in-service education for supervisors, encouraging participants to apply what they learn and evaluating the extent of application can be achieved by including such an application emphasis in your program design (Morrisey and Wellstead, 1980). Early in the program, have participants discuss their objectives for applying what they learn from your program, how to assess the extent to which they succeed, and how to write a few such objectives that are both desirable and feasible. Near the end of the program, have them critique and perhaps revise their implementation objectives and leave a copy with you. Let them know that you will send a reminder a few weeks before you send a reply form on which they can report on positive and negative results in their efforts to achieve their implementation objectives, other changes that resulted from participation in the program, and suggested improvements that might have made the program more helpful. You could reply with comments about their achievements and ongoing application, as well as use their progress reports to improve your future programs.

Formative Evaluation. The emphasis in formative evaluation is on use of conclusions by people associated with the program (instructor, participants, supervisor) to improve the ongoing process. Usually timeliness of findings and commitment to their use for program improvement are emphasized more than rigor of procedures for data collection and analysis and detailed attention to outcomes (Brinkerhoff, 1983).

To illustrate use of formative evaluation for program improvement, assume that you want to strengthen your use of questions to guide learning. One approach would be to assess discrepancies between desired and actual use of questions. Further assume that it would be satisfactory to use questions more in accord with the preferences of yourself, participants, and experts without testing in any detail how much this improvement contributes to learner achievement and application.

The basic evaluative process consists in making judgments about discrepancies between desired and current use of questions and then suggesting ways to reduce the discrepancies. An early step is to decide who can provide useful information about desired use of questions. Certainly, you can list your objectives and expectations about what you want to achieve through use of questions and what you consider to be characteristics of effective questions. Your participants can also state their expectations about uses of questions that occur in study guides, facilitating discussion, and self-assessments. You can also obtain expert opinion on use of questions in educational programs, from writings and available experts. Next, prepare a description of desirable standards for question asking composed of the generalizations common to all sources and those from each source.

Using the resulting criteria, describe your current use of questions. This description can be based on written questions you have used and your recollection of oral questions, supplemented by information from tape recordings, participants, and peers. Organizing this description of current practice in the same categories that you used for desired use of questions will facilitate the discrepancy analysis. As you make judgments about discrepancies, try to make explicit the assumptions, values, and additional information that you include in your rationale, along with the major discrepancies you identify. Next, from the resulting conclusions, prepare implications that suggest ways in which you want to improve your use of questions. Ongoing evaluation can indicate the extent and type of improvement you actually make.

A somewhat different formative approach is illustrated by the following example of evaluation of the selection, sequence, and pace of practice activities. These program aspects are somewhat more complex than the use of questions illustrated in the previous example, and two major criteria are achievement and persistence. In this example, you might begin with a description of practice activities, along with your rationale for selection, sequence, and pace. Your record of sequences of practice activities, progress during practice sessions, participant satisfaction, and persistence rate constitutes the baseline for evaluating what happens when you modify practice activities.

Assuming that you believe that practice activities could be greatly improved but that at the outset you are uncertain how, you might ask peers for suggestions, along with individual participants. The most promising changes in practice activities might then be proposed to the group of learners as a basis for selecting those to modify on an experimental basis. Next, prepare a set of forms to keep track of participant time devoted to practice activities, along with satisfaction. Combine this information with data on persistence and achievement and the descriptive information you have on the experimental practice activities.

The data analysis consists in comparing the time spent, persistence, and achievement under the new experimental practice arrangement with the results under the former arrangement. If there is some improvement, more detailed analysis of the process would be done to identify aspects that contribute to the results. Finding that the analysis of relationships was consistent with participants' opinions and your opinions about such relationships would be more convincing than either empirical relationships or subjective explanation taken separately.

In such a formative evaluation approach, the emphasis is on identifying and making improvements in the process, as an integral part of planning and conducting learning activities. By evaluating and making changes during a portion of an educational program, the participants can benefit from the improvements. In this naturalistic process, all concerned can be involved, changes can be made as soon as they seem promising, and the actual teaching/learning transaction can be both the proving ground for evaluation recommendations and the source of new evaluation questions for the next round in the cycle of approximations.

A widespread concern about formative evaluation for program improvement is what efficient and feasible small-scale procedures will yield desirable results (Deshler, 1984; Swierczek and Carmichael, 1985). One way to keep your evaluation manageable is to clearly specify the stakeholders who are the audience for your evaluation report and focus on the questions and issues important to them. In addition to yourself, such audiences may include the participants, a program coordinator, and policy makers from your provider or cosponsors. A second way is to use technology to collect, analyze, and report information, to save you and participants time. Such automation usually assumes a large number of program participants over time to warrant initial investment in the technology.

For example, in work and other organizational settings, there may be personnel or membership records that could be combined with ongoing formative evaluation data collected from participants and other people. If you are conducting management development programs, computer-generated summary information might be provided periodically to you and each participant, based on information from several sources. Personnel files might yield information from application forms, performance reviews, and special accomplishments. This might be combined with self-assessments, career plans, and anonymous ratings by subordinates and supervisors. Successive summaries based on accumulating information could be used for needs assessment, program planning, and identification of unexpected developments as well as alternative career choices.

In continuing higher education and other programs in which testing occurs, computer-managed instruction can provide periodic feedback useful to both you and participants. In addition to summary information on individuals' progress and their relative rankings on content mastery and coverage, test scoring can identify poorly worded questions, extent of guessing, and topics for more instructional emphasis. The evaluation results can also be keyed to self-managed and self-paced instructional modules that pertain directly to gaps or misunderstandings that become evident, so that learners can proceed from feedback directly to remediation.

A third example is the American Heart Association's microcomputer-controlled cardiopulmonary resuscitation (CPR) mannequin connected to videotape and audiotape equipment. Sensors on the mannequin result in feedback to someone in CPR training. This detailed individualized feedback, showing discrepancies between the programmed standards and the learner's performance, results in higher levels of learner performance in less time than traditional CPR training (without automation). The main audience for formative evaluation is the learner, but instructors can monitor progress and review summary information accumulated by the computer.

Formative evaluation for program improvement can sometimes be brief and oral (Stevenson, 1980). If you are teaching a small group in a program that extends over two or more days, you can devote a short time (perhaps twenty minutes) at the end of each day or session to program evaluation. In a conference or workshop format with concurrent subgroups, a leader and one or more participants from each subgroup can volunteer on a rotating basis to take part in joint evaluation meetings. In either case, the purpose is to assess program effectiveness and solve problems hindering learning, by discussing such topics as pacing, materials, group interaction, instructional procedures, and logistics. (If there are subgroups, just before adjourning for the day, members can tell their representatives about questions and concerns they would like to have discussed at the evaluation meeting. At the start of the next day's session, representatives can report on proposed solutions, and the participants can help decide on changes.) If such evaluation meetings are to be beneficial, you should take them seriously, be prepared to hear negative as well as positive comments, and be willing to seek solutions to problems that emerge. It helps to explain that improvements will be made where they can be but that some program aspects cannot be changed. Engaging in such evaluation meetings can also help participants learn to use evaluation more effectively in their future educational activities.

Guidelines for Conducting an Evaluation. In practice, a combination of formative and summative evaluation is most useful. External, summative evaluation provides the most convincing evidence of outcomes, which is of interest to administrators and policy makers as well as teachers and learners. (Such evaluation can be the most difficult and controversial.) But it is of limited value for you to know how successful your program is without also knowing what contributes to that success so you can preserve the strengths and reduce the weaknesses. That is the contribution of formative evaluation, in which people associated with the program analyze the process for purposes of improving it. This is much easier if there are important outcome criteria and measures against which to assess procedural modifications.

For any type of evaluation of your educational program, the following suggestions for conducting an evaluation can contribute to its soundness and to its fit into the ongoing educational program (Evans, 1983; Grotelueschen, Gooler, and Knox, 1976; Palola, 1983).

- Strive for fairness, objectivity, and credibility even as you acknowledge that evaluation is a combination of objective descriptions and subjective judgments.
- Explain evaluation plans and procedures to people likely to be affected by them.
- Provide clear instructions with all data-collection instruments and procedures.
- Recognize that evaluation can be disruptive, so be as organized and unobtrusive as possible, be accommodating, and minimize disruptions.
- As a part of the evaluation process, try to develop commitment to use of findings.
- Use pretesting and pilot projects to refine instruments and procedures.
- Look for strengths as well as weaknesses.
- Be alert to unexpected assumptions, influences, viewpoints, and consequences.
- Provide feedback from evaluation findings.
- Help participants learn how to use evaluation procedures as part of their own learning activities.
- In reporting evaluation findings, indicate implications and alternative courses of action.
- Anticipate consequences of plans, activities, and recommendations.
- Be willing to do additional analysis.
- Express appreciation to those who cooperate with or contribute to the evaluation effort.

As discussed earlier, evaluation serves several purposes. It enables participants to make informed decisions about their educational progress and helps you decide on program goals and procedures. These aspects of program evaluation are thus integral parts of the teaching/learning transaction.

Conclusion

Program evaluation can be used for planning, improvement, and justification. The evaluation procedures you select depend on evaluation purposes, audiences, and issues as you describe and judge the worth and effectiveness of selected aspects of your program. The aspects on which you focus depend on feasibility as well as your estimates of the points at which benefits warrant evaluation costs. The focus of evaluation can be any program-planning component (needs, context, objectives, activities, or evaluation itself) as well as related arrangements (participation, resource persons, finance, materials, facilities, records, and coordination).

Evaluation findings can help both you and participants make such educational decisions. However, it is important to be selective and focus on program aspects for which improvement or justification benefits exceed the costs of conducting the evaluation. Summative evaluation of program worth and impact focuses on outcomes and is useful for justification and accountability. Formative evaluation of program process and effectiveness focuses on procedures and is useful for program improvement. Guidelines for conducting evaluations include these: build on existing understandings, focus on what you want to analyze, design a basic study, collect and analyze data, and involve people and report findings in ways that encourage use of conclusions.

Like the other chapters, this chapter covered more aspects of its subject than you can deal with at one time. Which aspects seem most pertinent to what you currently do for evaluation? Which concepts are illustrated by your current evaluation practice? Are there any improvements you would like to make in your program evaluation? If there are, what are some initial steps?

It is usually desirable to start small. Perhaps begin with participant reaction forms or achievement tests or organizational records that reflect application of what participants learn in the form of improved performance. Critique this current evaluation practice and use a few ideas from this chapter to decide what few evaluation activities could be added or modified to provide a sounder basis for evaluation findings and increased commitment to use of the findings. This attention to evaluation can be a vehicle for your continued learning and improvement as an instructor; the participants and the provider organization are additional beneficiaries.

TEN

Helping Adults Apply
What They Learn

In your educational programs for adults, how important is it that the participants use or apply what they learn? If it is important, what do you do to help them deal with the facilitators of and barriers to application? This chapter reviews ways that you and others can assist with application and help participants reduce barriers in order to increase program impact.

In many educational programs for adults, encouraging and assisting with application is an important part of the teaching/learning transaction. There are various ways you can do so. You can encourage application by responding to pertinent participant aspirations, clarifying performance standards, and reinforcing and evaluating progress. You can also help to establish, in both educational and application settings, supportive arrangements so that time and resources are devoted to analysis of facilitators and barriers. You can help participants arrange to reduce barriers. Materials can also be used for practice and ongoing assistance with application strategies.

Encouraging Application

Usually participants want to apply or use what they learn in order to strengthen their performance in one or more adult life roles. When application is important to learners, there are several ways you can help. Your assistance makes learners more likely to achieve objectives that result in application and improved performance (Bandura, 1982; Barrows and Tamblyn,

1980; Bishop, 1976; Craig, 1976; Gage, 1978; Grabowski, 1983; Green, Grosswald, Suter, and Walthall, 1984; Knox, 1974; Lindquist, 1978b; Schein, 1978).

Attention to Performance Objectives. One of the best ways to encourage adults to apply what they learn is to help them find out what they are committed to apply. This entails helping them clarify educational needs related to performance they want to improve, in part by encouraging them to assume substantial responsibility for performance, standards, learning, and improvement (Argyris, 1982; Gross, 1977; Thayer, 1976; Wlodkowski, 1985a). An example of an approach designed to relate continuing education closely to performance is the practice audit. The typical steps are listed below.

1. Select aspects of role performance to be audited that are important to improve and can be analyzed to evaluate improvement.
2. Set essential standards for desired performance.
3. Make sure that participants accept the standards as desirable and feasible.
4. Analyze current proficiencies related to the selected standards.
5. Compare current with desired proficiencies to identify discrepancies as a basis for educational objectives (formative evaluation).
6. Provide participants with audit findings, educational activities designed to achieve standards, and encouragement to apply new learnings.
7. Repeat audit procedure, using the same standards as for formative evaluation.
8. Analyze progress toward standards—for example, by comparing the significant gains and losses with the changes that could have occurred.
9. Present findings to participants in ways that encourage self-improvement.

Attention to Incentives and Resistance. With any approach, you can increase application by attention to incentives and to resistance to improved performance. Incentives include benefits, such as occupational advancement or improved nutrition for less money, that are more likely as a result of participation in your program. Other incentives are positive feedback and reinforcement. Attention to resistance includes trying to reduce inhibiting factors such as inertia due to habits, competing time demands, and discouragement by other people who may be affected (MacNeil, 1980). To increase application, participants can begin early to discuss their interest in using what they learn (including importance and benefits), to analyze likely facilitators of and barriers to application in the setting where application is to occur, and throughout the program to devote time to exploring and practicing ways to use what they learn under conditions similar to those they are likely to confront (Mallory, 1981; Stenzel and Feeney, 1970; Stritter and Hain, 1977).

Encouraging participants to apply what they learn from your program may seem straightforward when the goal is skill enhancement, but it is also desirable and feasible when the goal is more diffuse, such as wellness promotion (Shea, 1981). Underlying an effective educational program that promotes wellness and health (in contrast with curing illness) are two concepts. One is that wellness is affected by personal practices and attitudes as individuals interact closely with other people who are part of their wellness system. The second is that individuals can take responsibility for their choices and practices that can enhance their wellness. Adults who participate in wellness education and apply what they learn are likely to believe that it is both desirable and feasible for them to manage their wellness better, to understand desirable practices that they are likely to internalize because those practices fit their personalities and needs, and to interact with people who are supportive and encouraging of such healthy practices. Some wellness programs include interrelated components, such as orientation of participants and people in their personal wellness system to improvements and contributions, assessment of the individual's past and current wellness condition and influences (in part as a basis for assessing improvement), increased understanding of stress and wellness along with personal potential for improvement as a basis for planning a workable program for improving personal stress management and wellness, practice to master procedures (such as fitness, relaxation, and diet) to achieve and maintain a high level of wellness, and ongoing personal and system reinforcement and inducements to solidify and maintain wellness-related practices.

Encouraging participants to apply what they learn entails dealing with resistance to change—theirs and that of other people in their application setting. A few ideas about identifying and dealing with resistance to change can help you become more effective in this aspect of helping adults learn (Hultman, 1980). People tend to be more open to changes they perceive as desirable and more resistant to changes they perceive as undesirable. The intensity of people's feelings about themselves, other people, and aspects of their environment is estimated by considering the strength and content of the attitudes, beliefs, and values they express by their words and actions. Understanding likely sources of resistance to change can help you to explore potential strategies for increasing support for a proposed change, to select those strategies to which people are most likely to be receptive as a basis for initial agreement, and to avoid issues that seem either irrelevant or emotionally charged. If you understand both factual and emotional reasons for resistance, you can initiate a negotiation process that can result in modification of the proposed change as well as increased support for it (Votruba, 1981). Dealing with resistance is discussed further under "Supportive Arrangements," later in this chapter.

Standards for Performance. As indicated in the second step of the practice audit, agreed-on standards of achievable best practice constitute an important basis for planning and conducting learning activities likely to lead to application. Task analysis and consensus by experts can contribute to agreement on essential standards of desirable role performance. Such analysis helps in the selection of realistic objectives. Usually the participants and other people associated with their performance are the main ones who agree on explicit standards and a timetable for implementation.

Such task analysis and agreement on standards occur infrequently and then in work settings. The description of current performance may be written by the person who does the work, by a supervisor, or ideally with assistance by a specialist in task analysis. Agreement on standards usually reflects several perspectives on achievable best practice which actually occurs and which most practitioners could be helped to achieve. Desirable performance should reflect state-of-the-art knowledge, as well as actual performance assessment.

For educational activities that take place in organizational settings (such as work or volunteer leadership), support for application can be increased by clarifying relations between learning activities and performance tasks. One way to do so is to prepare a task performance map (similar to a systems flow chart), which identifies subtasks and a desirable accomplishment sequence for success in the total task (Herem, 1979). A modified critical incident technique can also be used diagnostically to help potential participants understand discrepancies between current and desired performance and to increase commitment to improvements that education is likely to achieve (Stein, 1981). A critical incident is an activity of sufficient duration and completeness to permit inferences about relations among intent, performance, and consequences (Flanagan, 1954). Analysis of a critical incident should enable the actors and observers to identify performance and proficiencies (knowledge, skills, attitudes) whose presence or absence seems to be associated with doing well or poorly. The next step, identification of proficiencies likely to improve performance, goes beyond needs assessment to provide a link between learning activities and performance tasks.

Sometimes encouraging application entails clarification of performance standards, creation of appropriate educational materials, and a shift in who will help to implement the educational program (Crumb, 1981).

These aspects of encouraging application were illustrated when Mack Tuck redesigned an educational program for first-line supervisors in a manufacturing setting. Mack and his training staff arranged for learner-driven instructional models based on supervisory problems that occurred in the plant. The managers to whom the supervisors reported helped to select the problems that the modules addressed, to develop the instructional materials, and to monitor and assist their supervisors in achieving the instructional objectives. This role encouraged line managers and people from supporting departments to view production problems from supervisors' points of view.

Mack's educational approach was based on task analysis, development of agreed-on performance standards, and use of the standards for ongoing assessment and assistance until supervisors met the standards and were certified. Some task areas (such as administration, labor relations, and interpersonal relations) were common to all supervisors; other supervisory task areas were specific to each specialized type of production. The development and use of standards proved to be an educational experience for managers as well as supervisors, and the tasks, standards, and procedures for assessment and certification continued to evolve.

In the interpersonal relations module, supervisors practiced solving a difficult interpersonal confrontation through a simulation exercise. They practiced handling conflict in private with a coached antagonist, with an emphasis on conflict resolution within usual time constraints. The confrontation was videotaped for later playback. Supervisors then searched for alternative solutions from personal experience, reading, and consulting with personnel specialists and other managers. Mack had supervisors and their managers review and critique the video playback, and supervisors experimented with alternative courses of action until they were ready to evaluate progress. The task certification listings based on performance standards were used for evaluation. If progress was not satisfactory, the supervisor proceeded to another interpersonal simulation. If progress was satisfactory, the supervisor proceeded to another task area. Each module was designed to be completed in about four hours but was learner-paced. Mack guided the development and revision of standards, modules, and certification sheets, along with orientation of managers and monitoring of the entire process to ensure timely progress.

Reinforcement. Even if they know how to improve their practice, most adults require reinforcement and encouragement to do so. Effective reinforcement usually includes opportunities to practice and to receive feedback on how well the learner is able to achieve the standards. Method selection is important. Although teaching methods are similar in achieving knowledge acquisition, some methods (such as internships, role playing, case analysis, and action learning projects) are far more effective than more passive methods in producing application, transfer, and other performance-oriented outcomes. It is also important for participants to try to apply what they learn, in the context of actual or similar settings, and to discuss their efforts to do so. You can facilitate this process by arranging for opportunities for them to do so, by providing encouragement and support, and by enabling them to receive constructive feedback.

In addition to including principles that can be applied in various situations and having similarities between educational and applied experiences, there are practical ways in which you can increase the likelihood that participants will apply what they learn (Chasnoff and Muniz, 1985; Ehrenberg, 1983; Kelly, 1982; Leifer and Newstrom, 1980; Trost, 1985). Included are establishing positive change expectations before the program, providing opportunities for practice and feedback during the program, and arranging for support and reinforcement of positive performance after the program.

Before the program, you can let participants know pro-

gram objectives and intended benefits afterward, have participants communicate with other people (such as a work supervisor) who can help make learning activities beneficial, or ask
participants to engage in a task in preparation for the program
(such as brief prior readings or case analysis). Any such efforts
on your part help participants apply what they learn by emphasizing active learning, clarifying objectives, and increasing communication and commitment among participants and other
people with stakes in the educational outcomes.

During the program, you can use learning contracts to
help participants plan ways to apply what they learn, include a
session at the end of your program to explore probable implementation obstacles and strategies to deal with them, or help
participants form an informal support group or buddy system
of one or more people to encourage and assist implementation.
Such arrangements help participants to be aware of situations
in which new proficiencies are applied, to relate learning activities to probable applications, to practice active learning and
planning for implementation, and to receive reinforcement,
especially during the early stages of implementation.

After the program, you can provide timely follow-up
evaluation, periodically send additional brief readings or suggestions for further learning activities, request progress reports
to you and other people who care about the intended progress,
and suggest forms of incentive and recognition that might encourage persistence in implementation plans. Such procedures
provide participants with encouragement to use enhanced proficiencies, feedback about both learning and performance, and rewards for desirable outcomes.

Evaluation. Each of the foregoing suggestions referred to
feedback and evaluation. Three types of evaluation can contribute to application—needs assessment for planning, formative
evaluation for improvement, and summative evaluation to assess
impact on performance. Evaluation for application can also be
strengthened by involving participants in program development
decisions (especially agreement on standards) and by providing
timely feedback and involvement in decisions in ways that participants find useful (Clark, 1978). This can be especially effec-

tive when learning and action are combined (Argyris, 1982). This occurs when management development programs focus on improvement of problem solving and decision making in actual work settings (Byham, 1980; McNulty, 1979). In such instances, action learning combines organizational problem solving and personal development as administrators learn from their own experience with an actual problem, helped by and helping others in a similar situation.

Administrators are typically selected to be participants in an action learning program because of their promise for top leadership positions. As participants, they receive released time from their own organization to engage in an action learning practicum, in a host organization faced with a serious management problem and willing to work with the participant. Typically, each participant works with a different host organization. Because participants are away from the power structure of their own organization and they do not become part of the power structure in their host organization, they function similarly to a consultant seeking to evolve a solution from the resources of the host organization.

During a brief introductory period in residence with other practicum participants, each participant seeks an overview of what each host organization is trying to do and why, what seems to be interfering, and what might be done about it. Advisers assist small groups, each of which has completed several months of reading materials selected to complement its members' individual backgrounds. The prior readings and group discussions focus on topics such as information, risk, learning, value, decision, organizational system, and social change. Each adviser helps the small group of participants to become cohesive and to learn from one another and from materials, consultants, and people in their host organization.

During an extended period in the host organization, each participant observes, reads, and interviews in an effort to analyze the situation and problem and to evolve a paper solution in concert with members of the host organization. Periodically during this diagnostic period, small groups of participants meet, together with their advisers, to become familiar with one another's problem, host setting, and progress. Advisers, experts, and people from the various host organizations help participants discover management techniques, gain perspective on their problem, and critique suggested solutions.

A short consultation period follows, away from the host organizations, during which participants, experts, and advisers are available to help refine intended solution strategies. Then comes an extended implementation period during which each participant works with other people in the host organization who know and care about the problem and are likely to help with a solution. This implementation process includes gaining organizational support for a proposed course of action, followed by actions to achieve the best solution feasible. At the conclusion of the practicum program, a review with the adviser and other participants evaluates extent of success and lessons learned. In addition to assessing the organizational effectiveness of problem solutions, participants reflect on their enhanced proficiencies at information seeking, problem solving, personal development, and learning how to learn.

This example of action learning in organizational settings is similar to self-directed experiential learning in any setting in which the learner approaches learning activities with a problem-solving mind set instead of an information-receiving mind set. In such instances, participant commitment to application is likely to be present. Your special contribution may be to help participants place their applied goals in a broader context in which they consider implications of their goals, alternative goals, criteria for assessing desirability and feasibility of such goals, and implicit value judgments that are part of those goals. The focus of learning then shifts to examining the desirability of learning outcomes and intended performance. This action approach can be used in many programs (Argyris, 1982; Brookfield, 1986; Cooper, 1980; Darkenwald and Valentine, 1985a; DiMatteo and DiNicola, 1982; Gross, 1982; Knowles, 1975; Odiorne, 1984).

Supportive Arrangements

The foregoing section on encouraging application emphasized the learners, because they (and perhaps other people associated with relevant role performance) have the main influence on their use of what they learn (Knox, 1985). However, there are several types of plans and assistance you can provide that will encourage application. They involve arrangements for resources, facilities and materials, people, and analysis of the settings in which application is to occur.

Plans for resources in support of application are especially important because commitment of money and time is often a requisite for other arrangements. This is especially so for your time and that of other people who help conduct the educational program. Providing facilities, equipment, and materials (actual or simulated) to support practice and application usually requires money and staff time. People who can assist with application may be associated with your educational program or with the intended application setting or from elsewhere. They may be experts or others who demonstrate, model, or explain desired performance, or they may be peers or others who can discuss strategies for effective performance or feelings associated with doing so. The key point is that arrangements for resources, facilities, and people to support application are not likely to occur unless you have the commitment and make the plans and arrangements (Craig, 1976; Green, Grosswald, Suter, and Walthall, 1984; Klema, Casey, and Caple, 1984; Laird, 1978).

Another type of plan concerns analysis of application settings. Many of the ways in which participants want to apply what they learn would result in changes in performance that would affect other people in their group, organization, or community. Much resistance to change can result.

You can enable participants to reduce this resistance by helping them analyze the combination of facilitators and barriers likely to influence their efforts to change (Darkenwald and Larson, 1980; Deshler, 1984; MacNeil, 1980). Examples of facilitators include encouragements and rewards such as contribution to valued goals, availability of necessary resources, and recognition by people affected (including the learner) of the benefits from the proposed change. Examples of barriers include discouragements and punishments such as lack of essential resources or support, concern of other people threatened by the proposed change, and penalties likely to result from making the change.

Understanding these forces includes analyzing their interaction, including ways to reduce the barriers and perhaps strengthen the facilitators (Lindquist, 1978b; Schein, 1978). Typically the challenge for the learner is to overcome resistance to a change in performance, accomplish the change, and achieve a new equilibrium so that the changed performance persists.

Circumstances vary regarding how much you must be involved in the analysis of influences on performance change. What is usually important is that learners understand the combination of influences in their application setting and that they be able to deal with them effectively. This usually requires that you provide the planning and program time and assistance (Peterson, 1983; Redman, 1980).

These suggestions about supportive arrangements pertain not only to your plans but also to the flexible arrangements and ongoing assistance that participants receive during and sometimes after your program. An important form of ongoing assistance is helping participants assess discrepancies between current and desired proficiencies. Agreed-on standards of achievable best practice constitute the desired proficiencies. Ongoing evaluation that provides feedback, which reinforces current proficiencies and specifies the gap that remains, helps participants progress toward application in the form of proficient performance (Deshler, 1984).

One way to clarify discrepancies and to suggest ways learners can improve is to provide live or videotaped demonstrations of proficient performance. Opportunities for participants, during and after the program, to engage in learning tasks that call for application and to receive feedback on how their performance (perhaps simulated) compares with the standards will increase the likelihood of improved performance (DiSilvestro, 1981; Walter and Siebert, 1982).

Your provision and flexible use of varied materials can also contribute to application, especially after the program. During the program, materials (such as cases, simulations, or videotapes) can help participants try out new concepts or procedures. Afterward, familiarty with and access to such materials can enable learners to continue to enhance their proficiencies and improve their performance on their own (Chamberlain, 1980; Wilson, 1983). In addition, encouraging networking with other participants and people who can serve as consultants and in other ways help learners continue to improve can facilitate application during and especially after your program. In addition to planning for such ongoing assistance, you should be responsive to unexpected needs for assistance or opportunities to provide it. Flexible arrangements to encourage application allow you to respond to such opportunities.

Conclusion

Ultimately, participants' application of what they learn in your program depends on themselves and other people in the settings where that application might occur. However, there are various ways you can make such application more likely. One way is to emphasize and be responsive to the improvements that participants want to make, perhaps using a procedure such as a practice audit to identify mutually desirable changes. Other ways to encourage application are agreed-on standards of achievable best practice, procedures for reinforcement and encouragement, and feedback and evaluation of progress. Each of these practices can continue after your program.

You and people in the practice setting (work, family, community organization) can also establish supportive arrangements that contribute to application. Such a commitment is usually reflected in allocation of time and resources. An example is time to help participants analyze facilitators and barriers likely to influence their efforts to apply what they learn in your program and, as a result, to develop realistic strategies for application. Similar assistance would help participants assess discrepancies between current and desired proficiencies from time to time and use their conclusions to guide planned change efforts. These and other arrangements can be supported by providing materials for simulated practice of application strategies and offering suggestions that encourage past participants to try to apply what they learn and help them to be effective when they do.

If encouraging application is important to your program, did you discover in this chapter any promising ideas? If so, which ones might be included in a forthcoming program? Who else might help?

ELEVEN

Enlisting Additional
Resources for Program Success

In most organizations that provide educational programs for adults, there are some people who may help you. The evident example is the program coordinator or supervisor who made arrangements for you to help adults learn. Others include specialists in public information and marketing, counseling and personnel, finance and facilities, and library and publications. People with such expertise may come from outside your organization. Regardless of source or role, they can help you attract and retain participants, arrange for resource persons to help plan or conduct sessions, arrange for facilities and equipment, provide and prepare effective educational materials, and conduct useful staff development activities for you (Craig, 1976; Knox, 1982; Knox and Associates, 1980). This chapter briefly reviews such sources of program support to encourage you to draw on them to strengthen your program.

What types of program support and assistance have you received in the past? What did you have to do to obtain it? How satisfactory was it? As you read this chapter, note new ideas for program support that would strengthen future programs, along with why they would be desirable and how they might be arranged.

Encouraging Participation

When you help adults learn, your main concern is how you can benefit the participants. We tend to take for granted the process that influences their initial participation and ongoing persistence. Although other people may be mainly concerned with attracting and selecting participants for your program and with the counseling function, their efforts can greatly affect your program, and there are several contributions that you can readily make (Darkenwald and Knox, 1984; Darkenwald and Larson, 1980; Knox, 1979b; Knox and Associates, 1980; Okun, 1982; Redman, 1980).

One is to clarify how many and what types of adults your program should be serving. If the numbers and characteristics of the current participants are satisfactory, you might mention that to your program administrator or marketing specialist so that he or she is encouraged to keep up the good work. If not, you might discuss with that person ways to attract the numbers and types of adults with whom you would like to work and the contributions each of you can make.

Chapter Two reviews some of the reasons for and influences on educational participation. Related concepts and procedures can be useful when exploring ways to strengthen the marketing and counseling process. This is especially so when you want to attract and retain hard-to-reach adults and not just more of the type of adults who most readily participate (Darkenwald and Larson, 1980).

Marketing. The underlying concept of marketing is that it should produce a mutually satisfactory exchange of value. You and your provider organization receive enrollments, income, participation, and application on which your program depends. But what do the participants (and sometimes their supervisors) receive that warrants their participation? Almost by definition, the easier-to-reach adults have the highest motivation, the lowest barriers, and the most varied benefits of participation. By contrast, similar adults for whom your program is intended but who are harder to reach or to attract typically have less formal education, are older, are less recent participants, receive less encouragement to participate from friends and associates, recognize fewer benefits of participation, depend less on media and experts for pertinent information, are less optimistic about advancement, and are aware of fewer opportunities to participate. Several marketing concepts can enable you to attract and serve a higher proportion of such hard-to-reach adults. In some work settings where employees are required to attend, the targets of marketing may be the supervisors who send them and the managers who allocate resources for education and training as well as the learners themselves.

Clarifying the major segments of the target market you seek to serve can enable you to decide on a marketing mix most likely to attract and retain a higher proportion of each segment. Major elements of a marketing mix pertain to person, program, place and time, price, and promotion. The following questions suggest the types of information that will enable you to be more responsive to harder-to-reach adults.

- What aspirations, concerns, problems, or change events may contribute to a heightened readiness to learn?
- What educational needs could be well met by your program?
- What places and times would be satisfactory?
- What price would be feasible and competitive? (Take into account instances in which sources other than the learner, such as a supervisor or agency, are paying all or part of the fee.)
- What channels of communication are the adults most likely to use for information about such programs? (Hard-to-reach adults tend to rely heavily on oral communication from people they know and trust.)

Such ideas about marketing concepts and procedures can be useful directly, to guide your own efforts to encourage participation, and indirectly, to get assistance from marketing specialists and other people. The greatest influence on the decision to participate is comments by people who know about your program, such as current and past participants, people who help plan and conduct your program, and people for whom your program is a means to an end they value (such as supervisors, members of helping professions, and staff of referral agencies). There are many ways in which you can provide them with timely information about your program and request names and addresses of people who might benefit from your program whom you or others in your provider agency might contact.

Jan Chong discovered early that current high school equivalency participants were a key to increased enrollments. They knew about her program and about other people like themselves who might be interested. In addition to encouraging them to tell their friends, she provided a card or brief form to make it easy for them to provide names and addresses of potential participants. Jan encouraged both current and past participants to tell about benefits they received from participation and about how they had heard about her program. She also asked what information was especially influential on their decision to participate. When supervisors or other people helped them decide whether to enroll, she tried to obtain similar information from them also. Jan also sought such information about influences on and benefits of participation from an evaluation and from follow-up. Her supervisor used such information as the basis for human-interest stories for newspapers or television. Jan found that the stories attracted the attention of potential participants and helped them to crystallize their sense of the relevance of her program to their concerns. With the high turnover in her program, she realized the stake that she as an instructor had in helping with these marketing efforts.

In addition to your direct efforts to encourage participation, there are several ways other people can assist. Such people may be in various roles, such as continuing education coordinators and supervisors; specialists in marketing, public information, and public relations; and people engaged in counseling, personnel, and supervision who interact with potential participants. Listed below are some of the ways they can assist.

- Suggesting information and guidelines for marketing (perhaps helping plan ways to attract more or different adults).
- Helping prepare effective forms to collect information about

adults' needs, preferences, educational benefits, and ways of finding out about your program.

- Providing guidelines for promotion, publicity, and advertising (such as brochure content, format, cost, numbers, and use of mailing lists).
- Actually preparing copy for brochures, news releases, human-interest stories, or script-and-slide sets for talks to groups.
- Arranging with specialists to help with mailing lists, graphics, advertising, feature stories, or television appearances.

In most provider agencies, your interest in reaching more adults or serving more hard-to-reach adults is the starting point for an expanded effort. The foregoing section suggests when to ask for what type of assistance to make it happen.

In practice, most continuing education providers have at least one person who helps with marketing activities to encourage adults to enroll. As an instructor for an upcoming program, you benefit from this process and have information important to its success. Marketing messages influence the characteristics and expectations of the participants who enter *your* program. Your general familiarity with the participants in similar past programs can be augmented by summary information that you and other instructors accumulate from needs assessments, registration forms, and program evaluation.

Publicity pieces, such as brochures, can tell of the objectives, program features, and benefits that were important to past participants. You are the most likely source for this information. A marketing specialist would appreciate such information, along with information about how past participants heard about your program. Quotations from past participants in a brochure or a brief human-interest newspaper or radio story can also catch the attention of potential participants. You can suggest to a marketing specialist the participants who typify what you most want to accomplish in your program.

You can also compare participants' characteristics with your own expectations about whom you most want to serve, to identify whom you are missing. Specifying such underserved types of adults is easier if you can identify at least a few like them who were attracted in the past. Brief phone conversations or other means of finding out their reasons for enrolling and how they heard about your program provide the basis for contact with organizations, selection of mailing lists, and communication with contact persons likely to reach more people like them.

Even if you are convinced that attracting and selecting participants for your program is someone else's job and that you should be as little involved as possible, everyone is well served if you help clarify roles and make a few suggestions distilled from your understanding of the participants. For example, even instructors in mandatory in-service programs can give their program administrators useful ideas that can increase relevance so that employees participate more willingly and their supervisors are more willing to provide released time and other support.

Counseling. In addition to the summary information about participants' characteristics and needs that they can provide, people who perform counseling functions for adult learners can be of great help for persistence of current participants. In most continuing education providers, the counseling function is performed by various people. You and others who help adults learn typically make the major contribution to the counseling and guidance function as you assist participants with educational planning, study problems, and arrangements that directly affect their educational achievement. Some providers have specialists in counseling and personnel who are available to assist adult learners and to whom you can refer participants who would benefit from their expertise. Consider such referrals especially when participants' problems are more than you want to handle. Continuing education coordinators and administrators frequently perform counseling functions, such as assistance with registration, educational planning, and referrals. In addition, some providers have peer counselors, volunteers, or paraprofessional counselor aides who are sometimes able to relate especially well to participants.

Counseling functions include giving information (for example, about educational or occupational opportunities), assistance with planning, referrals, advocacy, and arrangements for supportive services (such as testing, support groups, and child care). You are probably in the best position to know about the counseling-related concerns of your participants and the counseling services available in your organization and community and to bring the two together.

Other people who help perform the counseling function can provide advice; receive referrals of special counseling problems; handle referrals; supervise volunteers who contact participants who stop attending; arrange for testing related to interests, learning style, study skills, and assessment of experiential learning; and conduct group sessions on topics such as career planning. Publicity about multiple program offerings can refer to counseling staff as a source of information and assistance for adults trying to select a program. In some communities there are educational brokering agencies that serve this function on behalf of many providers of educational programs for adults (DiSilvestro, 1981).

Such counseling services can reduce attrition. Although publicity about such services will reach some participants who would benefit from them, you are the most likely person to help your participants make that connection and, as a result, enjoy the benefits of a higher persistence rate.

When you perform the continuing education counseling function, it may include various ways of helping adult learners explore personal aspirations and available opportunities and make plans for their educational development (DiSilvestro, 1981; Hill, Miller, and Lowther, 1981). This counseling function is fairly familiar in conjunction with continuing education programs provided by educational institutions that offer assistance with selection of courses, career planning, values clarification, study skills, and solution of problems that interfere with study.

Counseling and coaching also occur in work settings when supervisors, trainers, and personnel specialists help employees exchange insights leading to understanding, shared goals, and plans of action to achieve them (Buzzotta, Lefton, and Sherberg, 1977; Schein, 1978). The intent is optimal results for the organization and optimal development for the employee. The resulting understanding and commitment can contribute to positive motivation as participants enter the program, persist, and apply what they learn. Counseling and coaching activities may include brief, informal supervisory contacts to make decisions to solve immediate problems, semiformal coaching sessions to assess recent progress and to explore plans for improvement in the near future, and extensive annual performance appraisal to assess last year's performance against objectives and to set next year's objectives. As an in-service instructor, you may work with supervisors as they counsel employees who are also the participants in your program.

The following four-phase approach to the counseling function seeks to avoid unproductive efforts by trainers and supervisors and instead aims to obtain the best results obtainable under the circumstances. In the precoaching phase, employee and supervisor use observations, records, and conversations to seek a similar understanding of employee performance before the actual coaching session. The second phase is a counseling session to identify improvement areas. The supervisor seeks to enhance the employee's autonomy by exploring connections between individual and organizational needs. Each of them describes the employee's performance and expectations, and they compare views and record growth goals to which both are committed. The third phase is action planning, in which supervisory control and structure are low enough to encourage employee self-discovery and growth. Both explore possible specific improvement plans, and then the employee writes down a detailed action plan regarding what to do, how, and when. Part of that plan is to agree on a review procedure and date, which is the fourth phase. Before that session, the supervisor and employee each review evidence of progress. This evaluation phase is similar to the needs assessment phase, in that each shares conclusions and rationale in an effort to achieve consensus on progress achieved and new growth goals. One by-product is educational needs assessment information that you can use for program planning.

Staff Assistance

Sometimes you may want some help in planning and conducting a program. Examples include workshops or management development series to which multiple experts and resource persons typically contribute. This section suggests roles, sources, criteria, selection, coordination, and evaluation considerations so that such arrangements for staff assistance will be effective (Brown and Copeland, 1979; Houle, 1972; Wilson, 1983).

Resource persons can perform various roles to help you plan and conduct educational programs for adults. Planning roles include member of a planning or advisory committee, identification or preparation of educational materials, source of ideas about program topics or procedures, and consultant. Conducting roles include presenter, discussion leader, demonstrator, panelist, and evaluator. In addition to people like yourself who teach adults, consider people in roles as consultants or paraprofessionals.

Usually, those who assist you in such ways do so on a very short-term or part-time basis. When you identify some staff assistance you would like, consider the many sources of people likely to be interested and able to provide it on a paid or volunteer basis. First, consider people who are especially able and interested in the topic or procedure on which you would like assistance, whether or not they are associated with the organization that provides the educational program you plan to conduct. Consider both what they can do for you and the program participants and the incentives and benefits likely to be important to them. Understanding how they perceive the opportunity to work with you will help you to locate able prospects and to be persuasive as you encourage them to consider doing so.

Potential resource persons who are associated with the organization that provides your program may be the easiest to locate and assess. If your program is provided by an educational institution, there may be people who teach pertinent topics who could be located through catalogues or administrators of their organizational units. For all providers, locate people whose good judgment and broad familiarity with people associated with the organization enable them to give you useful nominations of potential resource persons. Also consider people who have successfully taught adults about your topic before. Include in your search leaders and experts who have the desired content mastery and who relate well to adults, even if they have little or no experience helping them learn. Associations and clubs with kindred interests may be especially productive sources to explore.

Clarify major criteria about content mastery and about relating to adult learners, to help yourself locate able prospects and select those most likely to be effective. Useful mastery of subject matter content that you want taught is usually based on a combination of knowledge and experience. Useful people-oriented personal characteristics to consider include self-confidence, responsiveness, informality, humor, and enthusiasm.

The selection process entails both choosing the persons who are best qualified and gaining agreement on expectations and arrangements. Firsthand reports from people who have seen the candidates in action helping adults learn are especially valuable. In the conversation in which you finalize agreements with a resource person, information should be exchanged about expectations, working relationships, benefits, and arrangements. If you seek a resource person to complement your contribution, it is especially important that this be understood. Be clear about how and when the relationship will end and the basis for earlier termination.

Ongoing relationships with resource persons depend on whether supervision is provided by your supervisor or yourself and whether the resource person's performance is supervised directly or indirectly. Agreement on a general program plan and on educational materials helps clarify objectives and arrangements. Evaluation of objectives, materials, plans, and performance can contribute to useful adjustments as the program proceeds. Instructional performance can be evaluated by participants as well as staff and can include impact on participants' performance as well as the process of the educational program. Especially beyond an initial session, continued contributions by able resource persons depend on their assessment that the benefits they receive are worth their effort. You can maintain their cooperation by giving attention not only to extrinsic incentives such as money and recognition but also to intrinsic incentives such as professional opportunities and satisfaction from creative efforts and deepening personal interests.

Have you worked with other resource persons to plan and

conduct past programs? If so, how did it work? Did reviewing the ideas in this section suggest any improvements? If not, can you think of ways in which doing so in future programs might be well worth the effort?

Agency Support

There are several types of potential support and assistance from your provider agency, in addition to encouraging participation and persistence by learners and resource persons. These additional types of assistance pertain to resources such as finances, facilities, and materials (Boyle, 1981; Collins, 1981; Cooper and Hornback, 1973; Green, Grosswald, Suter, and Walthall, 1984; Houle, 1973; Knowles, 1980; Laird, 1978; Odiorne, 1984; Redman, 1980; Schein, 1978; Votruba, 1981).

In most continuing education providers one or more staff members handle financial procedures such as buying materials and paying staff. In small agencies, the director typically does so. You or your supervisor can find out from this person how much money, if any, is available for use for your program. In some programs, such as conferences and workshops, this is decided when the budget is set. As you plan your program, if sufficient funds are not available through your provider agency, consider alternative resources. Examples include facilities, equipment, or materials from cosponsors; volunteer assistance; and supplementary income from sale of materials.

As soon as you decide on the facilities and equipment necessary for a successful program, find out whether they are available and, if so, request them for your program. Consider both what is essential for the content and objectives and what would promote effective learning and interpersonal relations. If satisfactory facilities and equipment are not available, check with your supervisor or the person who handles facilities assignments about possible adjustments, including use of facilities outside the provider agency.

If your provider agency or parent organization includes a library or learning resource center, the library staff constitute another potential resource. They can help with suggesting, locating, and acquiring educational materials, including reserve materials and those available through interlibrary loan. These may include nonprint materials such as videotapes, slides, and computer programs. In addition, if your parent organization has a publications office, staff there can assist with the production of materials.

A written proposal is an effective way to acquire additional financial or nonfinancial resources. The proposal may be to your supervisor, to someone within the parent organization who can provide funds or other resources, to a cosponsor, or to an organization that provides grants or contracts. Depending on the size and complexity of the request, the proposal may be a one-page letter or a detailed proposal with much supporting documentation. A proposed plan and its implementation are strengthened by involving other people concerned with the proposed changes or improvement in the planning process to build support and commitment for the change. Important parts of a proposal include objectives and expected benefits; current people, programs, and resources; needed additional resources (including a budget); and a plan to achieve objectives and evaluate impact. Prepare a proposal so that it is most likely to be appealing to the people to whom the proposal is made (Buskey, 1981; Merriam and Simpson, 1984).

The support services available to you vary with type of provider. For example, in small organizations such as an association with a small staff, a community agency, or a local religious congregation, perhaps only part of one person's time will be devoted to coordination of continuing education, and little secretarial assistance may be available. By contrast, in a large continuing higher education provider, there may be many forms of assistance available, but unless you actively seek them out, you may not discover all of them.

The place to start is the coordinator who arranged for you to conduct your program. If a brief handbook for continuing education instructors is not available, your coordinator should be able to provide information about various support services in conversation. For instance, in addition to marketing assistance, mentioned earlier in the chapter, the people who

counsel and advise adult learners (including registration) can
provide useful information about needs and interests of potential participants and will welcome information about your program to enable them to interpret it well to adults who inquire.
In addition to library staff, who can assist with acquisitions and
circulation of print, visual, and electronic materials, there are
usually offices that can help with production and use of other
materials, such as slides, videotapes, and computer simulations.

Do you receive any of these types of agency support regarding finances, facilities, and materials? If so, how satisfactory
is it? In any event, what might you do to strengthen your program and its benefit to the participants through greater use of
such support and services?

Staff Development

Selecting able people to help you help adults learn is not
sufficient. A major satisfaction comes from what you learn in
the process. The challenge in teaching adults effectively reflects
both the limited preparation most practitioners have for doing
so and the unlimited opportunities for doing so better. Instructor growth as a benefit may be a major incentive, especially for
volunteers. This section reviews some of the ways in which you
and others can provide effective staff development opportunities for yourself and other instructors. Recipients may include
yourself, resource persons who work with you, and other planners of staff development activities for people who teach with
you in the total continuing education offerings of your provider agency (Bess, 1982; Bishop, 1976; Grabowski, 1976; Lindquist, 1978a; Nadler, 1982; Renner, 1983; Robinson, 1979;
Smith, 1982; Stritter and Flair, 1980). This section suggests
ways in which you can provide leadership to strengthen such
staff development for instructors.

In the same way that effective teaching should encourage
participants to make useful decisions about their learning projects, effective staff development activities should help instructors enrich and learn from their efforts to help adults learn
(Bartock, 1983; Gorham, 1985a; Roland, 1983). The ideas from

this book can be used to plan and conduct staff development activities with the instructors as learners and continuing education instruction as the improved performance.

There are various ways to help instructors of adults, including resource persons who assist you, become more effective. The orientation process can begin with a phone conversation, a confirming letter, a planning meeting, or a group orientation session. Attention can be given to specific objectives and procedures as well as generalizations about adult learning and teaching. Visits and observations at early sessions can identify effective content and procedures to be presented and strengthened, as well as aspects to be improved or changed. For multiple sessions or programs, a periodic review by yourself or perhaps your program administrator serves a similar function of evaluating current performance in relation to achievable best practice, to identify aspects to continue and aspects to change. In-service sessions can be used to present useful ideas and to enable instructors to learn from each other during and after the sessions. Pamphlets and other print materials are an efficient way to provide receptive instructors with guidelines and suggestions.

With so many potentially useful ideas about helping adults learn, it is important to assist yourself and other instructors in focusing on specific improvements that you or they want to make (Darkenwald and Knox, 1984; Knox, 1979a, 1979b, 1980b; Okun, 1982). Ways to do so include learning contracts, action learning projects, self-assessments, and participant evaluation of teaching. It is desirable to do so early enough in a program that the results can be used as feedback, and adjustments made and evaluated. It is also desirable to use criteria of effective teaching based on achievable best practice. The criteria for selection of resource persons may suggest applicable criteria, as do the major sections of this entire book. Select the criteria on which to focus from the various aspects of effective instruction. Consider aspects such as content mastery, understanding pertinent ideas about adults as learners, a perspective on continuing education in relation to the parent organization and other providers, planning and conducting learning activities that give attention to entry and persistence and application, and attention to an instructor's distinctive characteristics.

Some such staff development activities you may conduct for yourself or for resource persons who help you. Others may be conducted by your supervisor or people from related associations and university graduate programs that deal with continuing education and human resource development.

Although all guidelines for helping adults learn apply to staff development for continuing education instructional staff, several desirable proficiencies deserve special attention as objectives for staff development (Lippitt and This, 1980). In addition to explaining content, effective instructors model and guide an inquiry process that may include both technical information and learner values. This calls for a high level of instructor self-understanding so that the emphasis remains on learner growth. Related characteristics are personal security and previous experience as a learner as well as an instructor, which contribute to empathy and interpersonal effectiveness. Verbal communication is important, as reflected in use of words and images appropriate for particular learners. Understanding of pertinent concepts from the social sciences and humanities, combined with mastery of educational procedures, can enable instructors to have a rationale for selection of methods that combine impact with humanistic values. Such a combination of the "how" and "why" of helping adults learn depends on a high level of instructor proficiency and integrity.

In what types and extent of activities have you engaged for the purpose of increasing your effectiveness in helping adults learn? How useful have they been? What future staff development opportunities would interest you? What steps might you take to make them happen?

Conclusion

It may surprise you how many sources of support and assistance are available to you and your program as you help adults learn. Included are coordinators and specialists in marketing, counseling, personnel, finance, and materials. Most of these people in staff support roles (especially marketing and counseling) can help you attract and retain the numbers and types of adults for whom your program is especially intended. For all types of assistance, the leadership that you exert in identifying, selecting, coordinating, and evaluating such staff assistance is likely to be the major influence on the richness of support your program receives. In addition to such specialized services, you and your coordinator can strengthen the general support that your provider agency gives your program in the forms of finances, facilities, and materials. The provider can also assist you with staff development opportunities for yourself and those who help you plan and conduct your program. You can also take the initiative to help conduct staff development activities for others who help adults learn.

Such program support may not usually be thought of as part of helping adults learn, but it can be. Reaching out to use such assistance can enable you to enrich learning opportunities for participants and to enrich your challenge and satisfaction. With the multidisciplinary perspectives that adult learners appreciate, involving other resource persons, equipment, and materials can contribute to a more growthful program for all concerned.

TWELVE

Strategies for Improving Your Instruction

In my experience, most people who help adults learn care about content, participants, and results. You care about content enough to share it. You care about participants enough to be both supportive and challenging. You care about results enough to want your instruction and the total program to benefit the participants' lives. Your commitment to learning and growth for participants is likely to extend to similar benefits for yourself. It is almost a truism that effective instructors learn as much as the participants.

As we guide adult learners, we discover the maps and guidelines they are using, and we suggest more useful ones if they are available. The preceding chapters contain such guidelines that other people have found useful, guidelines that seem broadly applicable beyond limited content areas, providers, or audiences. Many of those guidelines were no doubt familiar. I hope they provide new insights and suggest new procedures you might use in your own instruction.

This brief concluding chapter is meant to explore promising directions for *your* own efforts to help adults learn and for the concepts and procedures for continued improvement available in the professional literature to all of us who do so.

The books and articles cited and listed as references in this book are but a fraction of what is available. A majority were published during the past decade, reflecting the growing interest in both continuing education practice and scholarship. Despite this wealth of available materials on the practice of helping adults learn, the overwhelming majority of people who do so are completely unaware of any such resources. Fortunately, many continuing education instructors who persist discover some basic concepts and procedures that work, and a few share their discoveries and add to the growing professional literature.

Some of your reading about the process of helping adults learn has no doubt confirmed what you already knew and served to fix established terms in your mind. This can be reassuring and at the same time can facilitate communication and exchange with other instructors. When your conclusions do not agree with those of other people you encounter through conversation or reading, that discrepancy can also be growthful. We tend to learn as much from differences as from similarities.

This chapter highlights some themes from preceding chapters and suggests how to make good use of any new insights gained that may enrich your practice. Thus, the emphasis is on *your* future directions as much as future directions for the field. The chapter also suggests directions for innovation, evaluation, and research by which you and others might discover new concepts and procedures that you can share with the rest of us. Therefore, this future-oriented concluding chapter parallels the opening chapter on teaching and learning, with its emphasis on the mobius quality of the teaching/learning process in which the stereotypical distinctions between teaching and learning blur, if not disappear.

The increasing amount of tested knowledge available about adults as learners can enhance the insights that each of us distills from personal experience. The resulting generalizations are useful to the extent to which we use our insights to appreciate the individual participants in each program we conduct. Underlying much of the detail is the fundamental concept of the developmental process by which adult proficiencies are enhanced. Thus the apt metaphor of adult learning as a journey and of our role as that of guides who help adult learners improve the maps they use in their explorations and discoveries. If we are successful, they become more active and reflective learners.

This role results in our twin tasks: to guide both the developmental process and content mastery. Consider which concepts of adult development and learning are pertinent to your content and teaching style. Think of several that seem to have the most potential for strengthening your instruction. How might you explore their implications and modify your practice accordingly, at least on a trial basis? Discuss this concept with colleagues or observe an instructor who exemplifies the approach you want to pursue or read more about the pertinent aspects of adult development and the corresponding instructional concepts and procedures other instructors have reported. Your inquiry and innovation should help you achieve greater individualization and responsiveness when you help adults learn.

The proficiency theory of adult learning, which undergirds this book, summarizes some of the available generalizations. The essential rationale of that theory is that by understanding developmental changes in discrepancies between current and desired proficiencies, we can better assess educational needs, guide learning activities, evaluate progress, enhance a sense of proficiency, and stimulate persistence in learning. Such generalizations can serve as tentative guidelines in efforts to improve your own instruction and for researchers and scholars to continue to test and refine such improvements. The result of such practice and research should be more powerful explanations that are more useful for us all.

Another use for your increased understanding of adult learners is in helping participants guide their own learning activities. Provision of learning-style inventories and other self-assessments can enable them to gain insights into both their learning goals and their preferred learning styles. How do you do this now? How might you strengthen the process?

Influences in addition to learner and instructor characteristics are situational, such as the relative attractiveness of various providers' offerings. We know more about preferred learning styles, values clarification, and needs assessment than we do about situational influences on adults' participation in educational activities. But ask yourself what contextual factors most affect the motivation and persistence of adults in your program? Perhaps a transactional understanding of widespread facilitators of and barriers to participation can be shared with participants to help them deal with such influences as well as used by yourself in making program-planning decisions.

Our general understanding of personal and situational influences on continuing education participation advanced in recent years when we discovered how major barriers to participation could be differentiated and separated from the lack of positive influences earlier identified as correlates of participation. We need more study of how to encourage and assist educational participation and persistence by hard-to-reach adults. As you gain insight into this issue from those who participate in your program, it is important to share your conclusions with the rest of us. Then, perhaps, we will make progress in solving this widespread problem of serving more underserved adults.

Your own contribution to planning and conducting effective continuing education programs extends far beyond being responsive to the participants. Surely you may adjust your teaching style and program emphasis to participants' preferred learning styles and expectations. But you should also be concerned with content, standards, and the effective organization of educational procedures. It seems evident that the varied aspects of your instructional role and procedures should fit together in a satisfactory way. Yet we know little about the relative effectiveness of various teaching styles and even less about the advantages in the elements of a teaching style given particular participant characteristics and program content. We can only estimate which relationships are crucial to your effectiveness. We can ask if there is an optimal level of content mastery for instructors working with participants of either high- or low-level proficiency. No one instructor can hope to answer this question. We must rely on studies of instructors at various levels of content mastery and participants of varying proficiency.

A greater understanding of the impact of teaching style and proficiency can guide our planning of teaching materials and procedures. Program planning receives more attention in research and other continuing education writings than most other aspects of helping adults learn. The many studies on effectiveness of instructional methods show most methods to be comparably effective for adults who persist to completion. The more important conclusion may be that methods are effective to the extent to which they encourage individual adults to persist until their objectives in a particular program are achieved.

Because the decisions you make are crucial to the success of your program, ask yourself some searching questions. What instructional methods do you typically use? Why? Might other ones enhance your program? If so, how might you modify your planning process to include some of these methods to the satisfaction of all concerned, at least on a trial basis? What criteria might you use for selecting other methods?

A troublesome planning decision is what type and extent of needs assessment and evaluation to include. Writings on this topic make the procedures seem so important and complex most of us respond by doing little but feeling guilty about it. But one of the most urgent continuing education research needs is to discover easily collected indicators of important educational needs, progress, and outcomes. To be feasible, such data should be efficiently collected as data from typical programs with the usual constraints on use of time, money, and specialized expertise. Until such indicators have been identified and efficient evaluation instruments developed to assess them, what do you use to estimate educational needs or achievement? Attendance figures and expressions of interest and satisfaction, perhaps. But how satisfactory are these tools? Have you come across any promising alternatives? Each of us can seek effective evaluation procedures and share them with colleagues.

Similar questions can be raised about crucial environmental influences on your program, especially on learner participation and application. Available writings suggest widespread influences, such as expectations of others and awareness of opportunities. How well do these generalizations fit your experience? Which influences can you or the participants do anything about? Again, as you identify influences that have implications for planning and program improvement, report your findings so everyone can benefit.

Major value judgments are being made, at least implicitly, when needs are assessed and objectives are set. Are you aware of these assumptions and judgments? If so, do they seem satisfactory? If you are unaware of such judgments, how might you discover them? Colleagues, participants, and coordinators can all contribute to the process of making implicit value judgments explicit and that process can have many valuable educational benefits. Sharing both your conclusions and the process you used to arrive at them can sensitize colleagues to implicit values in their practice and pose useful questions for evaluation and research.

As an instructor, you also plan for selection and development of program-related materials. Readings, worksheets, and handouts have always been important. But these tools are becoming even more so with increasing attention to individualization, technology, and learning at a distance. A major problem with materials has been their unrelatedness to other program activities—for example, prior readings that are not discussed in the sessions; visuals that distract from, rather than enhance, an oral presentation. A future challenge for practice and scholarship is to specify more useful guidelines for planning and using materials so they are integral parts of educational programs.

Such integration is illustrated by current attention to "high tech, high touch." As videotapes, computer simulations, and other applications of technology to continuing education have become more widespread, it has become even more important that deliberate attention be given to the human touch so that such materials will be *user-friendly*. Centuries ago, printing was a new technology, and even today, printed materials are barriers to learning for some potential participants. Phrases such as *computer literacy* reflect concerns about overcoming similar barriers to use of that technology. Television poses a different problem associated with its great familiarity, because its use for passive entertainment can interfere with its use for active learning.

Evaluate how you use technology in your program materials. Are they satisfactory, and how would you strengthen them? We would all benefit from evaluative critiques of all types of educational materials, critiques that alert us to pertinent effective items and guide our selection of them. Although such listings exist, they need to be more extensive and more widely used. How do you learn about and select such materials? What information do you need to make an informed decision?

Any preparation and planning is useful only to the extent it helps you engage the participants, guide the teaching/learning transaction, and encourage application. Various suggestions are made here for orientation, establishing a supportive and challenging climate for learning and achieving agreement on objectives. Now consider how your program responds to participants' interests and expectations. Are there ways you can more effectively help learners make a good beginning, with all the evident benefits of persistence and achievement? Your reports on what procedures work well and why would benefit the rest of us and contribute to more precise guidelines for testing by research. Of course, responsiveness is important at the outset of each program, but it is desirable throughout. What questions about how to be effectively responsive do you have now, and what answers have you discovered that you might share?

As the core of helping adults learn, the teaching/learning transaction contains strands from all aspects of planning and implementation and so is complex and dynamic. Participant time devoted to productive learning tasks is a central concern. For you, this includes ways you can encourage and guide the process for individuals and groups. A fundamental question is how you use questions. You should discover what major questions participants bring with them and what new questions arise during the program. Program content should help them answer those questions and discover even more useful ones. On another level, estimate how you use questions to provoke interest, promote sharing, and guide progression. Are you satisfied with your use of questions as tools to guide learning, and are you aware of new tools of this type that you might add?

There are other ways you can guide the sequence of exposure to new ideas and practice activities to improve progression. This book contains some guidelines. Many more suggestions are available from colleagues and in writings on helping adults learn. Until scholars have tested and refined these guidelines, each of us must proceed intuitively to sequence learning activities in ways that fit participants' preferences and his or her own teaching style. In the meantime, reports of procedures and rationales for pacing and sequencing of learning activities for effective progression and reinforcement could enrich the practice of us all.

Some of the most useful information can come from program evaluation. Make it an integral part of your program planning and implementation. Program evaluation can enhance feedback and reinforcement for participants as well as contribute to program decisions that you and participants make. What program evaluation procedures do you typically use, and how useful are they? Are the benefits to you, participants, and coordinators worth the time, money, and effort expended? In the process have you found any promising ideas about evaluation that might strengthen your program? This is one of the most critical areas of continuing education research. We must discover indexes of process and outcomes usable for evaluation activities that lead to improvement and justification of typical programs.

Reasoning related to problem solving is a pertinent and promising research area. We can use the resulting guidelines to help participants progress to higher levels of understanding (from fragmentary to comprehensive, to relationships within a given situation, to a more inclusive and creative perspective). Research insights into strategies that differentiate novice and expert problem solvers can directly influence and inspire our efforts to guide experiential problem-solving continuing education activities.

Another aspect of the teaching/learning transaction consists in the encouragement and assistance that participants receive to apply what they learn. You do so during the program and by follow-up activities afterward. However, the main responsibility does rest with the participants and the people they interact with in the context in which application is to occur. In work settings, these people might include supervisors, co-workers, and recipients of services. Your understanding of participant and organizational expectations enables you to build on positive influences that encourage application. There are barriers that discourage application. What are the main influences on application that affect participants in your programs? What do you do, in relation to those influences, to increase the likelihood of application?

Barriers to participation and application can be grouped as situational, psychosocial, informational, and institutional. Just recognizing which barriers discourage some participants from persisting and applying what they learn helps you, the participants, or other people work to reduce these barriers. What barriers seem to discourage application by your participants, and what more might be done?

Most organizations that provide educational programs for adults offer services that can contribute to your instructional role. Included are marketing, counseling, instructional materials, finances, and staff development. Which of these program support services do you use, and which additional services would be useful?

We know much about influences on continuing education and how to encourage participation, especially by those who may be hard to reach. You probably provide advance information about your program to a marketing or public information specialist so its availability can be announced to the adults for whom it is intended. There is still room to discuss other ways to encourage participation by adults who are not being served. What could be done in work settings, for instance, to increase interest and support by participants and their supervisors? A similar question can be raised about other support services, such as counseling and materials.

Your own development as a continuing education instructor is a case in which agency assistance is described. In best practice, such staff development activities should be excellent examples of helping adults learn—with you as the learner. In addition to distributing reprints and pamphlets about helping adults learn and arranging for you to attend meetings with people who instruct adults, assistance might be provided for your own self-directed learning efforts. The periodicals and books listed as references in this book contain many readings of potential interest. They are also publication outlets for reports you might write to share your insights and discoveries with the rest of us. This is the nature of the relationship between learning and teaching and learning.

References

Abt, C. *Serious Games.* New York: Viking Press, 1970.

Anderson, D., and Niemi, J. A. *Adult Education and the Disadvantaged Adult.* Syracuse, N.Y.: ERIC Clearinghouse on Adult Education, 1969.

Anderson, R. C., and Faust, G. W. *Educational Psychology: The Science of Instruction and Learning.* New York: Dodd, Mead, 1973.

Anderson, R. E., and Darkenwald, G. G. *Participation and Persistence in American Adult Education.* New York: College Entrance Examination Board, 1979.

Anderson, R. H. "Guidelines for Visuals." *Training and Development Journal,* Dec. 1979, pp. 30–33.

Anderson, R. H. *Selecting and Developing Media for Instruction.* (2nd ed.) New York: Van Nostrand Reinhold, 1983.

Apps, J. W. *Study Skills: For Those Adults Returning to School.* New York: McGraw-Hill, 1978.

Apps, J. W. *The Adult Learner on Campus.* Chicago: Follett, 1981.

Argyris, C. *Reasoning, Learning, and Action: Individual and Organizational.* San Francisco: Jossey-Bass, 1982.

Aslanian, C. B., and Brickell, H. N. *Americans in Transition: Life Changes as Reasons for Learning.* New York: College Entrance Examination Board, 1980.

227

Ausubel, D. P., and Novack, J. D. *Educational Psychology: A Cognitive View.* (2nd ed.) New York: Holt, Rinehart and Winston, 1978.

Bacon, M. "What Adult Literacy Teachers Need to Know About Strategies for Focusing on Comprehension." *Lifelong Learning,* Feb. 1983, pp. 4-5.

Bandura, A. "Self-Efficacy Mechanism in Human Agency." *American Psychologist,* Feb. 1982, pp. 122-147.

Barr, D. F. "More Needs Analysis." *Training and Development Journal,* Sept. 1980, pp. 70-74.

Barrows, H. S., and Tamblyn, R. M. *Problem Based Learning: An Approach to Medical Education.* New York: Springer, 1980.

Bartock, L. "Do-It-Yourself Faculty Development for Continuing Education Instructors." *Lifelong Learning,* Feb. 1983, pp. 6-7, 25.

Baruch, G., Barnett, R., and Rivers, C. *Lifeprints.* New York: McGraw-Hill, 1983.

Becker, S. "The Ten Sequential Steps of the Training Process." *Training,* Jan. 1980, pp. 40-42.

Beder, H. W., and Darkenwald, G. G. "Differences Between Teaching Adults and Pre-Adults: Some Propositions and Findings." *Adult Education,* 1982, *32* (3), 142-155.

Belasco, J. A., and Trice, H. M. *The Assessment of Change in Training and Therapy.* New York: McGraw-Hill, 1969.

Bell, C. R., and Margolis, F. H. "Pleasant Weather for Learning." *Training and Development Journal,* June 1985, pp. 30-31.

Bell, C. R., and Putnam, T. "Mastering the Art of Training Design." *Training and Development Journal,* May 1979, pp. 24-28.

Bergevin, P., Morris, D., and Smith, R. *Adult Education Procedures.* Greenwich, Conn.: Seabury Press, 1963.

Bess, J. L. (ed.). *Motivating Professors to Teach Effectively.* New Directions for Teaching and Learning, no. 10. San Francisco: Jossey-Bass, 1982.

Bigge, M. L. *Learning Theories for Teachers.* New York: Harper & Row, 1982.

Birnbrauer, H., and Tyson, L. A. "How to Analyze Needs." *Training and Development Journal,* Aug. 1985, pp. 53-55.

Bishop, L. J. *Staff Development and Instructional Improvement: Plans and Procedures.* Newton, Mass.: Allyn & Bacon, 1976.

Block, J. "Some Enduring and Consequential Structures of Personality." In A. I. Rabin and others (eds.), *Further Explorations in Personality.* New York: Wiley-Interscience, 1981.

Bloom, B. S., and others. *Taxonomy of Educational Objectives. Part I: The Cognitive Domain.* New York: Longmans, 1956.

Boshier, R., and Collins, J. B. "The Houle Typology After Twenty-Two Years: A Large-Scale Empirical Test." *Adult Education Quarterly,* 1985, *35* (3), 113-130.

Bowren, F. R., and Zintz, M. V. *Teaching Reading in Adult Basic Education.* Dubuque, Iowa: Brown, 1977.

Boyd, B. B. "Developing Case Studies." *Training and Development Journal,* June 1980, pp. 113-117.

Boyle, P. G. *Planning Better Programs.* New York: McGraw-Hill, 1981.

Brethower, K. S., and Rummler, G. A. "Evaluation Training." *Training and Development Journal,* May 1979, pp. 14-22.

Brinkerhoff, R. O. "Making Evaluation More Useful." *Training and Development Journal,* Dec. 1981, pp. 66-70.

Brinkerhoff, R. O. "The Success Case: A Low-Cost, High-Yield Evaluation." *Training and Development Journal,* Aug. 1983, pp. 58-61.

Brockett, R. G. "Facilitator Roles and Skills." *Lifelong Learning,* Jan. 1983, pp. 7-9.

Brockett, R. G. "Developing Written Learning Materials: A Proactive Approach." *Lifelong Learning,* Feb. 1984, pp. 16-18, 28.

Brockett, R. G. "The Relationship Between Self-Directed Learning Readiness and Life Satisfaction Among Older Adults." *Adult Education Quarterly,* 1985, *35* (4), 210-219.

Brookfield, S. *Adult Learners, Adult Education, and the Community.* New York: Teachers College Press, Columbia University, 1984.

Brookfield, S. *Understanding and Facilitating Adult Learning.* San Francisco: Jossey-Bass, 1986.

Brophy, J. E., and Evertson, C. M. *Learning from Teaching: A Developmental Perspective.* Newton, Mass.: Allyn & Bacon, 1976.

Brown, A. L. "Knowing When, Where, and How to Remember: A Problem of Metacognition." In R. Glaser (ed.), *Advances in Instructional Psychology.* Hillsdale, N.J.: Erlbaum, 1978.

Brown, C. R., Jr., and Uhl, H. S. M. "Mandatory Continuing Education: Sense or Nonsense?" *Journal of the American Medical Association,* 1970, *213,* 1660-1668.

Brown, D. "Rehabilitating the Learning Disabled." *Adult American Rehabilitation,* 1982, *7,* 3-11.

Brown, M. A., and Copeland, H. G. (eds.). *Attracting Able Instructors of Adults.* New Directions for Continuing Education, no. 4. San Francisco: Jossey-Bass, 1979.

Brown, M. G. "Evaluating Training via Multiple Baseline Designs." *Training and Development Journal,* Oct. 1980, pp. 11-16.

Brue, C. "Breaking the Ice." *Training and Development Journal,* June 1985, pp. 26-28.

Brundage, D. H., and Mackeracker, D. *Adult Learning Principles and Their Application to Program Planning.* Toronto: Ontario Institute for Studies in Education, Ontario Ministry of Education, 1980.

Bunker, K. A., and Cohen, S. L. "Evaluating Organizational Training Efforts: Is Ignorance Really Bliss?" *Training and Development Journal,* Aug. 1978, pp. 4-11.

Burge, E. J. (ed.). Special issue on adult learners, learning, and public libraries. *Library Trends,* Spring 1983, *31* (4).

Burton, W. H. "Basic Principles in a Good Teaching-Learning Situation." *Phi Delta Kappan,* Mar. 1958, pp. 242-248.

Buskey, J. H. (ed.). *Attracting External Funds for Continuing Education.* New Directions for Continuing Education, no. 12. San Francisco: Jossey-Bass, 1981.

Buzzotta, V. R., Lefton, R. E., and Sherberg, M. "Coaching and Counseling: How You Can Improve the Way It's Done." *Training and Development Journal,* Nov. 1977, pp. 50-60.

Byham, W. C. "The Assessment Center as an Aid in Management Development." *Training and Development Journal,* June 1980, pp. 24-36.

Caffarella, R. S. "A Checklist for Planning Successful Training Programs." *Training and Development Journal,* Mar. 1985, pp. 81-83.

Carkhuff, R. R., and Fisher, S. G. *Instructional Systems Design.* Amherst, Mass.: Human Resource Development Press, 1984.

Carnarius, S. "A New Approach to Designing Training Programs." *Training and Development Journal,* Feb. 1981, pp. 40-44.

Cattell, R. B. *Abilities: Their Structure, Growth, and Action.* Boston: Houghton Mifflin, 1971.

Cervero, R. M., Rottet, S., and Dimmock, K. H. "Analyzing the Effectiveness of Continuing Professional Education at the Workplace." *Adult Education Quarterly,* 1986, *36* (2), 78-85.

Chamberlain, M. N. (ed.). *Providing Continuing Education by Media and Technology.* New Directions for Continuing Education, no. 5. San Francisco: Jossey-Bass, 1980.

Chasnoff, R., and Muniz, P. "Training to Manage Conflict." *Training and Development Journal,* Jan. 1985, pp. 49-53.

Chickering, A. W., and Associates. *The Modern American College: Responding to the New Realities of Diverse Students and a Changing Society.* San Francisco: Jossey-Bass, 1981.

Chiriboga, D. A. "An Examination of Life Events as Possible Antecedents to Change." *Journal of Gerontology,* Sept. 1982, pp. 595-601.

Clark, T. "Creating Contract Learning." In O. Milton and Associates, *On College Teaching: A Guide to Contemporary Practices.* San Francisco: Jossey-Bass, 1978.

Claxton, C. S., and Ralston, Y. *Learning Styles: Their Impact on Teaching and Administration.* Washington, D.C.: American Association for Higher Education and ERIC Clearinghouse on Higher Education, 1978.

Collins, Z. W. (ed.). *Museums, Adults and the Humanities.* Washington, D.C.: American Association of Museums, 1981.

Connell, H. S. "Training Sales Managers on Motivation." *Training and Development Journal,* Nov. 1981, pp. 85-88.

Conti, G. J. "Assessing Teaching Style in Adult Education: How and Why." *Lifelong Learning,* June 1985a, pp. 7–11, 28.

Conti, G. J. "The Relationship Between Teaching Style and Adult Student Learning." *Adult Education Quarterly,* 1985b, *35* (4), 220–228.

Cook, T. D., and Reichard, C. S. (eds.). *Qualitative and Quantitative Methods in Evaluation Research.* Beverly Hills, Calif.: Sage, 1979.

Cooper, S. S. *Self-Directed Learning in Nursing.* Rockville, Md.: Aspen Systems, 1980.

Cooper, S. S., and Hornback, M. *Continuing Nursing Education.* New York: McGraw-Hill, 1973.

Craig, R. L. (ed.). *Training and Development Handbook.* (2nd ed.) New York: McGraw-Hill, 1976.

Cross, K. P. *Accent on Learning: Improving Instruction and Reshaping the Curriculum.* San Francisco: Jossey-Bass, 1976.

Cross, K. P. *Adults as Learners: Increasing Participation and Facilitating Learning.* San Francisco: Jossey-Bass, 1981.

Crumb, C. V. "Performance-Based Line Supervisor Training." *Training and Development Journal,* Sept. 1981, pp. 44–47.

Daloz, L. *Teaching Adults.* San Francisco: Jossey-Bass, 1986.

Darkenwald, G. G., and Knox, A. B. (eds.). *Meeting Educational Needs of Young Adults.* New Directions for Continuing Education, no. 21. San Francisco: Jossey-Bass, 1984.

Darkenwald, G. G., and Larson, G. A. (eds.). *Reaching Hard-to-Reach Adults.* New Directions for Continuing Education, no. 8. San Francisco: Jossey-Bass, 1980.

Darkenwald, G. G., and Valentine, T. "Outcomes of Participation in Adult Basic Skills Education." *Lifelong Learning,* Feb. 1985a, pp. 17–22, 31.

Darkenwald, G. G., and Valentine, T. "Factor Structure of Deterrents to Public Participation in Adult Education." *Adult Education Quarterly,* 1985b, *35* (4), 177–193.

Davies, I. K. *Instructional Technique.* New York: McGraw-Hill, 1981.

Davies, I. K. "Fitting the Media Key into Instruction." *Training and Development Journal,* Dec. 1984, pp. 22–27.

Davis, L. N., and McCallon, E. *Planning, Conducting, Evaluating Workshops.* Austin, Tex.: Learning Concepts, 1974.

Delbecq, A. L., Van de Ven, A. H., and Gustafson, D. H. *Group*

Techniques for Program Planning. Glenview, Ill.: Scott, Foresman, 1975.

DeNovellis, R. "The Personality Type Preference Indicator (PTPI)." *Journal of Psychological Type,* 1984, *7,* 29-31.

DeNovellis, R. "Understanding the Personality Type Preference Indicator." *Journal of Psychological Type,* 1985, *9,* 34-40.

Deshler, D. (ed.). *Evaluation for Program Improvement.* New Directions for Continuing Education, no. 24. San Francisco: Jossey-Bass, 1984.

DiMatteo, M. R., and DiNicola, D. D. *Achieving Patient Compliance.* New York: Pergamon Press, 1982.

DiSilvestro, F. R. (ed.). *Advising and Counseling Adult Learners.* New Directions for Continuing Education, no. 10. San Francisco: Jossey-Bass, 1981.

Dixon, N. M. "Incorporating Learning Style into Training Design." *Training and Development Journal,* July 1982, pp. 62-64.

Dixon, N. M. "The Implementation of Learning Style Information." *Lifelong Learning,* Nov. 1985, pp. 16-18, 26-27.

Dunn, R., and Dunn, K. *Educator's Self-Teaching Guide to Individualizing Instructional Programs.* New York: Parker, 1972.

Eble, K. E. *The Craft of Teaching: A Guide to Mastering the Professor's Art.* San Francisco: Jossey-Bass, 1976.

Eble, K. E. *The Aims of College Teaching.* San Francisco: Jossey-Bass, 1983.

Ehrenberg, L. M. "How to Ensure Better Transfer of Learning." *Training and Development Journal,* Feb. 1983, pp. 81-83.

Epperson, D. C. "Assessing Alternative Teaching-Learning Alliances." In L. J. Stiles (ed.), *Theories for Teaching.* New York: Dodd, Mead, 1974.

Erdman, J. I. "Teaching Writing as a Potentially Liberating Activity." *Lifelong Learning,* Nov. 1984, pp. 4-7.

Erickson, S. C. *The Essence of Good Teaching: Helping Students Learn and Remember What They Learn.* San Francisco: Jossey-Bass, 1984.

Evans, M. "Academic Evaluation in Individualized Education: Problems and Strategies." *Continuum,* July 1983, pp. 18-23.

Feeney, E. J. "Twelve Ideas Toward Effective Training." *Training and Development Journal,* Sept. 1980, pp. 14-16.

Feeney, E. J. "Beat the High Cost of Training Through LCI." *Training and Development Journal,* Sept. 1981, pp. 41–43.

Fetteroll, E. C., Jr. "16 Steps to Increase Your Effectiveness." *Training and Development Journal,* June 1985, pp. 68–70.

Fingeret, A. "Common Sense and Book Learning: Culture Clash?" *Lifelong Learning,* Apr. 1983, pp. 22–24.

Fink, A., and Kosecoff, J. *An Evaluation Primer and an Evaluation Primer Workbook: Practical Exercises for Educators.* Beverly Hills, Calif.: Sage, 1978.

Finkel, C. "The 'Total Immersion' Meeting Environment." *Training and Development Journal,* Sept. 1980, pp. 32–39.

Finkel, C. "Where Learning Happens." *Training and Development Journal,* Apr. 1984, pp. 32–36.

Fitzgerald, G. G. "Can the Hard-to-Reach Adults Become Literate?" *Lifelong Learning,* Feb. 1984, pp. 4–5, 27.

Flanagan, J. "The Critical Incident Technique." *Psychological Bulletin,* 1954, *51* (4), 327–358.

Flavel, J. H. "Metacognitive Aspects of Problem Solving." In L. B. Resnick (ed.), *The Nature of Intelligence.* Hillsdale, N.J.: Erlbaum, 1976.

Flynn, E. W., and LaFaso, J. F. *Group Discussion as Learning Process.* New York: Paulist Press, 1972.

Ford, N. "Recent Approaches to the Study and Teaching of 'Effective Teaching' in Higher Education." *Review of Educational Research,* 1981, *51* (3), 345–377.

Fowler, J. *Stages of Faith: The Psychology of Human Development and the Quest for Meaning.* New York: Harper & Row, 1981.

Franco, J. J. "Speaker, Know Thy Audience." *Training and Development Journal,* June 1985, pp. 20–21.

Gage, N. L. *Teacher Effectiveness and Teacher Education.* Palo Alto, Calif.: Pacific Books, 1977.

Gage, N. L. *The Scientific Bases of the Art of Teaching.* New York: Teachers College Press, Columbia University, 1978.

Gagné, R. M., and Briggs, L. J. *Principles of Instructional Design.* New York: Holt, Rinehart and Winston, 1970.

Gilligan, C. *In a Different Voice.* Cambridge, Mass.: Harvard University Press, 1982.

Gladis, S. D. "Notes Are Not Enough." *Training and Development Journal,* Aug. 1985, pp. 35–38.

Glustrom, M. "Educational Needs and Motivations of Non High School Graduate Adults Not in Participating Programs." *Lifelong Learning,* Apr. 1983, pp. 19–21.

Gold, L. "Job Instruction: Four Steps to Success." *Training and Development Journal,* Sept. 1981, pp. 28–32.

Gorham, J. "Interaction Analysis and Staff Development." *Lifelong Learning,* Apr. 1985a, pp. 8–10.

Gorham, J. "Differences Between Teaching Adults and Pre-Adults: A Closer Look." *Adult Education Quarterly,* 1985b, *35* (4), 194–209.

Grabowski, S. M. *Training Teachers of Adults: Models and Innovative Programs.* Occasional paper no. 46. Syracuse, N.Y.: Publications in Continuing Education, 1976.

Grabowski, S. M. (ed.). *Strengthening Connections Between Education and Performance.* New Directions for Continuing Education, no. 18. San Francisco: Jossey-Bass, 1983.

Gray, R. "Serving Adults with Learning Disabilities—Some Considerations." *Journal of Developmental and Remedial Education,* 1981, *4* (2), 3–5.

Green, J. S., Grosswald, S. J., Suter, E., and Walthall, D. B., III (eds.). *Continuing Education for the Health Professionals: Developing, Managing, and Evaluating Programs for Maximum Impact on Patient Care.* San Francisco: Jossey-Bass, 1984.

Gregorc, A. "Learning/Teaching Styles: Their Nature and Effects." In National Association of Secondary School Principals, *Student Learning Styles: Diagnosing and Prescribing Programs.* Reston, Va.: National Association of Secondary School Principals, 1979.

Gross, R. *The Lifelong Learner: A Guide to Self-Development.* New York: Simon & Schuster, 1977.

Gross, R. (ed.). *Invitation to Lifelong Learning.* Chicago: Follett, 1982.

Grossman, S. R. "Brainstorming Updated." *Training and Development Journal,* Feb. 1984, pp. 84–87.

Grotelueschen, A. D. "Program Evaluation." In A. B. Knox and

Associates, *Developing, Administering, and Evaluating Adult Education.* San Francisco: Jossey-Bass, 1980.

Grotelueschen, A. D., Gooler, D. D., and Knox, A. B. *Evaluation in Adult Basic Education: How and Why.* Danville, Ill.: Interstate, 1976.

Guba, E. G., and Lincoln, Y. S. *Effective Evaluation: Improving the Usefulness of Evaluation Results Through Responsive and Naturalistic Approaches.* San Francisco: Jossey-Bass, 1981.

Gubrium, J. T., and Buckholdt, D. R. *Toward Maturity: The Social Processing of Human Development.* San Francisco: Jossey-Bass, 1977.

Gueulette, D. G. (ed.). *Microcomputers for Adult Learning.* New York: Cambridge Books, 1982.

Gullette, M. M. (ed.). *The Art and Craft of Teaching.* Cambridge, Mass.: Howard-Danforth Center for Teaching and Learning, 1982.

Havighurst, R. J., and Orr, B. *Adult Education and Adult Needs.* Chicago: Center for the Study of Liberal Education for Adults, 1956.

Heffernan, J. M. *Adult Development and the Workplace.* Columbus: National Center for Research in Vocational Education, Ohio State University, 1983.

Hentges, K. "The Holistic Life Cycle Curriculum in Adult Education: A Proposal." *Lifelong Learning,* Oct. 1983, pp. 7, 16–17, 28.

Herem, M. A. "Help Your Learners with Task Performance Maps." *Training and Development Journal,* Jan. 1979, pp. 58–59.

Hill, R. E., Miller, E. L., and Lowther, M. A. (eds.). *Adult Career Transitions.* Michigan Business Papers, no. 66. Ann Arbor: Division of Research, Graduate School of Business Administration, University of Michigan, 1981.

Hill, R. J. *A Comparative Study of Lecture and Discussion Methods.* New York: Fund for Adult Education, 1960.

Holden, S. J. "Manufacturing Training—a Two-Step Process." *Training and Development Journal,* Sept. 1980, pp. 24-27.

Holtzclaw, L. R. "Adult Learners' Preferred Learning Styles,

Choice of Courses and Subject Areas for Prior Experiential Learning Credit." *Lifelong Learning,* Apr. 1985, pp. 23–27.

Horn, J. L. "Organization of Data on Life-Span Development of Human Abilities." In L. R. Goulet and P. B. Baltes (eds.), *Life-Span Developmental Psychology: Research and Theory.* Orlando, Fla.: Academic Press, 1970.

Horn, R. E. (ed.). *The Guide to Simulations/Games for Education and Training.* (3rd ed.) Crawford, N.J.: Didactic Systems, 1977.

Hortin, J. A. "Using Media with Adult Learners: Innovative and Practical Suggestions." *Lifelong Learning,* Sept. 1982, pp. 15, 30.

Houle, C. O. *The Design of Education.* San Francisco: Jossey-Bass, 1972.

Houle, C. O. *The External Degree.* San Francisco: Jossey-Bass, 1973.

Houle, C. O. *Continuing Learning in the Professions.* San Francisco: Jossey-Bass, 1980.

Houle, C. O. *Patterns of Learning: New Perspectives on Life-Span Education.* San Francisco: Jossey-Bass, 1984.

House, E. R. (ed.). *Philosophy of Evaluation.* New Directions for Program Evaluation, no. 19. San Francisco: Jossey-Bass, 1983.

Hultman, K. E. "Identifying and Dealing with Resistance to Change." *Training and Development Journal,* Feb. 1980, pp. 28–33.

Hultsch, D. F., and Deutsch, F. *Adult Development and Aging: A Life-Span Perspective.* New York: McGraw-Hill, 1981.

Hvitfeldt, C. "Traditional Culture, Perceptual Style, and Learning: The Classroom Behavior of Hmong Adults." *Adult Education Quarterly,* 1986, *36* (2), 65–77.

Ihlanfeldt, W. A. "Using Cognitive Mapping to Capitalize on Learning Strengths." *Training and Development Journal,* May 1981, pp. 99–104.

Jain, B. *Teaching in the Community College,* Units I, II. Springfield: Illinois State Board of Education, Adult and Vocational Education, 1981.

James, W. B., and Galbraith, M. W. "Perceptual Learning Styles:

Implications and Techniques for the Practitioner." *Lifelong Learning,* Jan. 1985, pp. 20–23.

Johnson, E. I. *Metroplex Assembly: An Experiment on Community Education.* Report no. 213. Boston: Center for the Study of Liberal Education for Adults, 1965.

Johnstone, J. W. C., and Rivera, R. *Volunteers for Learning.* Hawthorne, N.Y.: Aldine, 1965.

Jons, J. A. R. "A Skills Audit." *Training and Development Journal,* Sept. 1980, pp. 79–81.

Joseph, A. "Writing Training Materials That Turn People On." *Training and Development Journal,* May 1981, pp. 111–114.

Joyce, B., and Weil, M. *Models of Teaching.* Englewood Cliffs, N.J.: Prentice-Hall, 1972.

Kalamas, D. J. *Prepare to Work with Adult Learners.* Teaching Adults, module N-1. Prepublication copy. Columbus, Ohio: Center for Research in Vocational Education, 1986a.

Kalamas, D. J. *Plan Instruction for Adults.* Teaching Adults, module N-4. Prepublication copy. Columbus, Ohio: Center for Research in Vocational Education, 1986b.

Kaslow, F. W., and Associates. *Supervision, Consultation, and Staff Training in the Helping Professions.* San Francisco: Jossey-Bass, 1977.

Kearsley, G. P. "Designing and Implementing Distributed Education." *Training and Development Journal,* Dec. 1981, pp. 72–77.

Keaveny, T. J. "Developing and Maintaining Human Resources." *Training and Development Journal,* July 1983, pp. 65–68.

Keeton, M. T., and Associates. *Experiential Learning: Rationale, Characteristics, and Assessment.* San Francisco: Jossey-Bass, 1976.

Keller, J. M. "Motivation and Instructional Design: A Theoretical Perspective." *Journal of Instructional Development,* 1979, *2* (4), 26–34.

Kelly, H. B. "A Primer on Transfer of Training." *Training and Development Journal,* Nov. 1982, pp. 102–106.

Kirschenbaum, D. S., and Perri, M. G. "Improving Academic Competence in Adults: A Review of Recent Literature." *Journal of Counseling Psychology,* 1982, *29* (1), 76–94.

Klema, C., Casey, H. B., and Caple, D. "Training and Technical Manuals Can Be One—and the Same." *Training and Development Journal,* Jan. 1984, pp. 74–75.

Klevins, C. *Materials and Methods in Continuing Education.* Los Angeles: Klevins, 1978.

Knowles, M. S. *Self-Directed Learning.* New York: Association Press, 1975.

Knowles, M. S. *The Modern Practice of Adult Education.* (Rev. ed.) New York: Association Press, 1980.

Knowles, M. S. *Using Learning Contracts: Practical Approaches to Individualizing and Structuring Learning.* San Francisco: Jossey-Bass, 1986.

Knox, A. B. "Life-Long Self-Directed Education." In R. J. Blakely (ed.), *Fostering the Growing Need to Learn.* Rockville, Md.: Division of Regional Medical Programs, Bureau of Health Resources Development, 1974.

Knox, A. B. *Adult Development and Learning: A Handbook on Individual Growth and Competence in the Adult Years.* San Francisco: Jossey-Bass, 1977.

Knox, A. B. (ed.). *Enhancing Proficiencies of Continuing Educators.* New Directions for Continuing Education, no. 1. San Francisco: Jossey-Bass, 1979a.

Knox, A. B. (ed.). *Programming for Adults Facing Mid-Life Change.* New Directions for Continuing Education, no. 2. San Francisco: Jossey-Bass, 1979b.

Knox, A. B. (ed.). *Assessing the Impact of Continuing Education.* New Directions for Continuing Education, no. 3. San Francisco: Jossey-Bass, 1979c.

Knox, A. B. "Proficiency Theory of Adult Learning." *Contemporary Educational Psychology,* 1980a, *5* (3), 378–404.

Knox, A. B. (ed.). *Teaching Adults Effectively.* New Directions for Continuing Education, no. 6. San Francisco: Jossey-Bass, 1980b.

Knox, A. B. *Leadership Strategies for Meeting New Challenges.* New Directions for Continuing Education, no. 13. San Francisco: Jossey-Bass, 1982.

Knox, A. B. "Adult Learning and Proficiency." In D. Kleiber and M. Maehr (eds.), *Advances in Motivation and Achieve-*

ment. Vol. 5: *Motivation in Adulthood.* Greenwich, Conn.: JAI Press, 1985.

Knox, A. B., and Associates. *Developing, Administering, and Evaluating Adult Education.* San Francisco: Jossey-Bass, 1980.

Kohlberg, L. "Continuities in Childhood and Adult Moral Development Revisited." In P. Baltes and K. Schaie (eds.), *Developmental Psychology: Personality and Socialization.* Orlando, Fla.: Academic Press, 1973.

Kolb, D. *Experiential Learning: Experience as the Source of Learning and Development.* Englewood Cliffs, N.J.: Prentice-Hall, 1984.

Kopp, K. *Determine Individual Training Needs.* Teaching Adults, module N-3. Prepublication copy. Columbus, Ohio: National Center for Research in Vocational Education, 1986a.

Kopp, K. *Evaluate the Performance of Adults.* Teaching Adults, module N-6. Prepublication copy. Columbus, Ohio: National Center for Research in Vocational Education, 1986b.

Krathwohl, D., and others. *A Taxonomy of Educational Objectives II: The Affective Domain.* New York: McKay, 1964.

Krupp, J. *Adult Development: Implications for Staff Development.* Manchester, Conn.: Adult Development and Learning, 1981.

Krupp, J. *The Adult Learner.* Manchester, Conn.: Adult Development and Learning, 1982.

Laird, D. *Approaches to Training and Development.* Reading, Mass.: Addison-Wesley, 1978.

Landerholm, E. "Applying the Principles of Adult Learning to Parent Education Programs." *Lifelong Learning,* Feb. 1984, pp. 6-9, 27-28.

Langerman, P. D. (ed.). *You Can Be a Successful Teacher of Adults.* Washington, D.C.: National Association for Public Continuing and Adult Education, 1974.

Lasker, H. M., and Moore, J. F. "Current Studies of Adult Development: Implications for Education." In H. M. Lasker, J. F. Moore, and E. Simpson, *Adult Education and Approaches to Learning.* Washington, D.C.: National Institute for Community Development, 1980.

Lean, E. "Learning Disabled Trainees: Finding and Helping the

'Hidden Handicapped.' " *Training and Development Journal,* Sept. 1983, pp. 56–64.

Leifer, M. S., and Newstrom, J. W. "Solving the Transfer of Training Problems." *Training and Development Journal,* Aug. 1980, pp. 42–46.

Lenz, E. *The Art of Teaching Adults.* New York: Holt, Rinehart and Winston, 1982.

Lindquist, J. *Designing Teaching Improvement Programs.* Berkeley, Calif.: Pacific Soundings Press, 1978a.

Lindquist, J. *Strategies for Change.* Berkeley, Calif.: Pacific Soundings Press, 1978b.

Lippitt, G. L. "Integrating Personal and Professional Development." *Training and Development Journal,* May 1980, pp. 34–41.

Lippitt, G. L., and This, L. E. "Leaders for Laboratory Training." *Training and Development Journal,* June 1980, pp. 56–67.

Loevinger, J. *Ego Development: Conceptions and Theories.* San Francisco: Jossey-Bass, 1976.

Loewenthal, M. F., Thurnher, M., Chiriboga, D., and Associates. *Four Stages of Life: A Comparative Study of Women and Men Facing Transitions.* San Francisco: Jossey-Bass, 1975.

Loewenthal, N. H., Blackwelder, J., and Broomall, J. K. "Correspondence Instruction and the Adult Student," in A. B. Knox (ed.), *Teaching Adults Effectively.* New Directions for Continuing Education, no. 6. San Francisco: Jossey-Bass, 1980.

Loughary, J. W., and Hopson, B. *Producing Workshops, Seminars and Short Courses.* Chicago: Follett, 1979.

Lowman, J. *Mastering the Techniques of Teaching.* San Francisco: Jossey-Bass, 1984.

Ludwig, J., and Menendez, D. "Effective Communication Through Neuro-Linguistics." *Training and Development Journal,* Mar. 1985, pp. 44–48.

McAlindon, H. R. "Education for Self-Actualization." *Training and Development Journal,* Oct. 1981, pp. 85–91.

McLagan, P. A. *Helping Others Learn.* Reading, Mass.: Addison-Wesley, 1978.

MacNeil, P. "Organizational Barriers to the Administration of

Correctional Education: An Analysis of a Correctional School District." *Adult Education,* 1980, *30,* 208-221.

McNulty, N. G. "Management Development by Action Learning." *Training and Development Journal,* Mar. 1979, pp. 12-18.

Mager, R. F. *Preparing Instructional Objectives.* San Francisco: Fearon, 1962.

Mahler, W. R., and McLean, H. A. "Developmental Dialogues." *Training and Development Journal,* June 1980, pp. 126-130.

Mallory, W. J. "Simulation for Task Practice in Technical Training." *Training and Development Journal,* Sept. 1981, pp. 13-19.

Marlowe, H. A., Jr. "Social Intelligence: Implications for Adult Education." *Lifelong Learning,* Apr. 1985, pp. 4-5, 27.

Marshak, R. J. "Cognitive and Experiential Approaches to Conceptual Learning." *Training and Development Journal,* May 1983, pp. 72-77.

Maxwell, M. *Improving Student Learning Skills: A Comprehensive Guide to Successful Practices and Programs for Increasing the Performance of Underprepared Students.* San Francisco: Jossey-Bass, 1979.

Meierhenry, W. C. "Microcomputers and Adult Learning." *Training and Development Journal,* Dec. 1982, pp. 58-66.

Merriam, S. B. *Themes of Adulthood Through Literature.* New York: Teachers College Press, Columbia University, 1983.

Merriam, S. B. *Adult Development: Implications for Adult Education.* Information Series, no. 282. Columbus, Ohio: ERIC Clearinghouse on Adult, Career, and Vocational Education, 1984.

Merriam, S. B., and Simpson, E. L. *A Guide to Research for Educators and Trainers of Adults.* Malabar, Fla.: Krieger, 1984.

Messick, S. "The Nature of Cognitive Styles: Problems and Promise in Educational Practice." *Educational Psychologist,* 1984, *19* (2), 59-74.

Messick, S., and Associates. *Individuality in Learning: Implications of Cognitive Styles and Creativity for Human Development.* San Francisco: Jossey-Bass, 1976.

Mezoff, B. "How to Get Accurate Self-Reports of Training Outcomes." *Training and Development Journal,* Sept. 1981, pp. 56–61.

Michalak, D. F., and Yager, E. G. *Making the Training Process Work.* New York: Harper & Row, 1979.

Miles, M. B. "Changes During and Following Laboratory Training: A Clinical-Experimental Study." *Journal of Applied Behavioral Science,* 1965, *1* (3), 215–242.

Miller, H. L. *Teaching and Learning in Adult Education.* New York: Macmillan, 1964.

Milton, O., and Associates. *On College Teaching: A Guide to Contemporary Practices.* San Francisco: Jossey-Bass, 1978.

Moore, D. P., and Poppino, M. A. *Successful Tutoring: A Practical Guide to Adult Learning Processes.* Springfield, Ill.: Thomas, 1983.

Morgan, B., Holmes, G. E., and Bundy, C. E. *Methods in Adult Education.* Danville, Ill.: Interstate, 1976.

Morrill, R. L. *Teaching Values in College: Facilitating Development of Ethical, Moral, and Value Awareness in Students.* San Francisco: Jossey-Bass, 1980.

Morrisey, G. L., and Wellstead, A. R. "Supervisory Training Can Be Measured." *Training and Development Journal,* June 1980, pp. 118-122.

Mouton, J. S., and Blake, R. R. "Principles and Designs for Enhancing Learning." *Training and Development Journal,* Dec. 1984a, pp. 60–63.

Mouton, J. S., and Blake, R. R. *Synergogy: A New Strategy for Education, Training, and Development.* San Francisco: Jossey-Bass, 1984b.

Myers, I. B., and Myers, P. B. *Gifts Differing.* Palo Alto, Calif.: Consulting Psychologists Press, 1980.

Nadler, L. *Designing Training Programs: The Critical Events Model.* Reading, Mass.: Addison-Wesley, 1982.

National Center for Research in Vocational Education. *Manage the Adult Instructional Process.* Teaching Adults, module N-5. Prepublication copy. Columbus, Ohio: National Center for Research in Vocational Education, 1986.

Neider, L. "Training Effectiveness: Changing Attitudes." *Training and Development Journal,* Dec. 1981, pp. 24–28.

Newstrom, J. W. "The Management of Unlearning: Exploding

the 'Clean Slate' Fallacy." *Training and Development Journal,* Aug. 1983, pp. 36–39.

Newstrom, J. W., and Lilyquist, J. M. "Selecting Needs Analysis Methods." *Training and Development Journal,* Oct. 1979, pp. 52–56.

Oddi, L. F. "Development and Validation of an Instrument to Identify Self-Directed Continuing Learners." *Adult Education Quarterly,* 1986, *36* (2), 97–107.

Odiorne, G. S. "Setting Creative Goals." *Training and Development Journal,* July 1979, pp. 14–19.

Odiorne, G. S. *Strategic Management of Human Resources: A Portfolio Approach.* San Francisco: Jossey-Bass, 1984.

Okun, M. A. (ed.). *Programs for Older Adults.* New Directions for Continuing Education, no. 14. San Francisco: Jossey-Bass, 1982.

Olivas, L., and Newstrom, J. W. "Learning Through the Use of Simulation Games." *Training and Development Journal,* Sept. 1981, pp. 63–66.

Ostwald, S. K., and Williams, H. Y. "Optimizing Learning in the Elderly: A Model." *Lifelong Learning,* Sept. 1985, pp. 10–13, 27.

Palola, E. G. "Anxiety, Interpersonal Trust, and Adult Learning: Evaluation Theory and Practice." *Continuum,* July 1983, pp. 24–29.

Parry, S. B. "The Name of the Game . . . Is Simulation." *Training and Development Journal,* June 1980, pp. 99–105.

Pennington, F. C. (ed.). *Assessing Educational Needs of Adults.* New Directions for Continuing Education, no. 7. San Francisco: Jossey-Bass, 1980.

Perry, W. *Forms of Intellectual and Ethical Development in the College Years: A Scheme.* New York: Holt, Rinehart and Winston, 1970.

Peterson, D. A. *Facilitating Education for Older Learners.* San Francisco: Jossey-Bass, 1983.

Randall, J. S. "You and Effective Training—Part 5: Methods of Teaching." *Training and Development Journal,* Oct. 1978a, pp. 8–11.

Randall, J. S. "You and Effective Training—Parts 9 and 10: The

Art of Questioning/Evaluation." *Training and Development Journal,* Dec. 1978b, pp. 27-29.

Redman, B. K. *The Process of Patient Teaching in Nursing.* St. Louis: Mosby, 1980.

Reid, G. "Accelerated Learning: Technical Training Can Be Fun." *Training and Development Journal,* Sept. 1985, pp. 24-27.

Renner, P. F. *The Instructor's Survival Kit: A Handbook for Teachers of Adults.* (2nd ed.) Vancouver, B.C.: Training Associates, 1983.

Reynolds, A. "An Introduction to Computer-Based Learning." *Training and Development Journal,* May 1983, pp. 34-38.

Rhodes, D. M., and Azbell, J. W. "Designing Interactive Video Instruction Professionally." *Training and Development Journal,* Dec. 1985, pp. 31-33.

Richards, C. S., and Perri, M. G. "Do Self-Control Treatments Last? An Evaluation of Behavioral Problem Solving and Faded Counselor Contact as Treatment Maintenance Strategies." *Journal of Counseling Psychology,* 1978, *25,* 376-383.

Richardson, J. S., and Harbour, K. "These Are a Few of Our Favorite Things: Teaching Adults to Read—a Lesson Plan Model." *Lifelong Learning,* Sept. 1982, pp. 18-19, 31.

Rinke, W. J. "Holistic Education: Toward a Functional Approach to Adult Education." *Lifelong Learning,* Apr. 1982, pp. 12-14.

Rinke, W. J. "Holistic Education: An Answer?" *Training and Development Journal,* Aug. 1985, pp. 67-68.

Robinson, R. D. *An Introduction to Helping Adults Learn and Change.* Milwaukee: Omnibook, 1979.

Rogers, C. R. *Freedom to Learn.* Columbus, Ohio: Merrill, 1969.

Rogers, J. *Adults Learning.* Harmondsworth, England: Penguin, 1971.

Roland, C. "Style Feedback for Trainers: An Objective Observer System." *Training and Development Journal,* Sept. 1983, pp. 76-80.

Rosenberg, M. J. "The ABCs of ISD (Instructional Systems Design)." *Training and Development Journal,* Sept. 1982, pp. 44ff.

Rosenheim, J. H. "Case Study: Training—the Key to Success." *Training and Development Journal,* Sept. 1977, pp. 3-6.

Rothwell, W. J. "Bateson's Heterarchy of Learning." *Training and Development Journal,* July 1983, pp. 24-27.

Rubin, L. B. *Worlds of Pain: Life in the Working-Class Family.* New York: Basic Books, 1976.

Sanders, P., and Yanouzas, J. N. "Socialization to Learning." *Training and Development Journal,* July 1983, pp. 14-21.

Sawyers, L. *Equip, Participant's Book.* Philadelphia: Geneva Press, 1972.

Schaie, W. K., and Geiwitz, J. *Adult Development and Aging.* Boston: Little, Brown, 1982.

Schein, E. H. *Career Dynamics: Matching Individual and Organizational Needs.* Reading, Mass.: Addison-Wesley, 1978.

Scherer, J. J. "How People Learn: Assumptions for Design." *Training and Development Journal,* Jan. 1984, pp. 64-66.

Schwen, T. M., and others. "Cognitive Styles: Boon or Bane?" *Viewpoints in Teaching and Learning,* Fall 1979, pp. 49-65.

Shea, G. F. "Profiting from Wellness Training." *Training and Development Journal,* Oct. 1981, pp. 32-37.

Slaninka, S. "Writing as a Learning Process—Implications for the Adult Educator." *Lifelong Learning,* Mar. 1983, pp. 15-17.

Smith, M. E. "Self-Paced or Leader-Led Instruction?" *Training and Development Journal,* Feb. 1980, pp. 14-18.

Smith, R. M. *Learning How to Learn.* Chicago: Follett, 1982.

Snider, J. C., and Houser, N. P. "Guides to Growth in the Gray Classroom." *Lifelong Learning,* Jan. 1983, pp. 18-20.

Solomon, D., Bezdek, W. E., and Rosenberg, L. *Teaching Styles and Learning.* Chicago: Center for the Study of Liberal Education for Adults, 1963.

Solsbury, J. L., and Harris, R. L. "Video Cassettes Boost Sales at Lincoln-Mercury." *Training and Development Journal,* Mar. 1978, pp. 40-43.

Sork, T. J. (ed.). *Designing and Implementing Effective Workshops.* New Directions for Continuing Education, no. 22. San Francisco: Jossey-Bass, 1984.

Sork, T. J., and Buskey, J. H. "A Descriptive and Evaluative Analysis of Program Planning Literature, 1950–1983." *Adult Education Quarterly,* 1986, *36* (2), 86–96.

Squyres, W. D. (ed.). *Patient Education: An Inquiry into the State of the Art.* New York: Springer, 1980.

Stein, D. S. "Designing Performance-Oriented Training Programs." *Training and Development Journal,* Jan. 1981, pp. 12–16.

Steitz, J. A. "Issues of Adult Development Within the Academic Environment." *Lifelong Learning,* Apr. 1985, pp. 15–18, 27–28.

Stenzel, A. K., and Feeney, H. M. *Learning by the Case Method.* New York: Seabury Press, 1970.

Stevenson, G. "Evaluating Training Daily." *Training and Development Journal,* May 1980, pp. 120–122.

Stritter, F. T., and Flair, M. D. *Effective Clinical Teaching.* Bethesda, Md.: National Medical Audio Visual Center, U.S. Department of Health, Education and Welfare, 1980.

Stritter, F. T., and Hain, J. H. "A Workshop in Clinical Teaching." *Journal of Medical Education,* 1977, *52* (2), 155–157.

Sullivan, R. F., and Miklas, D. C. "On-the-Job Training That Works." *Training and Development Journal,* May 1985, pp. 118–120.

Swierczek, F. W., and Carmichael, L. "The Quantity and Quality of Evaluating Training." *Training and Development Journal,* Jan. 1985, pp. 95–99.

Tallmadge, G., and Shearer, J. W. "Relationships Among Learning Styles, Instructional Methods and the Nature of Learning Experiences." *Journal of Educational Psychology,* 1969, *60* (3), 222–230.

Thayer, L. (ed.). *Affective Education: Strategies for Experiential Learning.* La Jolla, Calif.: University Associates, 1976.

Thomas, J., and Sireno, P. J. "Assessing Management Competency Needs." *Training and Development Journal,* Sept. 1980, pp. 47–51.

Torrence, D. R. "How Video Can Help." *Training and Development Journal,* Dec. 1985, pp. 50–51.

Travers, R. M. W. (ed.). *Second Handbook of Research on Teaching.* Skokie, Ill.: Rand McNally, 1973.

Troll, L. E. *Continuations: Adult Development and Aging.* Monterey, Calif.: Brooks/Cole, 1982.

Trost, A. "They May Love It, but Will They Use It?" *Training and Development Journal,* Jan. 1985, pp. 78–81.

Tyson, L. A., and Birnbrauer, H. "High-Quality Evaluation." *Training and Development Journal,* Sept. 1985, pp. 33–37.

Vosko, R. S. "Shaping Spaces for Lifelong Learning." *Lifelong Learning,* Oct. 1984, pp. 4–7, 28.

Votruba, J. C. (ed.). *Strengthening Internal Support for Continuing Education.* New Directions for Continuing Education, no. 9. San Francisco: Jossey-Bass, 1981.

Wagner, P. A., Jr. "Adult Education and the Prison." *Adult Leadership,* 1976, *24* (8), 263–264.

Walter, T. L., and Siebert, A. *The Adult Student's Guide to Success in College.* New York: Holt, Rinehart and Winston, 1982.

Warnat, W. I. *Adult Learning in Inservice Training and Staff Development.* Washington, D.C.: Adult Learning Potential Institute, American University, 1980.

Weathersby, R. P. "Ego Development as an Aim of Higher Education." In A. W. Chickering and Associates, *The Modern American College: Responding to the New Realities of Diverse Students and a Changing Society.* San Francisco: Jossey-Bass, 1981.

Wedemeyer, C. A. *Learning at the Back Door: Reflections on Non-Traditional Learning in the Lifespan.* Madison: University of Wisconsin Press, 1981.

Weingand, D. E. "Continuing Education: ETN." *Lifelong Learning,* Oct. 1982, pp. 16–17, 25.

Whaples, G., and Booth, N. "Alternate Learning Environments: Providing for the Urban Low-Income Black Adult." *Lifelong Learning,* Sept. 1982, pp. 12–14, 27.

Whitbourne, S. K., and Weinstock, C. S. *Adult Development.* New York: Holt, Rinehart and Winston, 1979.

Wilkins, K. A. "Better Training with TV." *Training and Development Journal,* Dec. 1977, pp. 3–7.

Wilson, J. P. (ed.). *Materials for Teaching Adults: Selection, Development, and Use.* New Directions for Continuing Education, no. 17. San Francisco: Jossey-Bass, 1983.

Wlodkowski, R. J. *Enhancing Adult Motivation to Learn: A Guide to Improving Instruction and Increasing Learner Achievement.* San Francisco: Jossey-Bass, 1985a.

Wlodkowski, R. J. "Stimulation." *Training and Development Journal,* June 1985b, pp. 38–43.

Wortley, D. B., and Amatea, E. S. "Mapping Adult Life Changes: A Conceptual Framework for Organizing Adult Development Theory." *Personnel and Guidance Journal,* Apr. 1982, pp. 476-482.

Yager, E. "Quality Circle: A Tool for the '80s." *Training and Development Journal,* Aug. 1980, pp. 60-62.

Zemke, R. "Job Competencies: Can They Help You Design Better Training?" *Training/HRD,* May 1982, pp. 28-31.

Name Index

Subject Index

257